Being a Vet in the 21ˢᵗ Century

By

Paul D. Stevens

BVSc BA(Hons) MRCVS

For Anne

Always encouraging

FLD

Published in the UK by PillagePix Publishing
3 Ogston, Alfreton, DE55 6EL UK

First published in Great Britain 2019

ISBN : 978-1-9993661-0-0

Printed and bound in Great Britain by Clays Ltd, Elcograf S.p.A.

For Yvonne

Who assures me that the word 'practice'

is interchangeable with the word 'practise'.

and that 'practize' is a big no-no

This Page Left Blank Deliberately

No Really ! It was deliberate.

Contents

Author's note: In writing this book, I haven't dumbed down my language. I haven't written what I think you want to hear. I have said it all - how it is. I have left the long words in. No apologies... PDS

Introduction

Like many free-thinkers, I never usually bother to read a book's introductory chapter. There are many reasons. One is my indolent laziness. The other is that I want to get on and hit the important stuff as soon as possible. And so, I'm going to assume you are like me and want to get this over and done with as soon as possible. I've written the "Antidote to Introductions" which is far more fun. Let's "crack-on"…

Many people say they want to be a vet at some point in their lives. The unlucky few actually succeed…

In 2015, I surveyed over 250 vets and vet students as part of the Veterinary Personality Project (VPP) (Stevens, 2015). The survey had two parts - the first was designed to evaluate their individual personality types. The second part of the survey investigated their well-being and also their views on being a vet. Some of the data from the VPP survey was surprising. Both in terms of the vets' Personality Traits and also on the many revelations the participants revealed regarding their professional and personal lives. And their health. It seemed churlish not to include them all in this book.

The soft squidgy bits

Being a Vet in the 21st Century is all about the people. Particularly those young folks who want to become vets. (And their mums). It's about the people training to be vets and it's about those lucky ones who *are* actually *Being a Vet*. We are going to examine the career of *Being a Vet* and the many parts of the industry that affect a vet's life. But please note - we are not going to look at X-Ray machines, surgical techniques, or even Radiographs. We are not going to talk about fluffy bunnies or how 'wonderful' *Being a Vet* vet must be because vets "spend all day caring for cuddly kittens and poorly pets". No - we are going to look at what *Being a Vet* means for the *real* people who are actually physically involved in the day to day work.

We are going to discuss what *real people* can expect from a life working in the Veterinary Industry - both in terms of their satisfaction, and their happiness. We will touch on education - both at school and at university - and will reveal how changes of educational policy are impacting the lives of *new-vets*. We will reflect on the flood of venture capital that is having such an impact on day-to-day clinical vet practice, and we're going to 'do some economics' and historical social philosophy as it affects our clients - those troublesome owners of the animals we all care for so much. We'll look at *Being a Vet* through the eyes of the vets, the students and consider the aspirations of young folk who fancy a life of vetting. Then, maybe over a cup of coffee, we'll plumb our new-found knowledge about *vet-people* and see if it's possible to get a better fit. "Do the right people become vets?" How can we make sure they do?

Spoiler Alert !

We 'kick-off' in the first chapter - the longest one of the lot - with a psychological evaluation of our vets in terms of their Personality Traits - using scientific and academically derived psychological evaluations. Using that information, we discuss how to recognise those people who may be best suited to the veterinary life. With luck, we will help those people who may be at risk of *not being suited* to vet work by encouraging them to stop what they are doing - and think. Maybe they can take the opportunity to reassess their life-choices. It's never too late.

Through the eyes of these people - who we now hopefully understand better - we talk about how vets are made. Then we'll take a look at the business of vetting and also the changing relationship between 'the public' and so-called experts. It would be amiss of us not to look at how *Being a Vet* is changing and what the *new-vets* who graduate from university have to look forward to. The book concludes with a view on the future of an increasingly pressured veterinary profession. Oh yes. And we consider some ideas on how to be happy as a vet...

It's a thinly veiled warning...

TV, Social Media, Teachers and most "Influencers" present the vet profession with a sentimentalised blancmange made up of smiling & friendly vets, gentle cuddly nurses & people's adorable pets. This is all fantasy. Of course it is - just think about it for a moment:

As many as 5% of all vets have considered suicide. Many more are clinically depressed. Many are exhausted. We are going to learn that almost 40% of Vet Practices in the UK are now owned by corporate entities - largely funded by American venture capital. And that figure is climbing exponentially. Most *new-vets* are female - the men are long gone. And this major demographic change is having a significant impact on staffing and the vets' quality of life:

In reality, many *real-vets* work 10 or 12 hour days - often without a break. Many feel socially and professionally isolated. Practice managers now micro-manage their vets' every move and decision. And few vets receive much in return. Train-drivers and teachers get paid more than most vets. They get more support. They rarely get attacked.

This is not a manual on how to be a vet. Nor is it a grumpy treatise on how bad it all is nowadays. It is simply an invitation to stop and think:

Too many people have made choices that don't prioritize their personal needs, and are now suffering both physically and mentally. Too many young vets have donned their blinkers and jumped onto a veterinary *career escalator* at too young an age. They 'wake up' 10 years later in a stuffy consultation room in Rugeley - unhappy, stressed, and pretty much incapable of doing anything else in their lives other than *Being a Vet.*

It's not all bad though: Most vets have found their perfect job. They love every day of their professional lives. I salute them. But a very large proportion of working vets don't love every day. And that is a lot of vets.

Why am I writing this book? Surely no-one wants to read a depressing book when they can deceive themselves by reading about positive upbeat vets rejoicing in their every decision? Vets who wear muddy boots, drive a Subaru and carry a knowing smile on their lips. The answer? I am writing this book because no-one else is. The vet profession is injured. The people in charge (and the ones with the loudest voices) are running scared and seem to think a few glossy photos of smiling vets, serious surgeons, and cuddly puppies will heal its woes.

Being a Vet in the 21st Century is an antidote to this saccharine and misdirection. Being a vet has always been hard. It's hard to train; hard to do. But that doesn't mean *you* should do it. Just because you like a challenge and look forward to a struggle doesn't mean this is your only option. I want you to see vetting for what it is. And what it may become. You only get one life. I don't want you to make the wrong choices.

I hold my hands up: I have written a personal tract and not a dispassionate primer. But I have made every attempt to correctly reference its content. In the References and Bibliography sections, you'll find over 150 titles - most of them peer-reviewed research papers. There is some personal opinion - obviously. Most of which can be corroborated with a cursory internet search. And if not, then phone up a vet at 6.52pm on a Friday evening and ask them for their opinion on what you just read...

Dear Rosie (our aspirational (now) 16½ year old),

> *I am writing this book for you - you fortunate and lucky youth - who still has the time and opportunity to re-evaluate your choices. I am writing this book for your Mum because she has a duty to say to you,*
>
> *Why do you want to be a vet Rosie? Why?*

Rosie, *"There may be a better way for you to fulfill your dreams. Please stop and think."*

Instead of rushing headlong into being a vet, stop and consider some alternatives. How about one of these? :

→ Join an African Water Charity and improve living standards in a poor village. Help the inhabitants to embrace tourism, so they begin to recognize that killing their natural resources (elephants; tigers; forests) is a short term route to starvation and cultural desertification.

→ Or join an international Police-Force and slow down the international smuggling of animal-products. Or

→ Become a journalist and write about stray dogs in Romania who have their spines broken so they can be sold to misinformed, mis-educated and faux-sentimental do-gooders in the UK for large amounts of money.

→ Do a history degree and climb onto the managerial ladder. Then land the job of Boss of a large animal charity. You'll very soon be invited to be Animal Welfare Tsar and then maybe you'll have real impact on animals - not a vet degree in sight!.

→ Become a dog groomer.

→ Do science and learn *gene-splicing*. You'll have a greater impact on global animal welfare than you ever will as a vet working in Basingstoke.

→ *Become male*, and own lots of vet businesses. That will give you enough money to improve the working conditions of your employees. Then they will be happy, the business will be profitable, and you can do loads of Pro-bono welfare work from the deck of your yacht.

Spoiler Alert: Cuddly kittens and perky puppies will not be a feature of this book. But if you are strong enough to be a vet, then you should be strong enough to read this vision of vetting reality. There are *very* few people in the veterinary profession who are prepared to give you a real insight into what it's like *Being a Vet*.

Clarification Alert: In this book I am mainly talking about clinical vets. Namely the majority of university vet graduates who go on to examine and treat animals in their first 3-5 years after university.

Many vets opt for other roles after a few years of treating animals - management;

government inspection; pharmaceutical vet; etc. But pretty well all of them start off by being a clinical vet…

I have been a practicing clinical vet for the last 35 years. I have worked in many different vet practices in that time, and have owned two. To paraphrase *The Wonderful Wizard of Oz*,

> *I used to blow trumpets and whistles. I would wave flags and waft smoke.*
> *Now I have decided it is time to pull the curtain back…*

PDS 2019

Chapter 1 : Part 1

Do you have the right Personality to be a Vet?

You may be thinking this is a strange first chapter for a book that is hoping to inform you about *Being a Vet*. Here's why we are starting with personality:

*Being a Vet in the 21*st *Century* is a book born from my personal experience as a practicing vet. And it has to be said: *Vets are very different from the rest of the population.* (You, dear reader, may not know this - yet. (Which is really the point of this book. Durr). This chapter is going to show you that vets *are* a different sort of people.)

I'll start by admitting that I used to think vets were weird. I wasn't sure why. I knew I was a bit strange, and I thought that should explain why *all other* vets were strange too. This quote from a vet in Mastenbroek's (2010) research into the Vet Profession seemed to back my ideas up,

> *I'm not saying we're* [the veterinary profession] *particularly wonderful, we're just particularly odd..."*

They are in fact a special type of person with rare and unusual gifts. But it remains very important to recognise this *difference:* 'Being a Vet' and doing the work of a vet is extremely complex. I'm not just referring to the 'animal thing', but also the fact that being a vet is emotionally and intellectually *demanding*. A vet needs to have huge dedication and focus. This is not a job that you can half do!

And if you have decided to be a vet; or you are already studying; or you are just qualified; then to be *successful* and to *remain healthy and happy* enough to stay being a vet, you will need certain qualities:

And it comes as no surprise that there is no single 'quality' you need to be a happy vet. That would be too easy. There's little doubt though that being *different from the rest* certainly seems to be a factor. We are going to dig down into that idea by looking at personality, people's strengths and weaknesses, and the effects of 'being a vet't on their personal health and happiness.

Why do I say that vets are different?

When people ask me what it's like being a vet - and this happens *a lot* to most vets - I usually respond first by explaining the mechanics of the job: I talk about working in the surgery; meeting clients; the working day; the rewards and the costs. Sometimes I'll nuance my answers with funny stories; I'll talk about my team, the vets and nurses. I'll give glimpses… It was a lifetime of these questions that sparked my interest in writing this book: When trying to answer this question, I would invariably end up talking about the vets themselves. I'd say vets are amazing people with possibly the most difficult job in the world. I would nod sagely,

> *"but they are <u>all</u> a bit weird" I would say.*

I could never back this observation up. I just sensed it. Some friends say I was describing myself. And as I admitted earlier, I hold my hands up to that too.

Then one day, a friend wanted me to drill down into my "vets are weird" assertion. And I struggled to do so. I muttered something about 'being on the spectrum', the Asperger's Scale and 'borderline Autism'. I tried to create a coherent argument, but had nothing to back it up.

So one day, a couple of years ago, I decided to dig down into what 'weird' could mean. The first stop was to assume 'weird' is a description of a person's personality. I asked myself, *"What is 'Personality'?"* Does it actually exist, or is it just some *Psychobabble Quackery*? Can personality be categorized and measured? And if it *is* a science of sorts, and if it turns out vets share similar traits between them, then the big question could be,

> *"Could this knowledge help to make Being a Vet better?"*

Personality : The science of measurable traits

The investigation and classification of personality is a robust science. It really is. There are hoards of bearded folk in white coats who spend their careers watching people through one-way mirrors... They are scientists, and they are looking for research data that can be measured and *reproduced*. They are trained to deal with information that can be put into a graph or a table. It is this aspect of data which ensures that science is science. It must be *reproducible, applicable* and *reliable*.

I don't want to bore you with a justification of the science of Personality Traits here. Nor with too much detail on how it works. So I have put all that stuff in an *Appendix* at the end of the book. You are welcome to skim through that to give you a better understanding of this complex area.

It's worth noting at this point that many of my readers will probably be qualified vets who are trained in *hard science*. These illustrious and highly trained scientists will be most comfortable with research results that can be measured in laboratories. They want results that can be tabulated, and then verified using statistical and ethical academic tests. Part of the rigour of good science is that experimental results should be *repeatable*. I suspect many vets who have never considered the psychology of personality as a science will at this point be turning away, muttering,

> *"What utter nonsense. Where are your crystals, your divining sticks, your tarot cards?".*

Which is fair enough until you realise just how much scientific work has actually been conducted on the investigation and categorization of personality. I have read upwards of 100 *scientific peer-reviewed papers* on the subject as part of my research. Tedious it might be, but it is certainly rigorous. I have no doubt that it's as *hard* a science as any other - it's peer reviewed, statistically robust, reproducible, etc.

Weirdness - a history

My continued use of the word "weird" is not sustainable - unfortunately. It's obviously highly *subjective*, and possibly somewhat *discriminatory*. I suspect most vets will object to it. Which could be fun in a way… I promise that from this point, I will be less excitable and I will 'harden' the science: So, instead, let's say:

> *"a statistically significant proportion of the people working as vets share some specific personality traits in a higher proportion than do the general population"* Veterinary Personality Project, (2015).

There are currently 30-35,000 vets living in the UK, which is about 0.03% of the population (3 in every 10,000). Which is a tiny number: Even that fact alone tells us vets are indeed very special and unusual, and they have lots of things *in common*. I know I haven't yet made the argument persuading you of the *unusualness* of vets, but if we accept that vets are rare - at the very least - then a good starting point may be:

> *"Do you have to be different to be a vet? Or does being a vet make you different?"*

This is why determining a proto-vet's Personality Trait Profile could be amazing:

Wouldn't it be wonderful if there was a way of determining if a person were *suited* to being a vet before they *even started training*? I have to admit this is very close to my heart and has in fact been the driving force that has helped me to complete this book: I despair everyday in the vet practice when I see young vets apparently unhappy and stressed by their life choices.

So when a thirteen year-old Rosie touches her mum on the shoulder one day after school and says,

> *"I want to be a vet"*

then if we had a *pre-test* of some sort, her Mum could say,

> *"That's fabulous dear. Here take this test and let's see if Being a Vet will suit you…".*

Because the world is not yet using my *So-You-Want-2-Be-a-Vet Test,* the single-minded-Rosie has to spend the next 4 years at school cramming her A-Levels. And then the next 5 years blindly cramming at a university Vet School. She will wake up 10 years later - in a small examination room in *Rugeley* - realising that at the age of 24 years she's not in the least suited to a vetting life. The reality of vetting *always* comes as a complete surprise to the newly qualified! If Rosie had taken the *So-You-Want-2-Be-a-Vet Test* at the age of 14 years, she would have discovered *right at the start of her journey* that there was every likelihood she wouldn't be happy as a grown-up vet - even if she really *really really really did* want to be a vet and "help animals". If there were a reliable screening test, then she could take this information, and supported by her parents and advisors, she could have made her *first major positive mature decision about her future* - fully informed.

The So-You-Want-2-Be-a-Vet Test

Obviously this is not (yet) an actual test. But if it were, the first section would test your *personal* suitability to being a vet. Later sections would test *skills; tenacity; trainability; etc.* The starting point *should* be a person's personality. So, do I have the right personality to be a vet?

Let's cut to the chase. This is the main reason why you are reading this chapter after all!

> *The 13 year-old Rosie is asking, "Do I have the right personality to be a vet?"*
>
> *The 29 year-old vet Svetlana is asking, "Does my personality mean I am weird?"*
>
> *The 24 year-old newly qualified vet Sophie is asking, "Why am I so stressed and unhappy. Why do I hate every day so much"?*
>
> *19 year old Sam is asking, "How do I look with my new stethoscope around my neck?"*

Let's start by trying to determine what personalities vets *actually have.* The answers may give us an insight into *what works* and what doesn't… I'm going to start by investigating the personalities of current vets. If we can get an idea of what personality traits practicing vets favour, then perhaps we can better determine the answer to Rosie's and Svetlana's questions…

THE VETERINARY PERSONALITY PROJECT 2015

In 2015, I ran a survey which targeted practicing vets and vet students. I used the *Big5's* set of preferences. There are several accepted systems for measuring personality traits scientifically - I chose the one we call the *Big5*. The *Big5 Personality trait indicator* asks the subject (person) a series of questions, and five trait results are produced from their answers. The five traits are *measures* of Conscientiousness; Agreeableness; Openness to Experience; Neuroticism; and Extraversion. The Veterinary Personality Project (Stevens, 2015)(VPP) survey also asked the vets a bunch of other questions - questions relating to their work experiences, well-being, type of work, hopes and aspirations, etc.

The survey was answered by over 230 people. Which is not bad for a research work that wasn't supported by a big organisation. See the Appendices at the end of the book for a precautionary note on Self Selection Surveys. Also at the end of the book, I've reviewed the results in more detail. Here, we'll just deal with the interesting stuff.

Personality Traits of Vets (VPP 2015)

Have a look at the graphic of the VPP results for each of the 5 personality traits in our vets on the next page (Fig.1):

Here's an explanation of this graphic:

If you don't like graphs, then read on. (If that doesn't help either, then you need a new maths teacher!) The bottom scale is age groups. 18-21 year olds, then 22-25 year olds etc. The scale up the left is from 0 to 100 and measures the personality trait result - that is, how much a person has of each trait. A result of 50 equates to 50% of the population. For example, a Neuroticism score of 50 means a person is average for the population (not just vets - it is the average for about ½ million people globally who have completed the Big5 test so far).

Let's look at Conscientiousness (Definition: orderly; dutiful; self-disciplined; determined; competent; achievement-orientated.)

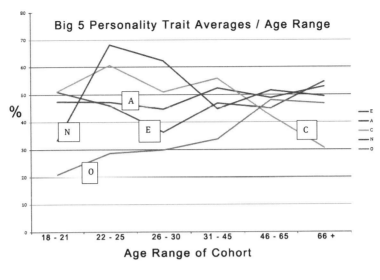

Fig.1. *VPP 2015 Personality Trait Results*

Conscientiousness (C) in vets

Look at the graph which shows the VPP results for vets: The 21 year olds show a Conscientiousness average of 50% - which is average for the general population. The 22-25 year old group have a higher result. These are the final year students and newly qualified vets. The first few 2 or 3 years after leaving University are *very very* hard. New vets usually feel a great responsibility in their new *professional* role and the vast majority will do just about anything, and make every effort, to do the job right. This then is evidence that this age group of final year students and working vets are perhaps making a conscious effort to *increase* their daily *conscientiousness*. They would do this presumably in order to do the job more safely and effectively? Perhaps in the hope that nothing goes wrong.

There is no doubt it's possible to 'up your game' with conscientiousness for a period of time. But inevitably, over time, a person will revert to their *innate* level of conscientiousness - especially when they get tired or stressed. Similarly, it is possible to artificially *subdue* one's Conscientiousness score when circumstances demand it. Again, there will always be pressure to allow one's C score to return back up to its norm value.

The graph shows that within the next age group - up to 30 years old - the levels of Conscientiousness are lower. They stabilise at a level lower than the general population (low 40s). Now that's something you wouldn't have thought possible - a vet (hero and all-round-good-egg) who is actually less conscientious than Mr Average ! (I have a possible explanation later in this chapter where I explain self-actualization. Or maybe these people are artificially reducing (subduing) their C levels in order to maintain their function in an environment that is hostile to high levels of conscientiousness.)

To maintain some element of mental and physical well-being, many vets (probably subconsciously) allow their average 'excellence' (*conscientiousness*) to be slowly eroded as the years pass. At some point, they find a level where it's possible to do the job "well-enough" and at a quality they are reasonably comfortable with. This erosion of the "need for quality" translates into the gradual decrease in *Conscientiousness* reported in *The VPP survey*. Obviously, it doesn't take much psychological knowledge to see that those vets that *don't allow* their conscientiousness to slip back to their personal innate levels are at risk of extreme exhaustion that comes from over-work - at best. There's a risk that exhaustion can lead to *fatigue and burnout or worse.* And this is the nub of this chapter's message. Later we talk about what traits can help you be a 'good' vet, but for that information to help, first a vet has to be happy and healthy: Fatigue, depression and burnout will always make a vet unhappy - however 'good at being a vet' they are.

Burnout is a term we'll talk about later in this chapter. There is also an Appendix at the end of the book to give you more detail. Suffice to say that Burnout is a measurable (and predictable) state of mind. It is a form of depression and it usually follows on from mental exhaustion. It is used by psychologists to signpost an increased risk of suicide and self-harm. *This* is why burnout is important.

Neuroticism (N). Possibly the most impactful Trait on being a happy vet

The name given to this personality trait is the only one of the 5 traits that has a negative popular association: (A 'neurotic' is regarded as having an uncontrolled nervousness, extreme anxiety, and they can appear unstable. Possibly even mentally ill).

But the term *Neuroticism,* as it is used in the *Big5* test, actually refers to the tendency to "*experience negative feelings*". The higher the N score, the more likely *minor events* are regarded by the person as being hopeless. Or indeed, a person can regard events as being more *important* than they should be. People with high Neuroticism scores are 'sensitive' or 'nervous'. They exhibit more self-conscious and anxious behaviour, and they generally

---

Personality Traits and Time

Our VPP survey is only a snapshot in time. It reflects fairly accurately what the vets in each age group prefer in terms of trait type. But we have to be careful in assuming that, for example, the 26-30 year group will take on the 31-45 year-old group's characteristics in 5-10 years time. This is not a so-called longitudinal study (those studies run over time and are employed in order to see how people change as the years go pass. We are not measuring that). The survey simply tells us what each age group currently contains 'today'.

There has been research to suggest that the type of person entering the profession is changing (Johnson, 2009). This research suggests that our 26-30 year-olds will never share the same trait scores as our older vets. This suggests that new vets are actually a significantly different type of person altogether...

---

have a predisposition to worry. Higher levels of this 'anxiety' can lead to envy, moodiness and can contribute to social isolation.

What happens as we get older?

In the work place, people with higher Neuroticism scores tend to be better in training - meaning they are easier to train up to a high level. This is even easier if they have a low Extraversion score (Chamorro-Premuzic, 2010). (Being 'better in training' is obviously a very very useful ability for vet students and for career-vets.)

High Neuroticism helps them cope with the intensity and high work-load of vet training and also with their lifelong 'keeping up to date' - which we call 'continuing professional development' (CPD). High train-ability is therefore good for students. It is also good for vets who take further qualifications (often embarked upon by vets in their late 20s and mid 30s once they have survived their first 5-8 years in the job). But let's remember that train-ability doesn't help a newly qualified vet as she struggles to make a useful diagnosis whilst holding a scratchy cat. Now that she's working, she needs a different set of 'strengths'.

Another feature of people with high N trait scores is they are easier and quicker to "arouse". This means that they perform well in jobs that are largely boring and repetitive, but which make occasional extreme demands of concentration and skill. These are jobs such as air traffic controllers, athletes, soldiers, and A&E Doctors. And vets. (It could be said that the bulk of vet work is mundane - or at the very least, repetitive. It is commonly interspersed with sudden and exciting life-or-death challenges.)

Easy-Box : On 'Well-being'

: the state of being happy healthy and comfortable.

It reflects the balance of good and bad in a life. It can be subdivided further into mental well-being, physical, social, etc.

Well-being is attributed to the balance between life's *demands* and *resources*

When the *demands* are low and the *resources* high, then everything is great. If it's the reverse - *demands* are high and there are low *resources*, then well-being becomes poor - which leads to stress. Which leads to illness and / or burnout.

Demands - these are the demands of life - in work or ones personal life.

Resources- these are the available sources of help, support, autonomy, self-determination, safety, etc. For example. *The Demand:* Your employer wants you to paint a room in 2 hours. *The Resources:* He only gives you a small paint-brush and thin paint and then turns his phone off. *The result is Well-being* plummets: You get tired. Angry. Frustrated. You know you will fail…

Well-being can be reliably measured. Rather like personality trait assessments, well-being is measured by asking questions. The answers attract a score - and the overall score gives an impression of a person's well-being. In the VPP, we used the UK National Health Service's Well-Being Self-Assessment Measure (now re-branded as Mood Self-Assessment).

The Neuroticism trait appears to be a particularly important one for the vet role: In the *VPP survey*, Neuroticism trait results are noticeably higher than the general population for the vet age groups up to mid forties.

Why is Neuroticism so important in vets? Health and Well-being.

We could put this question the other way around and ask why so many vets have high Neuroticism scores. A simple metaphysical answer to this question could be that,

> *"to be able to be a vet; or to want to be a vet, you need to have a high N score."*

I have no doubt that upon reading that comment, a host of practicing vets are running to their computer to find their own trait scores. Then they'll write (or *TwitFace*) a searing indictment of my opinions. I do love a bit of criticism…

Let's turn back to the *actual* N scores of those vets who are currently in their 20s and early 30s. Research has shown that N scores relate *directly* to well-being scores. And well-being scores are very closely related to mental health. If you read our Appendix on burnout at the end of the book, you'll also see that N is inversely related to a person's ability to *resist* burnout and also to other forms of mental strain and illness. (The higher the N score the lower a person's resistance to burnout.) Thus it appears that burnout and its related illnesses are *hard-wired* into some individuals. And amazingly we can measure

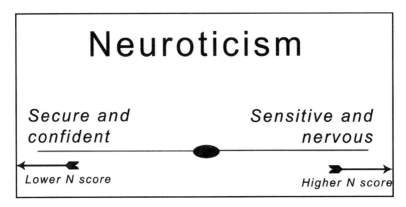

this through the *Big5* personality trait Neuroticism score:

> *The higher a person's score of N, the more susceptible a person is to illness and burnout.*

Burnout is only one measure of the 'failure of well-being'. Depression is another. Unhappiness another. And so on.

The remaining Personality Traits - A, E, and O.

Look at the graph (Fig.1) again - it's our VPP survey 2015 results for vets:

Agreeableness, Extraversion and Openness are noticeably lower for some age-groups of vet. In the analysis, the 2015 VPP survey suggested no direct links between these three traits and a vet's performance or their health or well-being. Having said that, these 3 traits do have some indirect influence on how a vet performs. To a small extent, these traits can be protective against the negative effects of other trait excesses. I'm not going to dwell on these 3 traits for long.

A note on generalizations

Let's not forget I am making huge generalizations throughout this book. There is no way that ALL vets are exactly the same. Some will be at one end of a scale and some at the other. I am talking about the MEAN = The average vet - the 80% bell-curve bunch of people - (ask your Maths teacher!)

Agreeableness (A)

Agreeableness is markedly low in our 22-25 year olds. The effect of *high* levels of Agreeableness is a person would be trusting; straight-forward; compliant; modest; tender-minded. *Low* Agreeableness is the opposite of these things: distrusting; pedantic; obstructive; disagreeable; etc.

Highly stressed newly-qualified vets in their first frantic years learning the job perhaps don't have the space in their day to be *nice* - even if their *innate* Agreeableness score is actually higher than they are feeling at the time. It's little wonder they occasionally snap and shout at their colleagues. Or can't find the energy to smile at Tyson's owner as he chews a hole in their arm.

The graph (Fig.1) suggests older vets may have found their innate agreeableness again after a few years on the job - or just that they are a different set of people Trait-wise. Interestingly, research shows that throughout a person's life, people with a high (innate) Agreeableness score are protected to some extent against burnout (Piedmont, 1993). This can be explained by suggesting that highly agreeable people are more easily satisfied "with their lot". They tend to be less likely to question their position or status, and so are more accepting of "their situation". This is a form of 'resilience' (more of which later in the book). Resilience helps vets to retain more physical and mental energy in the face of adversity - which then helps to get them through the day…

Extraversion (E)

The definition of high levels of E is a person is warm; gregarious; assertive; active; emotionally positive; excitement seeking. The *VPP survey* shows the average E in vets to be slightly lower than the general population. People with lower E tend to have higher N. Therefore a high score for Extraversion can be *protective* for burnout (because of the relationship that higher E means a *lower* N). The paradox here is that many people who choose a career based around animals are in fact, to some extent, rejecting human interaction (otherwise they may chose to be medical doctors? Possibly. There's no evidence for this one. *Ed.*). And so people who choose to be a vet are often less gregarious, less outward looking and are therefore more likely to have *lower* E scores.

Openness to Experience (O)

The definition of higher levels of Openness to Experience : Such a person is Inventive; liberal; artistic; action orientated - the higher the trait score, the more likely you are going to be *up for* parachuting / skiing / extreme linguistics.

This trait appears to have little impact on a vet's career success. It doesn't seem to matter much if a vet's trait score is low, high, or average. Having said that, vets with a lower O tend to be more consistent and cautious. They may be at less risk of boredom associated with the job's necessarily repetitive tasks. Take a look at the Ethics and Morals section later in this chapter for more on O.

Let's go back to Conscientiousness and link it with how clever a person is : General Mental Ability (GMA)

Conscientiousness is one of the two most influential traits for a vet's career and personal performance (the other is N as we just discovered). Remember, Conscientiousness is a measure of motivation; tidiness; personal organisation. Higher C scores are found in *perfectionists*. People with low C scores are easy-going; careless even.

Let's think about another aspect of being a vet that compliments the Conscientiousness trait category. In particular, a vet's **"cleverness"**.

> *"I wanted to be a vet but I just wasn't clever enough."* I've heard it a thousand times.

One of the measures of *intelligence* that psychologists use is GMA (*General Mental Ability*). This is the ability to reason; to plan; and to solve problems. It measures abstract thinking and the ability to comprehend complex ideas. People with a high GMA are able to *learn quickly* and also to learn from experience. They can predict the outcomes of 'good and bad behaviours' which is particularly interesting as this refers to moral and ethical issues (more later in this chapter). GMA is a great predictor of job performance - unlike the IQ test which is felt to be a bit wordy and too narrow in its investigations (Chamorro-Premuzic, 2010). GMA is a great predictor for jobs that are more complex, unpredictable and require independent judgement - that's *Being a Vet* then!

> *(GMA is not the IQ test!!).*

> *GMA and Conscientiousness have a strong relationship: High GMA scores - suggest a can do attitude. High Conscientiousness - a will do attitude.*

GMA is a great predictor of ability - and in parallel, Conscientiousness provides the *motivation* to perform and complete the tasks and solve the problems. These two factors in combination can be very powerful:- *"thus superstars are born".*

Many of you will be pleased to hear that women generally score higher Conscientiousness than men (Rubenstein, 2005). Within the *Big5* test, high levels of conscientiousness are associated with a sense of duty/responsibility, order and self-discipline. So women scoring higher C than men makes some kind of sense. Having said that, women's role in society has changed hugely in the last 60 years, so whether these new "social (and auto-perspective) freedoms" have any impact on vets' personality traits and their interpretations has yet to be seen (or measured).

Being a clinical vet - by which I mean actually doing the work - making diagnoses; dispensing drugs; performing surgery; writing accurate clinical notes; etc, you would *want* a vet to be highly conscientious wouldn't you? Most vets see themselves as such… But having a medium/high Conscientious Personality Trait score is slightly different from being *able* to be conscientious at work as we discussed earlier.

So, what personality should I have to be a vet?

This is the end of the discussion on *Big5* personality traits. (More stuff in the Appendices). So we should by now have an idea of what *real* vets working in the UK are like. We have also talked about which traits make for happier, healthier and more effective vets: So we can now make an attempt at answering the question above - albeit somewhat simplistically:

> **Medium Conscientiousness** is best. Not too low or you will find most of your patients will die and you won't care. And you won't bother trying to improve either. Also high C scores are linked with unhealthy *perfectionism* (read the later sections in this chapter) so we don't really want that either. Medium C means you will be a *good enough* vet. Doesn't sound sexy, but maybe it's sufficient?

> **Medium to low Neuroticism** is best. It means you will *care* but not too much. It means you will look after your well-being and will have a happier life.

> **Medium to high Agreeableness** means your clients will love you - if that's your *thing*. Higher Extraversion may keep you healthy by *getting you out more* - socializing etc.

If that isn't enough for you - and it shouldn't be - read Part 2 of this chapter coming up next for much more information on how people with these personality characteristics actually manage within the vet industry. We are going to talk about health and happiness of vets and we're going to do some psychology. It's interesting and a lot of fun. Trust me.

> *"Cripes, not more stuff about whinging and whining vets. I'm sick of reading about those unhappy young things. In my day we were tough. We just got our head down and got on with it. We just got thrown in at the deep end"*

If this is you, then Chapter 1 : Part 2 is a must-read. It will amuse and inform. It will appeal to your less than empathic approach to colleagues...

Chapter 1 : Part 2

Well-Being - Health and Happiness

Other aspects of personality as they relate to well-being and health

In the previous section we discussed Personality Traits as they apply to the vets who are working in the profession currently. We touched on the significance of how these traits influence performance. In this next section, we'll be more specific about the psychological, functional and health implications of a person's personal personality trait combinations.

Changing Demographics and consequences for Personality Traits

The School of Veterinary Medicine, Louisiana, USA (LSU) (Johnson, 2009) hosted some research on the changing traits of their first-year vet student-intake over a period of 12 years. They used the *MBTI* (Myers-Briggs Trait Indicator) trait assessment (not our *Big5* system unfortunately: see Appendices for more detail on our choice). Despite this, there is value in mentioning it here as it may make our discussion of difference and *change* over time a bit clearer.

LSU's work revealed a marked difference between their male and women students - in terms of the MBTI's *Thinking / Feeling* trait (These are opposite ends of the same trait. A person manifests *either* Thinking or Feeling. It's a bit like a see-saw with *Feeling* at one end and Thinking at the other. So if you have more *Feeling*, then you automatically have less Thinking. And vice versa.) Put simply, the men were biased towards Thinking. Women 'preferred' more *Feeling* traits.

To add to this bias in women towards *Feeling* traits, the LSU research also revealed that the women applying to vet university in 2007 were significantly different from those applying in 1996. Notably, they discovered that more women applying in 2007 'favoured' *Feeling* than those women applying in 1996.

Additionally, there were more women than men applying to Vet School in 2007 than in 1996. So this is a triple-whammy for women vets : they are women (!); there are more women vets now; and the women becoming vets have higher *Feeling* traits than women training to be vets in the past.

This is important because it means that *new-vets* are more *Feeling* than vets used to be. They have different priorities, and different ways of doing things. In fact, they are a different type of person altogether.

The significance of this information is that with more vets favouring the *Feeling* trait, there is a broad change in *new-vets'* relationship with their job. Here is the description of these two traits in the MBTI's own words (Martin 1997):

> *The test result:- I prefer the Thinking (T) trait :*
>
> When I make a decision, I like to find the basic truth or principle to be applied, regardless of the specific situation involved. I like to analyze pros and cons, and then be consistent and logical in deciding. I try to be impersonal, so I won't let my personal wishes--or other people's wishes--influence me.

> *Or this test result:- I prefer the Feeling (F) trait :*
>
> I believe I can make the best decisions by weighing what people care about and the points-of-view of persons involved in a situation. I am concerned with values and what is the best for the people involved. I like to do whatever will establish or maintain harmony. In my relationships, I appear caring, warm, and tactful.

The significance of this is that vets who have more *Feeling* traits will be more emotionally connected to their work and to clients than those favouring the *Thinking* trait. They may feel more affected when an animal is ill, or dies. These vets may be more expressive with client's animals - loving and petting them. They may squeal with delight when a puppy arrives in the waiting room. They often give their clients hugs when their pets are ill.

This all sounds fine in theory - the clients love them! But this will put them at risk. They are inevitably more susceptible to stress, emotional exhaustion and therefore to burnout. Such a vet can only be bubbly and cheerful for so long before their emotional batteries run dry:

> For example, vets often have days when they have to euthanase 3 or 4 animals. They may be treating 10 or 15 very ill animals whose owners are extremely worried and upset. The *Feeling* vet is going to actively support these clients by *sharing* the client's emotions. This can be very costly for them - from an emotional point of view. The risk is that these vets *overextend* their emotional giving to the client.

If the client were to *give back* to the vet somehow, then maybe the vet would be OK, but most clients are focused on themselves in these situations and their own 'pain'. They assume the vet will support them through difficult times. So these over-extended vets have to cope with their own emotional upset alone. *Resilience* is vital to their emotional health, but people who favour *Feeling* tend to lack this strength. Vets who favour *Thinking* traits are more protected from the risk of *emotional exhaustion* and *burnout* because they maintain an emotional distance from their work. They don't take on their clients' strains and emotional angst so much. These are the vets that clients describe as being a bit 'cold', 'distant' or 'hard'.

MBTI - Too Simplistic (more in the Appendices)

The *MBTI* really sounds like it describes a vet 'to a T' doesn't it? Loving and warm. Caring and cuddly. Who would not want their vet to be like that? But it is way too simplistic - people aren't just one thing or another! And more importantly, the *MBTI* doesn't correlate with mental health and well-being - and so is of little use to us in this book.

The *MBTI* is what the client *sees*.

The *Big5* reveals what the vet *is*.

So don't do a *MBTI* test - it won't help your decisions much.

Vets with high *Feeling* traits look like they love their job, and they love to cuddle the puppies. Because they are so lovely, no-one realises they are *flying on fumes* - eventually the engine will stop, and they will plummet to earth.

Notes on Self-Actualization - a supreme state-of-being

There is another way to look at vets which is less scientific, and more philosophical. It makes for a good read, and so I recommend you carry on. The ideas here can help us to identify and recognise some of the *different* (weird) behaviours of vets. In his book *Motivation and Personality* (1954), the psychologist Abraham Maslow devised an approach to determining a person's motivation. He created a theory that he called the *'Hierarchy of Needs'*.

His theory was that to be human, there is a sequential and additive series of needs. And each individual is comfortable with achieving different levels (Fig.2). The basic level is physiological - food, air, water - and all people have that need. The next one up is 'safety'. Meaning some people need to be safe from danger or threat. The next is 'belonging' - being a member of a tribe, or a family. See the diagram for more detail and also the Appendices. The top-most level is the 'self-actualized' state which can only be achieved once all the other levels have been satisfied. But not everyone aspires to the top level. Some are just happy to be loved (plus being safe plus having their physiological needs met) and have no need at all for esteem for example.

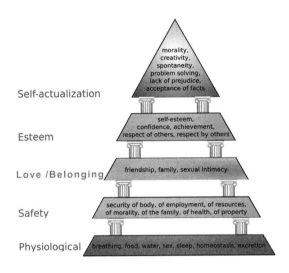

Maslow's Hierarchy of Needs

Fig.2 The Hierarchy of Needs.

Self-Actualization is a term psychologists apply to people who have achieved all the lower levels and now possess a certain *state of mind* and also a *personal relationship* with their world which cannot be much improved upon. Self-actualization suggests that they have achieved the absolute pinnacle of human *personal achievement*. To a degree, it is a 'liberal' term and it could be applied to characters like Superman/Clark Kent very well. Or Azlan or Mr Spock. Or even Albus Dumbledor. It doesn't refer to how sparkly your new car is, or how many horses you own. It's not about material possessions. Self-actualization is a *personal* state. It's about beliefs, values, morals, views, opinions…

Self-actualized people have some or all of the elements listed below: (If you know someone with all or most of the following attributes, then maybe they are self-actualized):

→ They know themselves. They know a fake when they see one. They are less affected by common desires, wishes or fears.

→ They live in the real world. They accept nature as it is. So they are not bothered by pus or faeces - useful for vets.

→ They feel guilt at their own laziness, thoughtlessness, temper, mental or physical ill-health, jealousy etc. And so they are intolerant of it in others. (Many vets reject the idea they could be ill - few seek help and many self-medicate in private.)

→ Self-actualized people may accept a compliment, but will ridicule it afterwards.

→ They are *ethical* by using fundamental principles. They don't follow the herd.

→ They focus on external problems, not their internal ones - which is not good if they are ill.

→ They can appear steady, aloof, calm, and a bit reserved - if you know a vet, you may recognize this.

Given the right motivation, this state of self-actualization can be achieved through hard work. But it isn't really like going to the gym where practise makes perfect. It is more the result of experience and education. It is a state that *is* the person and the person *is* that state.

Why self-actualized people may find Being a Vet attractive

Self-actualized people - or people on the road to achieving that state - may be attracted to the idea of *Being a Vet*. They like hard work. They like to be challenged. They seek roles where their skills can be recognised and they have a strong moral code. But the truth is that *Being a Vet* isn't always that easy, even for self-actualized people:

For example.

- The long hours spent working: Many vets, especially younger ones think about their work when they're at work *and* at home. Even after 30 years, my partner and I discuss clinical cases over the pancakes and coffee on a Sunday morning.

- Vets treat large numbers of animals every hour of every day.

- They have to speak to human clients every hour of every day.

- A vet must *accept* failure when a patient doesn't respond well to treatment.

- And *consider* their own failings when a patient doesn't respond.

- A vet works hard for little *external* reward - salaries are comparatively low for a trained professional.

- And very few clients seem to be grateful - especially for the small stuff that makes up most of a vet's day.

- A vet has to be constantly clinically excellent - a vet can't lose concentration halfway through an operation and pop out for a quick smoke or to check *TwittBook*.

If we propose that many vets share the attributes of a *self-actualized* person, it is easy to see that being forced to follow some of the elements listed on the list above would severely *test* their self-actualized position. For example:

> Working hard is fine for self-actualized people; but talking and explaining to other people is of less interest and so can be challenging;

> Accepting failure is OK for self-actualized vets because it is real to fail. Their problem comes when you have to justify and explain that failure to someone else;

> Working hard for low reward is OK at the beginning but can wear thin because recognition is important to a self-actualized person. Rewards are a form of recognition. (Note that esteem is just below the self-actualized level in the Hierarchy of Needs diagram above.

> Paradoxically, self-actualized people will actually *think less* of the person offering them recognition - despite them needing it. Crazy huh? We all know someone like this - just think about them and how they deal with their lives…

The role of *Being a Vet* is very stressful, and self-actualized people don't look after themselves well (they focus on external problems, not their internal ones). Which may explain why so many vets ignore illnesses in themselves; Why so many vets keep their mental-illnesses secret. Which is not sensible at all.

Impostor Syndrome and Perfectionism can affect a vet's well-being too

We all know what perfectionism is don't we?

- It's the girl who won't go on the play-ground swings unless she is wearing shoes that match her dress.
- It's the artist who refuses to release a painting until it is very very absolutely right.
- It's the scientist who cancels his experiment because he has been asked to substitute Bolivian copper sulphate with Chilean.

In 1998, a psychologist called *Sorotzkin* described a *perfectionist* as

"someone driven by fear of failure [who] strives compulsively towards goals beyond reach or reason."

This description suggests perfectionism is not a good thing. Psychologists have since tempered Soroztkin's somewhat extreme definition and now agree that perfectionists don't *have* to be addictive or obsessive personality types (Hagedorn, 2010).

Many 'normal' people have the belief that they must strive to be physically, intellectually or emotionally 'perfect'. Some are driven by a need to be accepted or loved by others. They think this is only possible if they present a *'perfect'* self to these unsuspecting others. Look at the young girls walking down the road with their perfect plastic make-up. Their perfect clothes. Their perfect way of walking… So the line between perfectionist and "normal" is very blurred.

Extrinsic factors affecting the development of a perfectionist are as important as internal trait influences. They include what is probably the most important factor - expectations: Cultural, social, or peer *expectations*. Namely, what you perceive others expect of you. Raised expectations of *self* are part of life from an early age - the perceived or real expectations of one's friends, parents, teachers, and policemen. *In the right sort of person*, pressures from the external expectations of others can have a large influence on that person's psychological development. So blame your parents, or your friends; or your fellow students.

Psychologists have recognised that many perfectionists come from "biased" backgrounds and childhoods. For example, perfectionism can affect a child who has overly didactic parents (teacher-types) who constantly seek only "the best" from their children. A variation on this are those children who are expected to fulfil their parents' dreams and desires: the kids of *Tiger Moms* or *Power-Moms*.

Psychologists have now realised that to be a perfectionist is not necessarily bad. Sorotzkin was too categorical and hadn't considered the possibility of a *scale* of perfectionism. Psychologists have now acknowledged this scale and have given names to various categories of perfectionism. These help to distinguish *healthy from unhealthy* forms of perfectionism:

> *Adaptive* perfectionists are people who strive for the "perfect" and rejoice in achieving it, but who *are able to tolerate* imperfections in their "perfect" (Stolz, 2007). Their self-esteem remains intact over the medium term.

> *Maladaptive* perfectionists on the other hand strive for the "perfect" too, but they *resort to harsh self-criticism* regarding any failure or imperfections in their achievements. In a word, they *beat themselves up* for not being perfect.

Note the "~ ive" at the end of the two words above. If the word used was "adapted", then it would suggest a person is stable within their perfectionism. Because the word used is *adaptive* then it becomes clear that with a bit of a push, healthy can become unhealthy; and vice versa.

Oh yes. For clarity, to be labelled a *Perfectionist* you don't have to be perfectionist at everything in your life - some people select areas of interest to be perfect in. They may be pretty slap-dash at other stuff. Take me for example - I'm a clinical perfectionist, but I don't care a fig about my clothes. These 'selective perfectionists' are generally well adjusted types - "normalish" in fact. It is only when a person wants to be perfect at everything that things can go wrong.

Maladaptive perfectionism is bad. It can lead to depression, anxiety, guilt, shame, worthlessness etc. It is in fact a predictor of suicide. *Maladaptive* perfectionists *worry*. (Sounds a bit like our people with high Neuroticism scores doesn't it?) 'Worriers' experience chains of negative thoughts and images concerning the outcome of future events. Obsessive Compulsive Disorders; Narcissism; addictive disorders; self-harm; workaholic behaviours; poor health and burnout are all possible outcomes of a drift towards *maladaptive perfectionism.*

Another distinguishing feature of the two types of perfectionism is their different approaches to realising goals. Both *adaptive* and *maladaptive* perfectionists often agree on their goals, but they achieve them differently.

Paradoxically, *Maladaptive Perfectionists* may often employ *avoidance tactics* to avoid even the smallest chance of failure:-

> Here's a Vet Example: Trudy, a three year qualified Vet is a pretty good surgeon. She is accomplished and she has very good surgical results. Recently, she has started to refer more of her complex cases to a referral specialist. It's not obvious why. We think this change followed an unusual run of difficult cases. Or possibly it was when a client reported Trudy's friend, also a vet, to the RCVS. (Royal College of Vet Surgeons - the vets' controlling body.) By referring more and more of her cases to a specialist, perfectionist Trudy has found a way to distance herself from possible failure. This way she is preserving her self-esteem. Unfortunately, over time, avoidance behaviour invariably has a negative feedback onto her self-esteem anyway. So her self-esteem drops nevertheless. (Hanchon, 2011)

The Impostor Syndrome

Which leads me to the connection between perfectionism and **The Impostor Syndrome:** The term "Impostor Syndrome" describes the feelings some high-achieving people experience of *being a fraud* (Sakulku, 2011). It is surprisingly common in high-powered professionals. These feelings tend to be particularly noticeable when performing high-tension / high responsibility roles:

- A person experiencing Impostor Syndrome will be unable to *accept* their own high-level achievements *as their own.*

- Often they will have a persistent fear of being exposed as phonies by colleagues or clients.

- They feel undeserving of praise and will reject or ignore any acknowledgment of their abilities by colleagues and clients.

- They write off any success as *luck*; or with a shrug of the shoulders.

This sounds similar to *maladaptive perfectionism* doesn't it? There is no doubt that perfectionism and Impostor Syndrome are two birds with a similar plumage. And they feed off one another. *Perfectionism* is an achievement ideal, but when it goes wrong, in steps the *Impostor Syndrome*. When a person feels they have not achieved their very best, and yet colleagues and clients still think they are wonderful, then *The Impostor Syndrome* rears its head.

So how is perfectionism and the Impostor Syndrome at all relevant to you being a vet?

Here's how:

- To be a good student, you are encouraged to be better than your class-mates. Competition is encouraged by the current university system (although it is just beginning now to recognise the damage this causes).

- To be a good scientist (a vet) you need to have perfectionist tendencies (science is a precise field. No precision? Then poor science!).

- To be a good vet, you need to have the highest standards - if you lapse just once, an animal dies or at the very least suffers unnecessarily.

- The RCVS demands consistently high standards of behaviour from you.

- The public will assume you are amazing. If you are not, the public are surprisingly quick to veer to the other extreme. They'll soon let you know that you are rubbish…

Some personal stuff:

> For my first twenty years as a vet, I wasn't my true self. In fact I was pretending to be a vet. If I met a client outside the practice I would be tongue-tied and squirmy because I assumed they would need me to know their dog's name, their name, or even my own! But once I was inside the surgery - as soon as I'd put my white coat on - clinical notes in one hand and a thermometer in the other - then I was King. "King Vet" in fact. I was in control; I was erudite, empathic, clear smile, firm hand-shake. I was amazing. Or so my clients seemed to think...

> And what a strain that was. I was classic impostor material. I refused compliments - in fact I internally despised those clients who thought I was amazing - I would ask myself, "What do they know?" "It wasn't my skill they were applauding. I only gave them some tablets! The dog was going to get better anyway... Silly people..."

So why do I now think I experienced Impostor Syndrome?

> I'm a maladaptive perfectionist when it comes to dealing with people. I desire, need and expect any social interaction to be perfect (I need to 'like' the person I'm talking to, and I need them to like me). But the problem is that I read too much into their behaviour. I think they despise me, or I bore them, or I am weak / or fat / or I stumble over my words / and so on. So like any other good maladaptive perfectionist, I practice goal performance avoidance - I avoid people in social settings. Rather than fail, and feel stupid, I don't go to parties. If I am forced into being in a room with more than 3 other people, I stand in a corner, head down - drinking too much. Drinking helps me to feel busy. I'm doing something useful (!) and this makes me feel less obviously a social failure... Pretty messed up huh? Which makes my ability to appear 'amazing' when I'm being a vet very difficult for me to understand. Clients seem to experience or see something special when they're with me. More fool them I say... Which is Impostor Syndrome. See?

So be warned - if you are a perfectionist to the point of obsession and if you are unable to accept being *just-about-good-enough*, then beware - your veterinary road's gonna-get a bit bumpy.

Ethics and Morals. Their relation to the Openness to Experience trait

As we saw earlier, people with a high *General Mental Ability* (GMA) have a better insight into outcomes of 'good and bad behaviours'. Meaning they have a broader view of the implications of scratching their neighbour's car; or of picking up a hitch-hiker (remember those?).

GMA, is the measure adopted by psychologists to measure a person's reasoning power; their ability to solve problems; to comprehend complex and abstract ideas; to learn quickly; and to learn from experience. It is a measure of a person's intellectual curiosity i.e. their ability and desire to understand their surroundings and environment.

Ethics and morals are a set of standards *within which* a person chooses to lead their life (work or leisure - more usually both). Most professional regulatory organisations have a code of ethics that they expect their members to adhere to: *The Royal Institution of Chartered Surveyors (RICS)* says this:

> Behaving ethically is at the heart of what it means to be a professional; it distinguishes professionals from others in the marketplace. They should,

> Act with integrity Always provide a high standard of service Act in a way that promotes trust in the profession Treat others with respect Take responsibility

The *Royal College of Veterinary Surgeons* doesn't use the word ethics any more in its Guide to Professional Conduct, but the document has a similar tone to the RICS when describing what is expected of a Vet:

> *Professional competence*
> *Honesty and integrity*
> *Independence and impartiality*
> *Client confidentiality and trust*

Professional ethics are essentially a set of guidelines formulated by committee. *Personal ethics* on the other hand are a reflection of an individual's *values*. They refer to a person's sense of *right and wrong*.

Research into *General Mental Ability* has found that it is *inversely related* to *deviance*. Sounds dreadful, but this actually means that those people with higher GMA are *less* likely to break local rules and laws - stealing from the stationery cupboard; or being racially abusive; or being overly aggressive in an argument. No one knows quite why this should be:- The somewhat simplistic suggestion is that someone with higher GMA is more *aware* of what they are doing and can *read* the consequences of their actions. A more nuanced explanation is that people with higher GMA are more aware of their *surroundings* and also of their 'place' within their society. They *understand* that a functioning society is largely based upon mutual respect and an inherent agreement to follow that society's rules. Therefore, they are more likely to remain within society's guidelines and so remain living within a set of ethics.

It is as simple as that. Most vets are bright people with high GMA and strong ethical codes both professional and personal. They have a willingness to conform with society's rules. Their conformity in particular resonates with our Vets' average to low Openness to Experience trait scores - conservative and somewhat conventional.

As part of our *So-You-Want-To-Be-A-Vet-Test,* GMA may be useful in developing a signalling mechanism for people who could make good vets. That is to say, those people who will be happy to adopt a life bounded by a strong set of ethics.

The "Animal Thing" - Asperger's Syndrome, Autism and other forms of f**ked-up-ness

What makes a vet choose to spend their careers dealing 'with animals' rather than people? Why don't these 'clever' and highly gifted people become medical doctors instead?

The answer is complex. But if all vets have one thing in common, it is that they primarily *choose* to take responsibility for the welfare of animals. If they chose to care for people, then they would obviously choose some other occupation. Why is this? Here are some dreadfully ill-informed stabs at a solution to that question.

The Animal thing: Attachment theory.

Much psychological research has been done on *Attachment Theory* - in particular the emotional attachments that young people develop with companion animals (Reevya, 2014). Reevya suggests that a child's early experiences of parenting combined with their personality type scores may lead to various forms of *dysfunctional* attachment behaviour:

> **Good.** Secure attachment - Children play with their carer (mum, dad, sibling, etc.) a lot. They seek comfort from their carer. These children are then able to develop trusting long term relationships as adults. They have high self-esteem.

> **Bad**. Resistant attachment - These children are distressed when their carer leaves them, and are not reassured by their return. Older children may be clingy and as adults, they are less inclined to form committed relationships with people. When their adult relationships break down (as they often do) they experience great emotional pain. These adults may be clingy with their own children.

> **Even Worse**. Avoidant attachment - Children are wary of their carers, and they do not seek out their carers for comfort. This is worse after the carer has been absent. As adults, they struggle to find intimacy in relationships, and they exhibit

very little distress when relationships breakdown. They usually fail to support their partners well.

Dreadful. Disorganized attachment - these children are confused and apprehensive of care-givers. This is the most extreme form of attachment disorder.

We are not here to investigate how these disorders are *created* in children, but it is no-doubt multi-factorial (due to lots of things). But let's blame the parents anyway - **Ha!**

Our reasons for exploring these disorders are that attachment-disorder affected children often use pets (companion animals) as *carer substitutes*. It is thought that animals represent a more predictable and stable 'attachment figure' for affected children (and indeed adults).

Whatever the cause of these attachment disorders, it's known that the higher a child's Neuroticism score, the more likely their attachment behaviour will tend towards *avoidant attachment behaviour*:- Children with high N scores will show disproportionately high levels of affection for animals - pets and other companion animals. They often become clingy and over-protective of their "charges". And yet, because of their attachment disorders, they often fail to recognise the *"pragmatic realistic reciprocity of their relationship"* (TeeHee) - Which translates as:

> The child may recognize certain pet behaviours as "loyalty" (reliability and security) - whereas in fact they are witnessing a simple pragmatic human-animal relationship of mutual advantage (I'll feed you and in return you'll bite the postman for me).

I'm not suggesting here that young vets (our up to 35 year olds) all decided to become vets at 14 years old because they had rubbish parents. But this issue does go somewhere towards answering a personal burning question of mine: Which is,

"Why do so many vet students cite their early teenage years as being Day Zero for their decision "To Be A Vet"?"

What is it that happens to these children to make them commit so entirely and thoroughly to the pursuit of this one highly specialized occupation at such an early age?

It's hard to work out why the Neuroticism scores of so many vet students and younger vets are higher than the population average. Why would someone who is prone to negative feelings, prone to anxiety, emotional instability, moodiness and sadness want to be a vet?

From the ages of 14 through to 23 years, veterinary students are expected to devote the vast majority of their waking hours to a narrowly focused pursuit of learning. They are expected to learn huge numbers of detailed facts and medical constructs. They are expected to understand how these facts support and explain outcomes. They are expected to learn physical as well as mental techniques, and they are expected to become extremely skilled in their implementation. As we learned earlier, people with high Neuroticism scores learn better and are easier to train. The truth of the matter may be that Universities are *selecting* for vet students with high N scores.

The animal thing: Autism and Asperger's - another theory to think about

Do people choose to be vets because they prefer relating to animals rather than to people? When they are beginning to build ideas of their career, does *Rosie*, our 13 year-old, first think,

> *"I want to care for things. I like playing Doctors and Nurses. I don't like people much. Therefore, I have chosen to care for animals."*

Asperger Syndrome (an *Autism Spectrum* syndrome), whilst being characterised by degrees of failure of *non-verbal communication* and *social interaction*, actually has little effect on a sufferer's normal language skills and their intelligence. So there is no reason why such people should not aspire to be a vet. Grandin et al (2010) has revealed that people on the "Asperger's Spectrum" relate more effectively to animals than they do to humans. Many also personally *benefit* from active involvement with animals.

> *"There seems to be a unique chemistry between people on the autistic spectrum and animals." (Mathews, 2013)*

I am not saying all vets, or all the people who want to be vets, have an autism spectrum disorder. That would be facile and lazy. But there can be no doubt that this issue must be included in our thinking about the personalities of the people who are involved in the veterinary profession. (More research and more surveys then? As you can imagine, there has been absolutely no research on this particular question!)

The Elephant in the room. Veterinary Suicide

Suicide. This subject could easily take up the entire book. The vet profession is aware that it has had a 'suicide problem' for years. Within the UK population, vets are over-represented (proportionally) in national suicide figures. The figures have dropped slightly for men vets recently and are now higher for women.

When I was a student, the high suicide rate was blamed (somewhat esoterically) on vets catching a disease called *Brucellosis* from the cows they were examining. Later, the high rate was attributed to the fact that vets have access to 'killing drugs'. Researchers have also looked at the *direct* effect on vets of having to euthanase 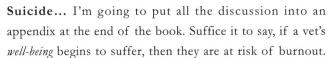 animals. In the last 2 or 3 years, more serious research is revealing multi-factorial causes (wouldn't you know it?). Just in the last 2 or 3 years, the vet profession has begun to address the issue more effectively:- First steps have included encouraging a national dialogue on depression and work-stress and their relationships with mental health.

Suicide... I'm going to put all the discussion into an appendix at the end of the book. Suffice it to say, if a vet's *well-being* begins to suffer, then they are at risk of burnout. If their burnout is not addressed, then more extreme forms of mental ill-health may appear. Invariably the next step is 'clinical-depression'. The number of young vets stating they have sought professional help for mental ill-health is sky-rocketing year-on-year. And suicide is invariably preceded by depression.

And suicide is not just for Christmas...

People with high Neuroticism scores are particular prey to depression and poor well-being. They are, unfortunately, highly represented in the national figures for suicide. Many vets, especially younger ones, have a high N score...

A Vets' Personality - a summary

In this first chapter we have talked about personality. We have shown that it can be measured and that we can take those measurements to help predict how vets address the world and their life as vets. We have looked into the types of people who are vets, and those that may want to become vets. In exploring these personality traits, we have discovered that both physical and mental abilities are intimately entwined with them.

So, let's take a look at our chapter title, *"Do you have the right personality to be a vet?"*

Hopefully, you are now reading this question differently from when you first read it. If I have done my work properly, you are no longer answering this question with,

> *"I love animals, so I <u>do</u> (have the right personality)",* or

> *"I love science, I'm intelligent and I'm very technical",* or lazily,

> *"I've always wanted to be a vet..."*

My purpose in writing this chapter is to persuade you that the most important process you should use in your decision (to be a vet) must be one of self-analysis. I want you to *ask yourself* these three questions:

> *"Will I be healthy and happy as a vet?"*
>
> *"Will vetting and me be a good fit?"*
>
> *"Will such a specialist role continue to satisfy me?"*

All three questions should now be attemptable (is there such a word?) after reading this chapter (and obtaining a *Big5* trait score). Further chapters will give you even more help in answering them...

These three questions are designed to probe the sense of *your own* "person" rather than what you *think*: I assume you want to spend the next 40 years or so of your life being physically and mentally healthy. I assume you want to continue to develop as a person - both socially and professionally. I assume you have taken time to read this chapter again. Maybe you have even considered taking a *'Big5'* personality test.

Ask yourself the last 3 questions again...

> *"Will I be healthy and happy as a vet?"*
>
> *"Will vetting and me be a good fit?"*
>
> *"Will such a specialist role continue to satisfy me?"*

Even More summary

I started this book wondering why most vets are a bit *weird?* We've gone some way to answering this question.

Apparent weirdness may be the degree to which a person has achieved *self-actualization.* These are those people who have achieved the upper reaches of pure amazingness. And being amazing, - a bit like the non-corporeal aliens in *Star-Trek* - they have a different view of mankind than do most people. Which can lead to them seeming a bit aloof, and way too calm. Or maybe it's due to a degree of attachment disorder. Or Asperger's. Or...

Combine this alien-ness with vets' generally lower than average Extraversion, and their higher than average Neuroticism scores, and vets begin to appear even more unusual.

My super amazing So-You-Want-2-Be-a-Vet Test:

What do we feel about being able to test young people when they first consider becoming a vet? At this point I have to acknowledge that our liberal society may regard pre-testing as being fascist and discriminatory. A bit like *'Pre-Crime'* in Philip K Dick's novel *'Minority Report'*. Critics will ask if such tests are the first tentative steps towards a eugenic nirvana? Could be…

But hey! We are here to challenge those established liberal ideas:- I am a scientist, and I think testing is good. I do tests everyday - trying to get a grip on disease. Why not use a test to see if a person is likely to be a happy and healthy vet? More importantly, remember that no test is 100% accurate. The results need to be *interpreted*. This is why we will always need Doctors and Vets. Results should not be just accepted as *black and white*. Many 'normal' people forget that medical and veterinary tests are only a guide. Just because a cat has a high Blood Urea Nitrogen doesn't mean it has kidney disease…

Once you begin to believe test results absolutely, then you are running the risk of being misled… *"The tyranny of medicalisation"*.

So I admit that I am very comfortable with testing *proto-vets*. No one is forcing them to follow the advice the Test comes up with! With my *So-You-Want-2-Be-a-Vet Test,* the results *would be read as guidance only* at the very most. At least until we find ourselves living in a totalitarian state - more of which in my next book!

So-You-Want-2-Be-a-Vet Test - More detail

My amazing test will be a series of questions:

So-You-Want-2-Be-a-Vet Test: Part 1: What are your Big5 Personality Trait Scores.

Neuroticism:

> If you have a high Neuroticism trait score, then you will be vulnerable to the pressures of the veterinary environment.
> A high N will help your training, and will help you become the well-informed and highly skilled animal carer you dream of being. Rushing from emergency to emergency…
> A low N will be better for your health.

> Which gives us the first paradox of veterinary personalities:- to be a great vet, you may need to have a high N. But that same high N may well make you unhappy and ill.

Conscientiousness:

> A high score will help you *become a vet* and will help you *be a vet* day to day.

> A low score will help you *avoid* burnout and ill health.

> Which gives us the second paradox of veterinary personality. To be a great vet, you'll benefit from a high C; but a high C may contribute to ill-health and unhappiness in the job.

Agreeableness:

> If you have a high Agreeableness trait score, it may help protect you a bit from the stresses of work. High A reduces your chances of *Burnout.*

> If you have a low Agreeableness score, then clients will hate you and complain constantly. It will help here if you also have a low Neuroticism score because, then you just won't give a damn what they think anyway!

Extraversion:

> High Extraversion can be slightly protective of stress. As E goes up, N goes down in most people - think about it...

> High Extraversion makes training much harder - not so good for vet students.

Openness to Experience:

> Not much effect overall... Higher O scores make you an extreme-skiing vet. Lower scores make you a moralistic gardening vet. Both work OK on the whole and have little impact. You can be either and it'll probably work out health and happiness-wise.

So-You-Want-2-Be-a-Vet Test: Part 2 : General Mental Ability

A high level will help with your training, your ethics, problem solving etc. It works very well alongside a high N.
A low GMA probably won't get you through the door. Sorry.

So-You-Want-2-Be-a-Vet Test: Part 3 : Tenacity.

We talk about tenacity in a later chapter. Suffice to say that without a good degree of this, you will struggle to excel.

There is no way to measure this currently. Just be aware of it. If something is hard, do you keep trying? Or do you say you're bored and go on to something else pretty quickly?

So-You-Want-2-Be-a-Vet Test: Part 4 : Resilience.

Resilience is having a 'thick skin'. It's gonna get tough - professors, teachers, clients, dogs, cats, your peers will all want to take a bite out of you at some point. Resilience gives you the ability to shrug it off. (Constantine, 2003)

Resilience is also the ability to *recover* from an insult on ones physical or mental structures. High Agreeableness can help here.

So-You-Want-2-Be-a-Vet Test: Part 5 :Animals

There is an argument to say you'll make a better vet, and be a happier person if you have a *practical* relationship with animals. One based on an ethical understanding of animals' needs rather than on your own personal needs (for animal interaction) - be they social, sentimental or emotional.

If you 'love' animals, you will struggle to achieve a distance from that emotion when you become a vet. As a vet, you will sometimes have to hurt animals to make them better. You will sometimes have to kill animals for their own 'good'. If you truly 'love' animals, every time you hurt them, a little bit of you will die too. Which may eventually make you unhappy; or ill.

Does my personality mean that 'Being a Vet' is the <u>only</u> thing I can do?

Absolutely not. Being a vet is a choice. And there are many other aspects to being a 'successful and happy' vet besides your personality. Things like your resourcefulness; your resilience; your gender; and your parent's annual income. They all contribute hugely.

There is something that we'll briefly touch on here that I call 'self-selecting behaviour'. That is to say *people with certain attributes* find themselves pushed or pulled into certain career roles based on their personal personality traits. A bit like Tony Bacon who decides to be a butcher. Or Uri Doktor who chooses a medical route…

For example, people with a high Neuroticism trait scores are very effective *in training*. And training to be a medic or vet are both incredibly intense. Thus people with high N may be attracted to these roles purely because they know *they will do well…*

People with both high GMA (*General Mental Ability*) and high Conscientiousness are in possession of the scientific version of a *Big-Mac Combo Meal - gone LARGE*. These guys will make great vet practitioners - in theory. All things being equal. Assuming everything else we talked about is OK.

Being a vet is rather like being a soldier tucked up in a fox-hole in no-man's land.

The background vibe of the day is stress. But in fact, most of the day is actually spent performing routine and repetitive duties. Every now and again there's an artillery attack - an emergency requiring intricate surgery; or a challenging case that needs extra research. Perhaps an urgent phone call to a referral vet for some advice. A vet needs to be comfortable spending hours every day doing the same thing they did every day last week. The same things they'll do next week too. BUT then. Maybe once or twice a week, they need to be able to quickly *arouse* themselves and become some kind of super-hero surgeon - at a moment's notice:- As we have learnt, people with higher Neuroticism scores are quicker to *arouse* and so again, may be attracted to these roles.

Self-selection goes some way toward answering the question why so many vets have high N scores.

The Perfect Vet

To get the job done, a perfect vet is easy to train and quick to arouse. They have a solid foundation of intelligence and conscientiousness…

To remain healthy, happy and productive is something else entirely. As we have already mentioned - and some of you will have already recognized this yourselves - that there seems to be a paradox to being a vet:- To be a good vet seems to imply there is a high risk of ill-health… Those people who are *really* attracted to being a vet are at a high risk of burnout (or worse) at some point in their careers.

These people can be helped. Particularly by the RCVS, the universities and the employers of new vets:-

The RCVS needs to be less controlling. It should be more trusting of its members to do a good job. The vet universities need to redesign their approach to teaching so that their students' well-being is maximised. Employers of new vets need to offer more support and understanding. The rest of this book explains why. And how…

Chapter 2

How to Make a Vet

"Vets get better by practicing. Please remember that skills can be taught.
It's a person's basic attributes that can't be learnt:
These are Tenacity - for a surgeon;
Empathy and compassion - for a therapist."

In this chapter we're going to see where vets come from. We will use what we've learnt from the previous chapter on personality and well-being and will talk about the *philosophy* of being a vet. And how the desire, that so many people have *to be a vet,* plays out in the real world.

Some questions we will try to answer here: What is it that makes people *want* to be a vet? What are the strengths that contribute to their successfully *making it*? What does *Being a Vet* look like from the bench in a university lecture room? What does it feel like, and what does it look like - to *actually be a vet* ?

Predestination - Square Holes for Square Pegs

It is generally accepted that a person *trains* in order to be a vet. They go to school and university, and are taught everything they need to know. Simple. But there is an argument that vets are not actually *made* at all: In fact, it could be said that vets are already vets - albeit part-formed - before they *even begin* to train. By this, I mean there is a group of young people in their second decade of life who have developed, or have been born with, a set of attributes that marks them out from the rest of society. This group of people have a highly definable set of characteristics and personal needs that are impossible to fulfil in any other activity - other than by *Being a Vet*. Which I have to admit sounds rather profound. And possibly a bit elitist.

This theory is sound - although we will try to ignore the deviant interpretations that proponents of eugenics placed on such ideas of predestination in the early 20th Century... In my defence, career predestination is an idea that can be applied to other groups in society:- Accountants, athletes, IT and computer geeks - they all fit the same thesis: These people are born to be what they end up being (or doing). For example, you may meet Robert at the age of 12. You 'somehow' know he's going to be a surgeon, or a lawyer or a plumber when he grows up. That's not to say these people don't work at attaining their goals - far from it. In fact people 'born' to a role are often the ones prepared to put *much more* effort into achieving it.

Jimmy the Athlete

A friend of mine told me the other day that his youngest son Jimmy decided to become a professional athlete at age 7. He is now 21 and earning the big-bucks playing hockey.

Pre-destined people still have to make many compromises on their journey: Jimmy, as an aspiring athlete, *feels* a *need* for competition; a *need* for winning; and probably a need for public approbation. As Abraham Maslow has shown us in the previous chapter, Jimmy is *driven* to fulfil his personal *needs profile:* Many athletes like Jimmy are on their way to achieving *self-actualization* at the same time as they seek athletic prowess. Jimmy achieves his goals by being self-driven - albeit with a little help from his parents and perhaps some pushing from his coach. Jimmy has a determination to perform and to succeed despite anything life throws at him.

This is not to say Jimmy can't compromise and stray from his chosen career-route: Pragmatism is a vital skill that "driven" people need to develop: Working afternoons in an *Off-Licence* gives Jimmy enough money to get him some new running shoes. Or to buy a ticket to the Olympics to watch some of his heroes.

It's the same with *proto-vets* (people who want to be vets or will be vets, but haven't started to train yet). They have a vet-shaped hole in their *being* and they will work very hard to fill it.

If you agree with this theory of pre-destination, then you will recognize that *Being a Vet* is actually a specific career *framework* which is designed to precisely fulfil the abilities and needs of those same people who end up as vets. This last sentence is a bit circular I admit.

Rather than being a job that is filled by people who *would be good* doing it, it is a *job created by the people* who can do nothing else nearly so well! An absurdist simile for this is "what do people with one leg and a longing to be in dangerous high places do for a living"? Answer: They become one-legged high-wire artists.

One end-result of this somewhat extreme (predestination) view is that very few vets, once they are established in vet practice, move to any other professional role successfully. This is very important for us because for many vets, it means *once a vet, always a vet*.

"You can settle the bill any time, but you will never leave."

High achievers. Self-driven and also driven by mum

It's a 'given' that most vets are "high achievers". On the podium of success, they stand comfortably alongside athletes, CEOs of large businesses, and leading politicians. What marks them out from these other high-achievers is that they step out onto their (very specific) career path particularly early on in their lives. Nearly half have made *the* decision to be a vet by the age of 11 or 12 years old (BVA, 2017). Some are ridiculously young. Laura Muir, a 24 year old vet student who is also incidentally *(sic)* an Olympic Athlete has known she wanted to be a vet since she was 5 years old! (SimplyHealth, Undated.)

These are *driven* individuals. Driven by their parents obviously, but mostly driven by their own *internal need to succeed*. They are people who could be leaders in whatever field they chose - it just so happens that this cohort have a set of additional *needs* that are likely to be filled only by a life in vet medicine.

Drive and direction.

How do they maintain these two energies throughout their difficult years into adulthood?

> **Alison** is 17 years old. She is driven, focused, and she knows exactly where she wants to be. She is in her pre-university year and is the perfect example of a *proto-vet*. Her Mum drives her hard every day. Mum checks on what Alison has learnt each day and makes sure she does her homework every night. Mum has arranged some work-experience at the local vet practice, and Mum drives her to her job at the saddlery shop every Saturday morning. Alison doesn't see much of her friends these days. She doesn't have time for a boy-friend.

> Young high-achievers will often receive a lot of unquestioning support from their peers and their families. This support is mainly focused on academic achievement and comes in the shape of *time and space* - so they can study and develop their knowledge. Their friends understand their reluctance to go out every night.

Competition - For high-achievers, it's the winning that counts, not the race.

Let's not forget, we are talking about an elite group here, and just like Jimmy in his athletic training, it's all about the winning. *Proto-vets* not only seek to be intellectual winners, but they also fulfil their need for winning with more traditional pursuits: Many are physically very active. Both team and solitary activities will feature highly in their week.

And as with all focused athletes, a high-achiever's success can be counted on the bodies of those that lost. But if you remember this book's previous section on self-actualized people, these super-achievers definitely aren't psychopaths. Far from it. Their motivation is not to hurt those that lose. Their motivation is to win. They look at their class-mates - the people they are in competition with - and they see office-workers, marketing-consultants and dentists. They see second-leaguers. But one of the important characteristics of our *proto-vets* is that they don't look down on their class-mates: Self-Actualized people - and those on the road to achieving that state - demonstrate the characteristic of needing to win whilst having little interest in the defeated.

Our high-achievers know that they are winning by becoming a vet. And by becoming a vet, they are winning…

Caring and vulnerable - is not the veterinary stereotype - but is mainly true.

So we have a group of elite teenagers - intellectually and physically able warriors. They have a *need* to prevail, and they *need* to succeed. But as we noted above, they aren't Teutonic or Wagnerian *Valkyrie*. They don't wear Viking helmets and certainly don't pillage. In fact, the absolute opposite: They exhibit compassion and caring. Look again at *Self-Actualizers* (in the Personality Chapter or Appendices) -

> *They live in the real world. They are less interested in abstraction or stereotypes. They accept nature as it is. Which means they can understand how other people feel, and so can empathize.*

Appreciation seekers

And, here's the dangerous bit for our *proto-vets*. And in fact for all practising vets: Giving out care and compassion to animal owners and clients doesn't come for free. For compassion givers to be able to continue *giving*, they need their fuel tanks filling back up - and often. Possibly the best fuel for a self-actualized person is *appreciation* - namely *being* appreciated. This is the kindling that keeps their fires alight. Vets and *proto-vets* like to be liked. In fact self-actualized people (and vets) often seek out situations specifically where they may find respect from others. It may appear a bit like showing off:

> In the full waiting room one evening, Phil the Vet sweeps out of his consulting room and says to a worried lady in the corner,
>
> *"Yes Ms Pleezd, my surgery on Mitzi means she's going to be fine. It was a close thing, but we pulled her through- and she'll soon be as good as new."*
>
> Phil feels *revived* when Ms Pleezd is so grateful and appreciative. Paradoxically, he will think *less* of her for being so effusive.

Yes - vets need plaudits and appreciation in order to enable their giving. No - they tend not to value the person appreciating them.

Social skills - vets seem to have a different set...

We talked in the Personality Chapter about 'Attachment behaviour'. There is some evidence that children who experience childhoods lacking sufficient "unquestioning love" go on to seek roles in life specifically where they will be specifically able to claim *respect and appreciation* from people (Reevya, 2014). Meaning they claim appreciation by virtue of their profession: roles like doctors and nurses, vets and footballers. For young people making their early life-choices, caring roles like medicine and veterinary science are increasingly attractive because such professions appear to be closely associated with an automatic gratitude and appreciation.

Another explanation maybe that many vets' parents are teachers - busy being 'intellectual' and supportive to their school-students. They exhaust their supply of devotion and commitment whilst at work - meaning there is little 'love' left over for their own children. After a long day, the only thing left over for their own child other than some 'critical' career suggestions and is an "*attaboy*" for homework well-done. No? Just me then...

Maybe some vets come from broken families where they had to compete for attention and love from a succession of 'fathers', or 'mothers'. And so on and so on. Enough with the 'fag-packet hypotheses'...

Middle Class brats

The previous section detailed some suppositions about parenting skills. What *is* fact is that most *proto-vets* come from affluent (middle-class) families: University costs and fees are very high these days. Training to be a vet is more expensive than ever. Not least because a vet doesn't begin to earn money for another two years compared to the majority of graduates. Their family's money and support are vital to their success. Vets -

if they truly are approaching the state of *self-actualization* that we have spoken of - are less interested in money than most people. Thus, because vets are not paid an equivalent wage to other professionals, then vets need to have a family behind them to offer financial support well into the first decade of their careers too. The average debt that a vet leaves university with is eye-watering.

Perhaps there is a link here between the affluent families issue and with these kids having some gaps in their social skills... Affluent mums and dads are mostly out at work earning the money. This means the *proto-vets* may develop a less parent-orientated 'view of their world...

Vet Moms and their blind enthusiasm

The thing about *Being a Vet* is that everyone knows what it is. 'Perhaps more accurate to say that most people have a strong, yet simplistic view of what being a vet is. Pretty well all parents want their children to be successful - of course. And so by definition, some more *active* parents will seize on anything that fits *their own ideas* of what success is:

> You're a Mum. You're sitting at the kitchen table. Reading the Sunday Times as delicate wafts of *Waitrose Medium Roast* drift past your elbow. Rosie, your 13 year old (who we've met before), sits across the table from you, chewing thoughtfully on a piece of toast. Tim, your 16 year old, is draped on the sofa next door nursing a hangover. You and Tim are still reeling from your screaming match last night.
>
> →Rosie flicks the corner of your paper. "I'm going to be a *Director of Marketing* at *Celebrity First Impressions* when I grow up."
> "That's nice, Rosie", you say. "Tell your brother I want a word with him about cutting the grass."
>
> →Or Rosie flicks the corner of your paper. "I'm going to be *Generic Drugs Intervention Program Practitioner* when I grow up."
> "Really? That's nice Rosie", you say with a smile. You put the paper down. "You finished with the Times Supplement?"
>
> →Rosie flicks the corner of your paper. "I'm going to be a *vet* when I grow up."
> "That's great Rosie. You do love your animals. I'm glad you're thinking about your future. What a wonderful thing that could be. You have to be clever and work hard at school - but that's no problem eh? Let's do some research..."

This is the exact moment when our *proto-vet* is presented with their first 'decision opportunity point'. Obviously this single point in time is pivotal. It is the moment when parental and peer approval *may* force a vague throwaway comment such as " I'm going to be a *vet* " from a hazy teenage fun-idea into an achievable aim. Why so pivotal. Why so potentially dangerous? It is important to remember that by their very makeup, driven by their very specific personality traits, *proto-vets* are chasers: They are like greyhounds:

> Give 'em a rabbit to chase and
>
> Convince them to chase it and
>
> Chase it they will - until they catch it, or they break a leg trying.

Like the greyhound, *proto-vets* will twist and turn, following every skittering change of direction, every jump and every dive. They will certainly catch the rabbit eventually - because that's what they do. And like greyhounds, they often don't know what to do with the rabbit when they've got it. They have lost sight of *why* they are chasing. Our high-achieving proto-vets concentrate solely on the catching - and the winning. Rosie - once she is convinced she has to work work work - will be so focused on the task that she will forget to ask, the '*why*' question... Ever again...

The Why Question: **Why am I chasing this rabbit? Why do I want to be a vet?**

Many vets graduate from university at the age of 23. They look around at their new life. They wonder *what it is* that they have actually won...

Whoops. Wrong kind of Role Model. My Bad.

Why are Pushy Vet Moms so dangerous?

We've all seen those TV documentaries that show highly-driven 14 year-olds. Up at 5am - in the pool by 6am for 2 hour's swimming training before Dad drives her to school. Mum collects her at 4.30pm for the trip to another pool on the other side of the city where she is competing in a junior league race at 6pm. Home by 8pm for 2 hour's homework and food. Bed by 10.30pm. I watch these families open-mouthed. I wonder how they find the time. Or the energy. Don't they ever flop in front of *Hollyoaks* or X-*Factor*? What about *Harry Potter*, or *The Hunger Games*?

It appears that our group of elite teenagers find little interest or challenge in such mundane occupations:

> *Hollyoaks* is full of defective fictional characters - not interesting; *Harry Potter* never made a valid decision in his 'life';
>
> *Katniss Everdene* - although set up to be a feminist role model - actually was no more than a pawn in someone else's plans (a man wouldn't you know it?).

Our young swimmer has better role models:- Maybe other athletes in her training group. Or her coach perhaps. Maybe a recent UK Olympic 400m freestyle winner. Or the Woman's 100m Sprint champion. She dreams of sporting glory every minute she's not asleep. And also when she's asleep too. *Proto-vets* are no different except they are dreaming of *vetting* glory - whatever that may be.

Significantly, *proto-vets* are even more immersed in the river of aspirant-success than our young swimmer is: She only spends maybe 4 hours a day swimming. *Proto-vets* not only spend their evenings and weekends with animals and with their studies, but they also study vet-related valuable stuff all day at school as well. Working in the science lab at school, listening to a teacher expound on Boyles Law, learning English and Maths, or dissecting a shark's egg - they all lead *directly* towards becoming a vet. These 15 hour days represent a total immersion in their pursuit of veterinary excellence.

And pushy vet-moms are dangerous because if it all goes wrong, *proto-vets* have been left with no alternatives. The whole of their lives will have been focused on the pursuit of vetting - practical and academic. Our 16 year old swimmer is lucky. When she realises she is just not good enough to win, then she can easily become a kid again. She has managed to maintain a healthy life balance despite all her mom's pushing. She has spent 6 or 7 hours each day NOT swimming. Doing school stuff that has zero relevance to her dreams: Boring stuff like hanging with her mates; breaking some windows; tagging the back-wall of the gym; feeling up Brent in the boiler room. Remember that it's boring stuff that keeps a mind healthy.

On the other hand, if *proto-vet* starts to struggle on her vetting-quest for some reason or other, pushy-mom just pushes some more: Mum gets a tutor. She organises more training. Mum just wants their *proto-vet* to get into Vet School. When *proto-vet* gets in, then Mum will stop pushing because she knows the university takes over the pushing from there on…

Pushy vet-moms' greatest failing is they don't give their kids the space or desire to ask *'why?'*. They are too fixed on their encouraging mantra of,

> *"More learning is directly proportional to more vetting glory. My love…"*

Some Advice to the Moms of proto-vets - Keep 'em healthy: Back off bitch!

STOP pushing.

No, seriously folks, you really *must* distract your *proto-vet* for a few hours each day. Make them watch *Corrie* with you and then discuss it with them afterwards over the washing up. Sit and eat a meal with them. Or lock them in a cupboard under the stairs with no light. That's Harry Potter isn't it? See where he ended up! Didn't do him any harm…

And when the A-Level exams loom on the horizon, don't let your *proto-vet* drop their outside interests. Use <u>all</u> your energy to encourage them to keep riding that horse every weekend; encourage them to stick with their boyfriend (even if he is a *spotty-waste-of-space*). Or give them some cash so they can buy pizza for their mates. Keep 'em healthy because it helps. Remember they are still kids. And it only gets harder from here on…

Why did you want to be a vet?

Most answers to this question are invariably vague and unclear:

> *"Because I liked animals."*

> *"It sounded exciting."*

> *"Durr."*

> *"Sorry, I've got a full surgery to do…."*

Unfortunately many *proto-vets* are never properly asked the *'why'* question by anyone in their life - ever.

> **"Why do you want to be a vet."**

> **"Why?"**

"Why do you think that?"

"Why?"

As we have already mentioned, the *why?* question doesn't get asked because most people involved think they *already* know the answer themselves. They think they 'know' what being a vet is - and it feels obvious to them why someone else would want to be a vet.

> *'So you want to be a vet Rosie. Amazing huh?*
> *Helping all those animals.*
> *Heroic stuff.*
> *Saving Lives.*
> *People love vets.*
> *Being on TV.*
> *Loads of money too!"*

Rosie's answer to the *Why?* question is assumed, so why bother asking her the question at all?

Athletes at the weekend

Intellectual athletes work hard and play hard. *Proto-vets* don't like empty time: They choose hobbies in which they can excel. They swim; they race bikes; play tennis; and they train horses. Most of them play *individualistic* games - although a small number of them do participate in team games - but only games where they can shine as individuals. For example, rugby, which is full of giant egos; hockey which is full of bruised shins.

This preponderance of individualistic activity is actually changing as more and more women enter the profession. Over 80% of graduating students are women currently:

Team Work

Back-in-the-day Vets were the über-meisteren within their vet practices. Meaning that 95% of the work was done by the vet himself. Or at least that's what he thought… He felt he was generating all the income for the practice - single-handedly. A few vets were aware of their team - receptionists, nurses, support staff, etc. Older vets would invariably neglect the value of their input.

This has now changed: The *medicalisation* and *industrialization* of veterinary practice means it is imperative that a vet has trained help. Someone to do the finance; someone to care for the animal's recovery; someone to service the MRI machine. The modern vet team now *includes* the vet. More recently still, management and HR (Human Resources) practice now includes *the client* as part of the team along with the receptionist, the business owner, and the animal. They are all working towards the common aim of creating health and happiness for client and animal - the customers. Read the forthcoming chapter on The Client - and look out for the bit on *Cooperative Medicine.*

The high numbers of women currently working in the profession becomes relevant here: Women are better team-players than men (Bear, 2011). Forgive me, but it's true. Teams with women in them function better. Maybe this is because women are less willing (than men) to win by beating up the loser.

How are vets made? The work of training to be a vet

Proto-vets work hard - every available hour and every available day. From the age of 14 years old. 13 Years. 12 years old. *"It is absolutely vital to be totally focused."* - their internal voice tells them… Strict learning schedules and regular exams become the norm. Exams, with their inherently competitive nature encourage our *proto-vets* along their chosen road, *"That's exam number 7 completed. Now onto number 8…"*
And *proto-vet* school kids have to be better than 'normal' school kids - because they are going to vet-school. And 'entry places' at vet-school are *always* over-subscribed, so they *have* to be the best.

This is invariably the first major *competitive* target young people have ever had in their lives:- *Getting into Vet School*

> **"Rosie, if you get into Vet School, you will have beaten everyone else. It is the hardest course to get into. It would be amazing if you got in. Work harder!."**

Applicants to Vet School need to be straight-A students (Americanism alert). Interestingly, there are some 18 year olds who choose a Veterinary education simply because they are bright and are good at exams. (We have learnt that they may well have higher Neuroticism traits and a high GMA.) These students don't have a veterinary vocation as such - many will have never handled an animal in their lives. But they do excel at the training - especially the theory and intellectual aspects of the long course. They invariably fall by the wayside somewhere through the 5 years as they realise their mistake. Or shortly after graduation.

Training to be a vet is very difficult - on some measures possibly the most difficult professional under-graduate course of them all. But completing the course doesn't get you academic accolades - or riches - or even much kudos these days. It just makes you a vet… Whoops.

Rosie F*cks up her A-Levels

And if Rosie misses a grade; or becomes ill in May (as many students with high Neuroticism trait scores do); then she and Mum will spend Rosie's 18th summer touring all the vet universities to try and wheedle a university place. They will smile, persuade, beg, and glad-hand a university place for Rosie - one way or another. Mum will be phoning local practices, trying to get work-experience that can go on Rosie's CV. They'll beg borrow and steal written references from vets, farmers, doctors, teachers, stable-owners, and Gerald next-door - to help their cause. Charity work at the week-ends helps pad-out the CV. Private tuition just in case Rosie has to do a re-take. Whilst her school friends are getting paralytic in *their* Fresher's Week, Rosie may begin to feel she's lost the race. Incredibly, it begins to look like her friends have won, and she has lost…

What choices do *proto-vets* have when they f**k-up their A-Levels?

1.   Keep trying.
2.   Give up and do zoology at Bangor.
3.   Pick grapes in Aus'.
4.   Sit at home and feel like shit.
5.   Do six months as a *runner* at Dad's film company.

To paraphrase: Do you remember that time when a very young Batman fell down a water-well? As his dad drives him to hospital, he asks his son this rhetorical question;

> *"Why do we fall Batman?*
> *So we can learn to get back up again"*

So what does Rosie choose from our 5 options above? Option 1. *Keep Trying* of course…

Hurrah! Rosie gets a place in vet school. Of course she does!

It's the first year; first semester; first week. Day 3; It's a Wednesday. *"Heads down everyone. There's a lot to get through…"*

Vet School - Yay!!

University vet-courses have changed. In fact they are still changing - very rapidly . Especially so as more and more universities set up new Vet Schools within their science departments. The structure detailed below ("Back in the day") remains the backbone of most vet courses in the longer-established vet schools. The newer vet schools are mixing it up a bit. Pretty successfully according to reports. The long-established, historically more conservative, schools are having to play catch-up. *Nottingham (UK) University* was the first in a developing wave of new vet schools. In 2006, Nottingham were in the enviable position of creating a course from scratch: They could do what they wanted as long as their students were spat out at the end of year 5 with a set of minimum skills recognized by the *Royal College of Vets* in London.

Nottingham University (The Big Thing - not just the Vet bit) is a very successful university. Its leaders have built very close relationships with funders, and with 'industry'. They have a strong income flow (money), and they have put all their marketing and student know-how into their new veterinary product: With *'Millennials'* (more of whom later) in mind, the Vet Department have created a vet course that introduces animals and animal interactions from day one. This is a key innovation and it is what marks Nottingham out as different! No more dry sciences for the students in their first 2 or 3 years of study. *They* get their brown coat* at the end of the first week.

---

* Unsubstantiated facetiousness - Number 11

I wonder if the students get their *scrubs* and *brown coats* donated by the veterinary corporations and pharmaceutical companies? And when I say brown coats, I actually mean dark-green boiler-suits with bright and shiny breast pocket logos.

CVS, the large consolidator business who are buying large numbers of private vet practices, are now in partnership with Keel University to build a new Vet School. CVS will inevitably become involved with vet training and vet education. No one is sure how this will turn out. We assume they will consider *creating* a new type of vet who will be designed specifically to fit into their own various business models. Watch this space. Go… BigBusiness

---

The University of Nottingham's marketing department have done a sublime job: If you do a search for *"cute kittens"* on *Google*, at the top of page two of your results you'll find the Nottingham Vet School! Nice job… (Correct at time of writing.)

Joking aside, this is an inspired way of maintaining engagement with 'Millennial' students. It's a great way to sell the course to proto-vets too. After all, animals are supposedly why they all want to be there in the first place. I have a suspicion that Nottingham have realized that their students don't want to be scientists at all. No! They want to be vets who treat animals and make them better. So Nottingham have made a course that is instantly recognizable as training for animal-care and animal-healing. It is a course that constantly reminds the students of the purpose of their study - to be a vet.

Let's take a look at the Nottingham course structure - it is very well-balanced. It is very modern. Very now… It seems to be listening to its students:

Nottingham students are not educated vertically - in a progressively more clinical (more 'animally') sequence of subjects that build upon foundations of pure-science - like what I was *(sic)*. They are now taught from year one with their future patients always in mind. They are taught *what they will need to be a vet*:

Modular courses - A4 sheets with tick-boxes.

Outcomes and learning objectives... Those three (4) words send a shiver down my collective spines: Blah!

The modern approaches to veterinary education are built around modular systems - each module relating to a body system (e.g. gastro-intestinal; reproduction; and so on). And within each module, students are taught the anatomy, physiology, function, etc. of that body system. *'Normal'* healthy body systems are taught in the first 2 years.

From **Year 3** onwards, the format is repeated, but this time in clinical subjects: For example, the module is the gastro-intestinal system. Students are taught its *pathology*, *disease* and appropriate *clinical approaches* and *treatments*. They then move on to the next module - The Respiratory System. And so on.

Alongside these 'veterinary' modules, students also receive training in the soft-skills that are increasingly recognised as being a necessary part of *Being a Vet*. These personal and professional skills are taught for a few hours each year. (Not nearly enough, but still better than none at all I guess). Soft skills are things like *communication*; *empathy*; *ethics*; *business*; *avoidance of litigation*; etc. They even make an attempt at teaching *Resilience* to the students.
'Clinical skills' are how you practise as a vet.
'Soft skills' are how you survive as a vet.

Year 5 : aka. Extra Mural Studies

The final year of university is now largely spent off campus at privately-owned associate (or foster) practices - several of which are now co-funded and even staffed by the universities. Time spent in these businesses, hospitals and practices is designed to develop not only student observation, but also practical and communication skills.

Information I have gleaned from the *VPP survey* suggests system is not working too well as of yet. Students continue to complain they don't receive sufficient training in *any* of these areas: Here are some outspoken ideas and opinions on current teaching practices from students and *new-vets* collated from the *VPP survey 2015*:

- *"There are now so many students in each year, there just aren't the opportunities. There are only so many legs to be bandaged, or veins to be catheterized.*

- "The animals being treated belong to the public and the practices we visit are [mostly] commercial enterprises. That enterprise wants [needs] the client to come back, to spread the 'good word', and spend more money. This means the practices aren't prepared to risk a student messing up a procedure."

- "The vet students doing their Extra Mural Studies (EMS) are under the supervision of "university clinical staff"."

The "university clinical staff" mentioned in the last quote are mostly highly skilled specialist vets (Diplomats and Specialists), many of whom, in addition to their teaching role, are in fact building their *own private clinical practices* within the university setting. So obviously this creates a conflict of interest. As a result, many specialist vets are too busy doing their own work to be very effective at *supervising* and *mentoring* the students as well.

Let's do a Back-In-The-Day® Box

Back in the day, Vet Students in their **first year** kicked off with pure sciences. Anatomy, physiology, biochemistry. Exams every 8 or 9 weeks (every two weeks for anatomy) which often counted towards the year-end final exam. **Year two** - pure science still - maybe some parasites in grubby opaque and flocculent formalin jars. Desiccated and wrinkly intestinal worms on stained microscope slides. Statistics and genetics maybe.

Year Three - Animals and how to care for them - housing, feed, handling, breeds, species, crops. Then the beginnings of disease and some pharmacology.

Year Four - Back -in-the-day you were sent out to buy yourself a brown coat (for farms) and a white one for the small animal hospital. Your aunt buys you a pink stethoscope for Christmas. Teaching of basic surgery techniques; lots of sickness lectures.

Year Five - All out sickness. More theory, more animal experience, a bit of contact with the public - maybe a 2 week stint doing prelim. consults at the small animal hospital.

EMS - extra mural studies. Holiday activity requirements : 12 weeks of animal contact (farms, kennels, charities, etc) in the first 2 years - that's about half of each summer holiday. Then 26 weeks clinical-based EMS (practices, slaughter houses, etc) in the final 2½years - which is all of your summer holiday and half of the Easter holiday. Each year.   Nowadays? All change…

It seems obvious then that the line between teacher and practitioner is too blurred - and unfortunately it's the students who are most affected. Many students feel they are losing out to their teachers' personal and commercial priorities.

Several respondents told this story:

> *A student asks a 'supervising' vet, "Can I have a go please?" And the response is often, "That is the university's responsibility. Go and ask them."*

…Currently, students are receiving few opportunities to 'practise on animals' before their graduation as a fully legal vet. They repeatedly say they receive little or no 'safe' clinical engagement experiences before being released onto the public.

Practical-skills teaching is severely weakened when it relies purely on observation. There is no substitute for holding a scalpel and cutting through the muscle yourself. It is easy to see that the current EMS model which offers only observation exercises is therefore flawed. For students to attain a decent range of basic skills, universities should re-consider teaching directly - on their own premises and in their own time. A recent UK study (Brennan, 2010) noted that those Medical (human doctor) Students who had more clinical experience before their transition (from student) to junior doctor suffered significantly less transition stress. This is pretty obvious I guess, but it is good to see it written down. Vet students similarly need more clinical experience before they graduate. And yet a SPVS (Society for Practicing Veterinary Surgeons) survey confirms a decline in vet students' practical experience: They report that in 2008, 86% of vet-students qualifying had performed a cat spay. By 2015, this figure had dropped to 50%. A similar decline was seen across a range of main-stream 'everyday' vet activities.

The 5th and final year at Nottingham University continues with clinical observation and self-study. It leads ultimately to the FINAL EXAMS at the end of the course.

A gradual drift towards technician

The other universities in the UK, realizing the appeal of Nottingham's *problem orientated approach* for *'Millennial'* students are following suit (Simon Sinek (2016) on Millennials in the Workplace - see References section.): They are drifting away from pure science foundation years to a more integrated, job focused and applied approach to teaching. This increased focus on *Being a Vet* and a decreased focus on *the processes of veterinary science* has the unfortunate / fortunate effect of creating *practitioners* rather than *scientists*. The upside of this is that the course fulfils *Rosie's* dream of *Being a Vet*. The downside of this change is that if Rosie decides to embrace another branch of science later in life, she will be hampered by having a limited foundation in her pure scientific knowledge.

Despite their focus on creating narrower, job focused, and practical skills objectives, most universities are still struggling to produce vets with a *working* balance of theoretical and practical skills (not to mention 'soft skills').

Teaching soft skills at university - important but not at the cost of self-confidence

Role play - a flawed and yet popular system used to teach soft skills to nearly-mature experienced adults. Students pretend to be vets or clients, and they act out common scenarios.

This is fine for the students who have high Extraversion trait scores, but what about the one with low E scores? The shy ones. The ones who struggle to speak in front of groups?

Another failing of role-play is that it fails to endow the players with sufficient emotional engagement to the imaginary situation: There's no substitute for the reality of having a client so angry with you that you fear for your safety.

Soft Skills:-
Communications;
Resilience;
Team skills;
Empathy;
Time management;
Dealing with criticism

All very difficult to teach. Many of these skills develop with time and experience - you just have to wait....

EBVM - Evidence Based Veterinary Medicine

EBVM - a theoretical approach to vet practice that involves collating as much data and evidence from academics and specialists as possible in order to create a bunch of guidelines for practitioners to follow: relevant to diagnosis, treatment choices and outcomes. The EBVM approach to medicine enables a vet to rely less on their own intuition when approaching a case, and more on what the EBVM guidelines dictate. It's like having a flow-chart on the wall, or an algorithm in a diagnosis App. in your phone - you put the information in at one end and the answer / advice / protocols are spewed out at the other.

It's true that these new vets who have been trained using EBVM approaches are pretty impressive - especially at the theory. They do seem to fully understand animal diseases, and how to treat them. EBVM turns out to be a very powerful clinical tool - particularly useful for the less intuitive, less bright, and less Educated practitioners who increasingly rely upon it in order to succeed (my email address later…).

What some of these *new-vets* do lack are the skills to also form a healthy and balanced personal relationship with their job: They seem to struggle at living with the day to day application of all that knowledge and the EBVM tools. As a result of these failings, a large number of vet students report that on graduation, they are afraid. Very afraid. Many report a lack of professional self-esteem necessary to get the job done. There is increasing evidence that this new (black and white, and dogmatic) approach to training creates many vets who are showing signs of being paralysed with a 'fear of failure' (a recognized Millennials issue (Sinek, 2016)). Which may make them practice in an automatic manner - more like a technician…

And *Millennials* also seem to lack *resilience*. And as we suggested in Chapter 1, resilience isn't something you can teach easily. As Constantine (2003) reminds us, resilience is something that can be developed only with good support and help. It is something you learn - usually within in a supportive environment!

Students I have spoken to recognise the need for a rebalancing of their relationship with university work. Many did not realize just how much effort it would take to get through the day. Most students right up to graduation are mentally stuck in the *"I wanna be a vet"* stage. They just haven't had the opportunity to ask, *"How* can I be a vet?"

The First paid Job : The first year

I have to tell you that you will feel absolutely amazing when you land your first job. It is when all those desperate years of study meet with your life's dream. Hey! You don't feel remotely ready. But Wow! Someone has recognised you as a vet and has given you a job! Epic! And although the first days and weeks and months are probably going to be horrific and scary, underneath it all you will have an immense satisfaction that you have *made it*. You are *Being a Vet* - and someone is paying you to do it. Amazing. Huge smile.

The first Practice

The world has changed a lot in the last 30 years. Ask any vet who qualified in the 1980s about their level of practical skills at qualification, and they will tell you,

> *"I was bloody awful. I didn't know a thing about anything.*
> *"I'd only done a few cat spays at Uni. and 5 or 6 castrates in my local practice.*
> *I scrubbed into a Pyo once and the vet let me stitch it up. Did a few calvings and a*
> *bunch of sheep docking."*

How did these 1980s students become the confident and wonderful vets we see now? Possibly much of it has to do with their first practice (and maybe a little of it is due to their resilient personalities). Often landing their first job in the same practice where they did their *EMS* (Extra Mural Studies') during their final 2 years at university, their new employers gave them a very slow introduction to the big world of vetting:

- Their first few weeks were spent 'out back', doing minor surgeries, x-rays.

- Never meeting the public.

- All closely supervised by 'proper' vets and some amazingly experienced nurses.

As a newly qualified vet, their first solo farm visit was to a cow with 'wooden tongue' that had already been diagnosed by a proper vet. The cow just needed a daily injection. Their second visit maybe, was to change the dressing on a pony's leg. These *new-vets* wouldn't meet the public unaccompanied, or see a new case for a good few weeks.

Newly qualified vets were recognised by the practice as being pretty useless. But the bosses knew that with a bit of care, they would flourish in time. Their advanced training would begin to show through the fog of their fear and confusion. Many older vets now recognise that it was this caring support in their first job that enabled a smooth and faultless entry into clinical work. Their hands were held by a "proper vet" throughout their first days in the job. There was always an experienced and willing vet with time to spare: to help and to guide them. Within a few weeks, the new vet was confident enough in their own abilities that *they* decided when they were ready to go it alone.

But what is it like *now* for a *new-vet* in their first practice? Late in the second decade of the 21st Century?

Vet practices are run much more carefully manpower-wise than they were. The modern veterinary business is a finely tuned HR (Human Resources) triumph - which translates into normal English as meaning being chronically understaffed. And so the 'newly employed vet' is seen as a godsend. The whole practice is desperate for a day off.

The *new-vet* on their first day at work will be shown where to hang their coat. They will be shown their consultation list for the day and how to use the computer. They are probably doing their first proper shift that afternoon: Seeing clients and their animals. Incredibly, they are treating animals - on their own; on their first day. Of course there will be an experienced vet nearby - but they are often so busy and so 'fully booked' themselves that they will have little free time to support 'the new vet'. In fact, I have heard on occasion these more experienced vets asking,

> *"What's in it for me?' Why should we established vets pick up the pieces when it's the boss' penny-pinching that makes them employ a new-grad in the first place?"*

The boss is on holiday, or sitting on a committee somewhere. Some experienced vets can't or won't help. The *new vet* is straight into the hot water - sink or swim.

Let's remember Vets *have* courageous personalities. They are high-achievers. Players of sports. Accomplished 'doers'. Our *new-vet wants* to fight their way through the day. To be as good as any other vet in the practice - which to you and me is obviously a ridiculous thought. But it's how *new-vets* are. It's how they think. They will forge ahead, whatever the cost.

New-vets have an additional problem. The profession is increasingly scared of client litigation - particularly 'client complaints' to the regulatory body - the *Royal College of Vets* (RCVS) in London. *New-vets* are petrified because they perceive that a RCVS disciplinary procedure will result in their name being removed from the register - which would mean they can't be vets any more. And having their name removed would be worse than 'losing a leg' for our high-achieving professionals. They have just spent the last 5 or 10 years being better than their peers. Competing with other vet students on their course. Competing with themselves. Trying to get <u>on</u> the register. To be removed now would be a disgrace. Embarrassing. Life-ending. The thought makes them feel nauseous. It would be like admitting they were less than perfect!

Vets in the 80s and 90s could have their names removed too. The system is the same. What has changed is that *new-vets* seem to *expect* to be sued. Vets in the 1980s never considered it for a moment! *New-vets* report being disproportionately scared (*VPP 2015*). It's almost as if anticipating litigation is part of their training!

Having your name removed from the RCVS Vet Register doesn't sound all that bad for a non-vet. But you must remember that the vet only knows *how to be a vet*; has only ever *wanted* to be a vet; only *knows* being a vet; has *no experience of anything else…* For them to be "struck-off" amounts to being stripped naked and tied to a tree outside the hotel where their University 5-year reunion is being held. Then to be pelted with their patients' dead bodies by a bunch of grey-haired celebrity vets who are shouting,

" You are worthlessness. You are an obscenity to the vet profession."

Attendant on this fear of litigation is a fear that they will be 'found out' by their peers. They fear their colleagues and friends will see them for what they are - a bad vet! (See *Impostor Syndrome* in the Personality Chapter.)

Vets and being defensive

This elevated awareness of client complaints and resultant litigation contributes to many vet's concern that their clients are actually out to get them. Every day they meet clients who seem to take pleasure in picking holes in their methods and their diagnoses. Criticising the prices they are being charged. Complaining about the other practice staff.

It almost feels some days that the clients are off-loading their own personal problems onto the vet. One way or another, many vets feel targeted. For many vets it is only 'by the grace of god' that they haven't been hauled up in front of the be-wigged *Disciplinary Committee* at RCVS Towers in London. Vets once expected to go through their career receiving only the odd informal complaint (normally delivered to them by a harassed receptionist). *New-vets* now have a finely honed-suspicion of their clients. This attitude *seems* to be based on what they have been taught, and on what their vet-friends tell them.

As we will learn later, *Millennials* hang out together for mutual support (possibly because they have reduced access to more mature mentors). Vet-friends supporting each other is great. But it shouldn't be exclusively the only support available. The downside of vet-friend support is that such isolation from a more mature experienced view inevitably can lead to a hysterical fear of doing some thing wrong. *New-vets now expect* to be *got* by the RCVS. They think if they let their guard down for a minute, they are *finished*.

It is a fact that Vet Practices receive disciplinary letters from the RCVS more regularly than in the past. In fact, to satisfy disgruntled clients' demands, the RCVS has recently doubled the size of its disciplinary department to cope with all the complaints. This cannot be a healthy situation. It has arisen partly from the breakdown in the once solid 'marriage' of trust between client and professional: The vet / client relationship has become very fragile: The mutual trust that existed for so long has been stretched to breaking point. (See the Chapter on *The Client*)

Human nature being what it is, this increased fear of disciplinary action has led to vets practising *'defensively'*:- Every day, every hour, every consultation, every phone call - vets now take extra special care to,

>*Say the right thing.*
>
>*Do the right thing.*
>
>*Never take risks and in so doing, avoid ever making mistakes.*

This means vets now take more samples, do more tests. They use drugs that are specified as 'best practice in the EBVM handbook*'. This inevitably leads to a fear of missing something, and higher fees for the client. More to complain about…

Proper vets who are practising defensively will rarely allow a vet student to stitch up a bitch spay: Because it will break down 3 days later in a sea of pus. Therefore vets recognise it is just 'safer' to do it themselves. This is 'defensive vet medicine'. And this is one reason why students can't learn much from visiting veterinary practices any more. They just don't get the opportunity to practise on animals.

*(The EBVM Handbook doesn't actually exist but probably will do soon. It effectively stipulates that all vets HAVE to practice vet medicine exactly how the academics recommend. And the RCVS is complicit in a deceit: Vets are being led to believe that the RCVS will consider disciplining any vet who makes a mistake and who hasn't followed this virtual (non-existent) guide. (See Glossary: EBVM. STOP PRESS.))

See the problem here? The RCVS expects a *new-vet* to follow guidelines that don't actually exist. Confusion and fearfulness are inevitable.

Is there a cure for this tendency toward defensive medicine?

Unfortunately there is not much to be done about vet-clients' legalistic and pedantic attitude while Society continues to develop as it is (see Chapter on *The Client*). And not much to be done about the RCVS' approach to their members. One solution may be to help the affected vets directly. The profession needs to get *new-vets* as *resilient* as possible as soon as possible after leaving university. Resilience really can't be taught - despite the universities' attempts. It is the employers who can help the most. Namely be *supporting* the *new-vet* more effectively. Employers *must* tell them they are doing fine. Tell them things don't matter that much. Make a joke. Tell'em that they'll be OK. Give'em a hug.

Here today, gone in 5 months...

The vet profession is struggling to find enough decent vets to fill vacant jobs. Ask any practice-owner… To make matters worse, the statistics suggest as many as 50% of *new-vets* will change their jobs 3 times or more in their first 2 years of working as a vet

(Robinson, 2013). This is a huge number! It points to enormous dissatisfaction with first jobs.

Many employers are no longer able or willing to devote energy and resources (money and time) to providing a caring introduction for *new-vets*. The *new-vet* is not seen as having any long-term value to the business. Young people *going over the top* in the First World war were called Cannon-Fodder…

'Private vet practice' is aping big business and so has adopted more competitive business models. With computerization comes more efficient accountancy and financial planning. This means businesses and their managers focus on profit margins as opposed to the simple idea of doing a 'decent' job. Which was pretty well the only measure of success back in the last century.

Practice was easy then. It was almost impossible to fail financially as a vet. It probably still is. But now vet businesses are not all owned by vets these days. Most are owned by 'big-business' and they measure success by the weight of their wallets. Veterinary managers use 'big business' techniques: They set targets, they measure profit and loss; customer satisfaction; etc. They don't like to see their employees standing around chatting over a coffee.

Practice Managers and owners of veterinary businesses who are (mostly) not vets themselves find it hard to believe that a vet can graduate from university after 5 years intensive training, and still not be able to stitch a cat's leg properly. These *be-suited* and *be-BMWed* smooth-talkers don't seem to understand that a new vet will need their hands holding for *another 2 or 3 years* before they become positive and reliable generators of money. Because of this lack of understanding, many *new-vets* find themselves in jobs with little or no support. No one knows - or cares - that they are not coping. They are expected to start working and generating income the moment they first walk through the door. They are rarely missed when they leave.

PDP - Professional Development Phase - for *new-vets*.

PDP is a monitoring process for vets qualifying after 2007. It is supervised by the RCVS: Newly graduated vets have to regularly register their 'veterinary' activities online. This forms the basis of an assessment of their *'Year One (and Two) Competences'*. Its aim is to confirm that *new-vets* are advancing their skills in the first two years of Being a Vet. The system, which is not currently compulsory, is designed to guide and measure the *new-vet* in their first year.

It is, in truth, an attempt to encourage employers to support their *new-vets* more by offering them formalized mentoring. Unfortunately, the system doesn't motivate the employers much to help their *new-vets*. Many see it as just more red-tape in a business which is already drowning in bureaucracy. So they have little interest, and often just leave their *new vets* to complete it by themselves:

Many *new-vets* will end up completing their PDP in isolation (without employer input); Or they fail to complete it; Or it takes 2-3 years to complete. Some commentators have accused the RCVS of naiveté and degrees of Ivory-Towerness: Giving *new-vets* even more targets and obligations to complete - on top of juggling a challenging, possibly isolating, and highly stressful job - is crazy. It just creates more stress. Has no-one told the RCVS *new-vets* are exhausted already?

So rather than perform a radical re-think of what they are doing, the RCVS are considering making the PDP regime compulsory! *LOL (Laugh Out Loud - Denotes Ironic amusement).*

> This re-think will probably be along the lines of the medical profession. *New-vets* would have to complete a series of 'rotations'. Their performance in each rotation would be assessed and verified by external parties (the universities presumably) - for a fee of course! *LOL*. Only then would those graduates we have called *new-vets* be 'fully qualified vets', and so be allowed to practice unsupervised. This sounds like a good idea - bureaucratic and costly maybe… The obvious benefit of this system is that it *protects* the new graduate vet for their first few years.

> And the 'rotations' idea would allow them to develop skills and better resilience at their own pace. But I'm not sure *where* this would all happen. Where would these vets be working when they are *doing their rotations*? Would they get paid much? Almost certainly not - *LOL*. There's a real risk that they would become 'interns' - those unfortunates known universally by business owners as 'cheap slave labour'.

"Who will pay for these rotations?"

> The *new-vets* themselves will pay - of course! They will pay by working for free; or for very reduced wages and more poorer work conditions. Knowing how business works, I'm afraid this is inevitable. A side-effect of this 'rotations' idea is it would contribute to the current dearth of vets looking for work in the UK - because new-graduates will not be available to work unsupervised for another few years yet. Therefore, the chances of 'rotations' being compulsory are pretty-well nil. Sorry… Business just won't support such a thing.

Or maybe the RCVS' idea is that these 'rotations' will be under the *direct* auspices of the universities. Meaning *new-vets* will graduate after 5 years and then be automatically enrolled as MA students at the same university for another couple of years. This 'new course' would be developed into some quasi-qualification perhaps - and so justifying the university charging the student even more fees!

It's all a bit of a mess - this conflict of interest between the RCVS, the Universities and Business.

Things do have to change!

Being 'thrown in at the deep end', which many of the older vets who sit on RCVS committees seem to think of as a 'rite of passage', can no longer be sustained in this finely-tuned commercial world. "**In at the deep end**" just doesn't suit the changing vet industry, and certainly doesn't suit the changed personalities of our more recent graduates. They are a totally different set of people from the 'grey-hairs' who are currently making policy (see the Personality Chapter).

The new graduate -a summary.

Some *new-vets* spend their days like 'rabbits in the headlights'. Probably most. Others - the lucky and enviably fearless confident types who are looking great in their blue 'scrubs' - striding purposefully between cases - do better at first. They ride the wave of their 'confidence'. That is, until they really balls-it-up late one Thursday evening when they are tired, and they get a bit over-confident with a choking cat: Pushing-the-(veterinary) envelope is not a good plan when you barely have the skills to write the address on the front:

The first year as a vet is like walking a very high tightrope - for the first time. And the rope is never tight enough. It wobbles a bit. You've learnt the theory on how to walk the rope at Vet School. You know how to balance. You've put on your sticky thin-soled rubber shoes. You've got the 'gear'. There's a safety net below you. It looks a long way down, and it has a few holes… Even so, the best advice for *all new-vets* is,

> *"Go slowly, one step at a time."*

Don't try *to look like you know what you're doing*. You don't! And stop trying so hard. And for God's sake, Don't run!

Self-deluded

Back-in-the-day *new-vets* were generally regarded as being a lot of effort to employ and also to mentor. But most employers had the feeling it was worth it in the long-term.

Graduate Academy - New support structures

A large veterinary practice company with hundreds of practices across the country has instituted a 'graduate academy' which is designed to offer their new graduate employees a structured 'introduction to work' plan. Recognizing the issues we have just spoken about - the lack of support and control - the employer is seeking to help the new-vets' progress through their first year of work with more clinical success, and particularly, with more confidence.

It offers free time month for personal and professional development. This business recognizes there will be a benefit to their graduates, and therefore to the company - a happier more confident vet is more likely to stay with the business. In addition to financial incentives, new graduates on the scheme receive a guaranteed one day a month CPD (Continuing Professional Development -training), a dedicated clinical coach, and the opportunity to work in other departments of the business. New-vets are not required to work in the out-of-hours Rota or on their own as part of a Rota for the first few weeks of their employment.

Good support and understanding can lead to new graduates feeling valued and cared for.

In the last 2 years or so, more and more corporations are instituting graduate support programs. There are some complaints from new-vet participants that the CPD and training offered by large employers is all about improving profits rather than developing professional skills. But hey, it's still early days. A more caring approach still has to be a positive thing…

Back-in-the-day, *new-vets* usually held on to their jobs: There was very little job-jumping. Employers (boss-vets) would employ a *new-vet* (with a sinking feeling and a wry smile) knowing they had 12-18 months of hard work ahead - not only doing their own duties, but also mentoring *and* coaching the newbie. They were confident that within a few years, those vets would be useful and effective. They would be earning a secure place in the practice. They would have a 'client following', and they would be reliable.

But modern employers and practice-managers *need and expect new-vets* to appear totally competent and rounded professionals from *Day 1*. Because Day 1 is when they see their first hamster! And as Simon Sinek reminds us in his *YouTube* video (2016), *Millennials* need to appear confident - even when they're not. Millennials are good at appearing smooth and assured.

New-vets, during their training, are not encouraged to view themselves as pieces of clay ready to be moulded by their new practices. EBVM gives them the illusion that upon graduation, a vet should be complete and ready to *vet the beans out of life*. It would be better to include mouldability into their training.

Because they are Millennials they are unable to declare that they know absolutely nothing! But 'inside', many are scrunched up in a corner, shivering. And not a little afraid...

Going to the slave market to pick up some new-vets

A modern phenomenon in the vet industry is the recruitment agency. Recruitment agents seize the best *new-vets* straight off the graduation podium. These *be-suited-fast-talking-low-voiced-men-in-suits* 'sell' their victims into the corporate veterinary businesses. It's a bit like slavery, but with a smile and a comforting hand on the shoulder - instead of chains and a stick.

This system unfortunately runs the risk of making *new-vets* a *commodity*. Bought and sold at a profit. The result of this de-personalisation is that employers may also see them as being cheap and disposable. Some short-sighted employers just *use up* their *new-vets* rather than developing them for the long term. Another aspect of a throw-away society. And it's not just the large corporate practices who work this way. Increasingly, private practices entranced by big-profits are copying this approach too.

I have to admit I am made very uncomfortable by the image of a *new-vet* working away at a long list of consultations in their first weeks of work. Many *must be* play-acting 'the vet' whilst secretly drowning in feelings of inadequacy, Impostor Syndrome, and fear. Their vet colleagues (if they are lucky enough to have some) *should* be their role models - reliable, competent, and confident. In many cases they are absent - on holiday, or at a branch-surgery somewhere.

As we said earlier, 50% of *new-vets* change jobs in their first two years after university. Scary numbers, but perhaps not surprising, having read all the facts above. In the VPP survey, the *new-vets* cite poor management and a lack of mentoring (often promised at the interview - *with a smile and a firm-handshake* - but never actually forthcoming). They mention a lack of control over their personal working hours (e.g. no opportunity to work *part-time*, or only weekdays, or weekends, etc.). They talk of a consequential decline in self-confidence. Of the 50% who change jobs within 2 years of graduation, many can expect to work in another 2 or 3 practices before they find 'a good fit'. As of 2017, a ridiculously high number (~25%) of new graduate vets are actually *leaving the profession altogether! (BVA, 2017)* PDP unfinished. What's wrong there then?

Vets - Years 3 to 8 after university

The survivors of their first few years of vetting will develop more confidence - hopefully. It may all still be an act - but they have learned to be better actors. Some may begin to *believe* their own acting - which definitely helps with their *well-being*. With steadily improving vet skills - and much more importantly, their *client skills* - the stresses and strains of the role have eased a bit. At last, they are able to stop and take a look around - at their life and at their profession. This is the period when many vets make life-changing decisions. Maybe they become veterinary teachers; Or take a job in industry; Or they go part-time and have a family. Let me remind you that over 25% of UK graduates will have left the profession by this point. Some may start an *Advanced Practitioner* RCVS qualification (an approved further education qualification), whilst a few will simply move jobs. A few will investigate practice ownership - perhaps by buying into one of the various franchise veterinary businesses.

A Note on Surgeons - Tenacity

In *'Complications'*, the book about his first years as a junior doctor, *Atul Gawande* relates a principle that one of his surgical professors adhered to when choosing young doctors for his surgical rotation.

Manual skills can be taught, tenacity can't.

Most surgeons believe their success is due to practise. Not their innate skills. They believe that surgeons are *made*. To be a good surgeon, a candidate needs to be conscientious, stubborn, bone-headed and industrious. (All of which add up to tenacity). Gawande's professor would always favour the tenacious candidate over a manually gifted one.

Tenacity is the will to battle-on through adversity. To continue, to fight and persevere until the job is done - to think like *Henry the 5th*; or *Hugh Glass* in the film *The Revenant 2015*: There's no way back after the first cut…

> Let's consider a surgeon and the act of surgery: He stands in front of an anaesthetized body, scalpel in hand.
>
> Surgery is not like climbing a mountain. Nor is it like painting a picture. Or running a race. It's not like diagnosing hepatic cirrhosis, and then prescribing tablets and a special diet and then waiting a few weeks to see what happens. It's not like changing the spark-plugs in your car. It's not like arranging a loan, and then spending the money on a 'thing' - and then taking it home:

When a surgeon lifts his scalpel, and makes that first cut, he has entered into an unbreakable contract: He has to know, and to have absolute faith, that he can complete the task and close the hole back up. He has to believe he can allow the body to reawaken, fully re-assembled and functional. He has to be sure that whatever fate throws at him over the next few hours, he will be able to cope, to adjust and continue to a conclusion which includes a live patient. A surgeon can't stop halfway through to check his phone, take a rest, or have a coffee. Exciting huh? Sounds pretty scary if you think about it:

Our surgeon is 60% through dissecting an invasive tumour from around the left carotid artery. 3 hours in and his back is stiff and aching; his fingers are throbbing; his eyes itch and that nagging pain behind his left temple is starting again. He has two choices... No he doesn't. He either continues; or he continues. There is no one to defer to. No one is around to help. In fact, he wouldn't defer anyway - even if there was someone. Surgeons don't do that sort of thing! Surgeons make mistakes, sure. But they NEVER question their ability to Surg'.

That is what *tenacity* is: The surgeon's faith in his own abilities gives him the faith to make the first cut. And it is *tenacity* that means the tumour is in the shiny dish 6 hours later. Tenacity is one of the reasons why Vets Are So Good.

Tenacity transformed

Let's remember, vets are not doctors. They are veterinary *surgeons,* and so all vets need to possess the tenacity of a surgeon. Yes, they are still human. Yes they catch flu; they get stomach bugs. But they always turn up to work. Vets will think, "If I don't do it, then who will?". They 'power themselves' through the day - ignoring the discomfort, the headache, the pain. And yet somehow they still manage to do their job effectively. As you can imagine, many pay a high personal price for this conscientiousness. This isn't just one day a fortnight. Or one hour in a day. This is 6 days a week, 10 hours a day. There are no figures for the number of days vets take off work, but I know it could be counted on the finger of a single (tired) hand.

What is particularly interesting for us here - is that this is no longer true.

Recently - maybe the last 9-10 years - I have noticed vets beginning to take more days off sick. I don't know why as yet. Maybe it's that young vets are more sickly than older ones. A more likely explanation is that *proto-vets* are being taught team-skills in university.

Once upon-a-time, a vet would think themselves as THE leader. As indispensable.

> *"If I don't go into work, then who will cure all the animals?"*

But when a vet begins to consider themselves more a team member and less as a leader they may think,

> *"Well, the manager will find someone to do my duties won't she? I'll take the day off."*

Then again, this tendency to taking days-off *may* be part of the *Millennial* effect: Many young vets view their commitment to their work differently. Many decide to prioritize their own health over their job. Maybe they say *"it is in the team's best interest that I stay at home feeling sorry for myself"*. Or maybe young vets are actually different personality types, and so have different concerns and priorities (Johnson, 2009). Or maybe they possess lower *tenacity* which leads to stress *avoidance…*

Which is interesting because the vet profession has become mainly female over the last 20 years. And females generally favour non-surgical areas of practice (Baxter, 1996). They begin to call themselves medical practitioners rather than surgeons. The vet (official) job title - *Vet Surgeon* - may soon be a thing of the past… You must have noticed that more and more vets call themselves veterinarians (originally an *Americanism)*. And if there are more vets with a lower interest in surgery, perhaps that points to a population of *new-vets* with decreased tenacity. Which naturally leads to more sick days. A somewhat viscous circle! *(sic)* (See the Epilogue (including How to be a Happy Vet).

Tenacity vs. Perfectionism

And let's not confuse tenacity with perfectionism. We have established in this book's *Personality* chapter that vets are high-achievers, and they are usually conscientious. *Perfectionism* is a natural part of this construct. Perfectionism is the tool a vet uses as their guide to conscientiousness. But it is very important to remember that it is *totally* possible to be tenacious *without* being a perfectionist:

> It's morning surgery. The first appointment is at 8.30 and Consults end at 12.30 with a 15 minute break half-way through. 10 minute appointments means there are 21 appointment slots. Sophie, the vet, will see at least 21 animals (some owners bring extras so it could be more).

> 8 x Vaccinations and health checks. Each animal/owner as a worming/flea discussion. 8 introductions to the 'new' practice health program. The patient is weighed. Oh, and an examination of the animal, a discussion of the findings, formulation of a treatment plan and an injection. And tablets to collect from the dispensary.

4 x post-op checks and stitch removals.

2 x old cats 'not been eating' for over 3 days each - they need blood tests, hospitalization and fluids at the very least. Thankfully Sophie has a nurse who can do the 'back-room' stuff. The treatment plan will need explaining to the client - including bespoke printed cost estimates. Consent forms to be printed, explained and signed. Sophie has to help the nurse take the blood samples - up to 3-4 minutes each depending on the cat.

2 x dogs with diarrhoea, and 3 dogs with itchy skin - one chronically infested with parasitic-demodex.

A vet has to be good to finish on time. A vet has to be very good to finish on time *and* get a 10 minute break. Most will spend their breaks phoning clients with blood sample results and updates. It is tenacity alone that gets the vet through the morning:

And then there's a 20 minute drive to a branch surgery which starts at 1.50 and runs until 4.30.

Another 16 appointment slots. More vaccinations, re-bandaging, diarrhoea and itchy skin. Thankfully, animals needing blood samples and similar procedures can be sent back to the main surgery where Olga, the other vet, is already struggling with a full afternoon.

Tenacity keeps Sophie going through the afternoon. If she's got the energy, she may drive back to the main surgery to help the floundering Olga - who is struggling to keep up with her own consultations. Olga has just admitted a fat Labrador with suspected pyometra (a possibly fatal uterine disease) into the kennels.

Tenacity means Sophie has the fat Labrador on the operating table by 5.45pm, and the infected uterus in the stainless-steel tray by 6.15pm. Tenacity gives her the energy to explain to the dog's owners about post op care. She discusses their options - overnight at the practice or a trip to the Out-Of-Hours clinic.

Tenacity is the power Sophie draws upon as she drives back to the surgery at 9.30pm after she's made dinner and put her kids to bed, so that the clients can pick up their Labrador and take it to the Out-of-Hours clinic in their own car.

It is Tenacity that gets Sophie out of bed the next morning at 6am. She feeds the kids again, takes the dog out, and is at work for 8.20 for another busy day of operations and more consults.

A note on *Perfectionism and conscientiousness:*

You've just read Sophie's day. Obviously Sophie doesn't exist. But the day does. It is the daily reality for thousands of vets across the UK. Tenacity is defined thus on *Google,*

"the quality or fact of being very determined; determination"

Google also lists these synonyms of tenacity:

persistence, pertinacity, determination, perseverance, doggedness, tenaciousness, single-mindedness, strength of will, firmness of purpose, strength of purpose, fixity of purpose, bulldog spirit, tirelessness, indefatigability, resolution, resoluteness, resolve, firmness, patience, purposefulness, staunchness, steadfastness, constancy, staying power, application, diligence, assiduity, sedulousness, insistence, relentlessness, inexorability, inexorableness, implacability, inflexibility;

If you read Chapter 1. on *Personality*, you will understand that vets are all these things. From the age of 8 years, when they first decided to be a vet, they have developed a steely will to achieve and to succeed. Becoming a vet is so very hard: Not just the academic achievements (school, homework, work experience, university); Not just the financial costs; but also the personal costs that must be paid (relationships, physical and mental health, stress, geographic mobility, etc.). There can be little doubt that when you see a vet student walk proudly back to mum and dad waiting in the audience after collecting her degree from the University Vice-Chancellor, you are watching a very determined person. There are few people more so in this world.

Sophie's working day is hard. Tenacity and determination get her through it. It is clear there is no place for perfectionism. There is little time for conscientiousness. How can Sophie be her true conscientious self when she has only 10 minutes per animal?

To call a client in; say hello; find out what's wrong; examine the animal; explain all the options; discuss their costs; explain drug side effects; check doses; take samples; dispense treatments; give injections; advise on revisits; advise on drug compliance; say good bye and see the client back to reception. (Plus or minus sporadic requests from nurses and receptionists for help). Honestly: This is real! Sophie only gets 10 minutes for all that. Hard to believe…

And if Sophie gets behind time - which she will - then the waiting room fills with clients and their animals. There is no other vet to help. Vet surgeries are not like Tesco's where a *shelf-stacker* can be directed to open a till and help with the rush. There are no vets in the back stacking shelves waiting to be called. If Sophie is running late, then she has to catch-up. She has to empty the waiting room somehow, so she can get to the afternoon surgery at the branch practice. So inevitably she begins to miss some elements of her animal examinations. Perhaps doesn't examine the ears of *all* the dogs. *Maybe* she doesn't bother offering a skin-test when she is 80% sure she knows what the cat is suffering from. *Maybe* she doesn't tell the client *all* the side effects a pain-killer may have. *Maybe* she doesn't engage with the client so much - she keeps her head down. She doesn't smile.

This is Sophie being less conscientious. Sophie's perfectionism catches up with her at the end of the day as she falls onto the sofa at home. She asks herself, "How can I be perfect *when I can't even be conscientious?*" This is not good for Sophie. She has spent her life being conscientious. Being the best she can be. She aspires to be perfect. And because she has tenacity, she has usually been able to achieve it in the past. But in this job, she can't. And it isn't her fault: She would like 20 minute appointments instead of just 10. But the boss won't allow it. Sophie is in pain...

The psychologist Abraham Maslow reminds us that our mental health suffers, and our behaviour becomes dysfunctional when we can't be who we are meant to be ...

How are those Vets who are qualified 8 years plus doing?

You are now 30 years old. If you are still vetting, you've made it! Welcome to the fun bit.

You've found a good job. "Your clients" love you. They ask for you rather than the other vets - and you like that. You are working the *right* number of hours / days / weeks for your personal needs. You have sufficient *control* over your day to help you be content. The money is OK. But it was never about the money was it? You are valuable to your employer and you have been allowed to negotiate enough clinical freedom to practice your own sort of vetting. Your colleagues are all pretty good. At home, you are in a safe, supportive and loving environment.

You are happy. Nice one.

Chapter 3

The Busyness of Business & Introducing the Business of Education.

Veterinary warriors defending all the vulnerable animals

Not many 16 years olds realise that being a vet is a commercial service. They are blissfully unaware that *Being a Vet* is a money-driven occupation. Even more *un-thought-about* is the fact that a vet's role is largely *customer-facing*. *Proto-vets* mostly imagine themselves *be-booted* - striding around farms curing horses of colic or leaning on gates discussing cows and their calves with a strangely-attractive farmer's son. Or they dream of being *be-blue-coated,* standing in front of a grateful owner whilst holding a beautiful purring and fully recovered pussy-cat in their arms. They lightly kiss the cat on its head, and pass the grateful, sleek creature over whilst quietly sniffing back a shared tear of compassion. *Proto-vets* imagine themselves standing around an operating table with their respectful colleagues, collective chins in hand as they discuss the patient who doggedly refuses to reveal the secrets of their malady.

Even those already embarked on their veterinary career have spent little or no time fully considering the mechanics of being a vet (Robinson, 2013). Very few of them have asked the following questions,

> *"Where does the money come from?"*

> *"Does the answer to that question have anything to do with me?"*

We have mentioned that many high-achieving school and university students follow a blinkered academic path towards fulfilling their veterinary career dreams. Rushing along that road they risk forgetting their dream-destination, and instead become consumed entirely with the single aim of achieving academic success. So they forget to make any critical appraisals of their destination - aka. *Vetdom*. That is, until graduation by which point it's a bit late.

High-achievers (not just vets) love to have a goal. They thrive on achieving targets. Having a goal means that they can use their amazing problem-solving skills. They can practice finding their way around obstacles in their path, and they can excel at the same time. The goal is the thing that drives them but it's the getting there that excites them.

Excellence usually comes from being single-minded - and that can become a problem too. It is easy for their academic goals to become all-consuming - becoming the *'be-all-and-end-all'*. Success or failure for our high-achievers is measured by how close they get to their target.

If high-achievers have a fault, it is that they don't stop and take the opportunity to step aside from their journey in order to *reassess* their goals. They simply keep battling forward - pushing aside whatever is put in their way. Vet students are like elite athletes - if there is a finish line, they will give absolutely everything within their abilities to cross it first. When they do cross the line, they rejoice - obviously. Two minutes later, high achievers are thinking about the next goal, the next race.

Because high-achievers are so goal-oriented, they take little notice of distractions along the way, and pay little heed to ideas that may divert them from their *'work'*. I call this 'mindless' pursuit of academic achievement the *escalator of excellence:* The only way is up. You can't get off. The only other way off the *escalator* is to turn around and run back down - and that feels like failure.

Particularly worrying is that many high-achievers regard the act of *even considering* an alternative to their chosen path as an admission of failure. To consider an alternative is to question a 'lifelong-commitment' to their project. With *Proto-vets*, once they have committed to achieving their goal - to *Being a Vet* - there seems to be little hope of swaying them from that journey. These excellent people give themselves little time for reflection, and even less for the (facile) idea that they could deviate from their chosen path. The *escalator of excellence* runs ever upwards, and they give little or no thought to getting off...

If you talk to a first-year vet student and suggest to them that they are in reality just training to be *customer-service operatives*, most will give you a look of pity. They pity you because you are incapable of grasping the enormity of the task they have chosen to pursue. They're sorry for you that you fail to understand that the Veterinary Profession is on hold until they qualify.

Commercial Veterinary Business

Few *proto-vets* or *new-vets* thank you when you challenge them on their choices. Their journey started with a dream, and they have spent all their efforts attaining it. Most will reject any suggestion that they are destined to end up being just a cog in someone else's machine.

But it is foolish to minimise the fact that vetting is primarily a business. The truth is this: A vet offers a service for money. This isn't a new thing. Obviously. Vets have always been paid for their services - usually directly by the owner of the animal. Much like the medical doctors of old, vets were consulted on various aspects of illness, and were paid for their opinions, advice, and for the potions and lotions they dispensed. Here in the UK, the *medical profession* became a public service in the 1940s, paid for by the government. This was the point at which human patients began to forget that their relationship with the doctor remains, in essence, a commercial one.

Unlike Human Medicine, vetting never did become a public service (Fig.3). Vets still work in a world where they are paid *directly* by the consumer of their services. Namely, the public. As our society has matured into a "consumer society", universities are recognising that the public are now buying services from veterinary businesses (as opposed to the previous relationship which was that vets treated animals and people paid them for that service - a subtle difference). Consequently, Business is becoming part of the university curriculum for vet students:

Universities teach about *Capital* & *Profit* & *Loss*. They ask students to consider the *real* costs of vet procedures: to consider the equipment; the costs of the nurse's time; the vet's time; the building; the receptionist; taxes; the accountant. To consider advertising costs and practice insurance. Universities teach how to create services & products that *appeal to consumers*. This is a good thing and should be encouraged.

There is an argument that the business aspects of vetting should be the *first* thing ever taught to a student: The more a vet student understands about the mechanics of this interaction with the client, the better will be their understanding of the role they are training for. It may even prompt them to reconsider their choice of career. Which is something I would like every vet student to do at least once a year during their training.

Unfortunately, most vet schools still spend too little time on teaching business. They include just a few hours each week for a couple of weeks each year. Which patently can't be enough. The universities argue that if they spend more time on teaching business, there is less time for teaching clinical work. But the reality of *Being a Vet* is all about the commercial relationship with the client.

The patient : NHS doctor interaction	The client : vet interaction
The patient is seeking a personal service.	The client is seeking a service for his animal and for themselves
The patient makes no direct financial payment	The client is required to pay directly or via insurance
Patients feel they have less recourse for complaint as they have not paid directly	The client has a personal relationship with the financial transaction.
Patients are more sanguine with respect to their medical outcomes	The client will, and should, advocate for their animal's health outcomes.
They understand NICE's procedures, and that the NHS operates under financial restraints - they are more tolerant of delays.	The client is charged high fees and costs. Client expectations are therefore high.
NHS is faceless and therefore it is hard for an individual to feel they can approach it as an individual.	The vet is a person who is responsible, always present, and always in. There is only a receptionist standing between the vet and the client's complaint.
Patients have no understanding or knowledge of the true costs of care.	Clients have little awareness of the real costs of care, and this may lead to confrontation and misunderstanding.

NICE = National Institute for Care and Health Excellence

Fig.3 The Client : Patient : Medical Interaction

Old school versus The Now - A different kind of student

There are two extreme views on the *purpose* of *veterinary education*:

To teach science or,

To teach Service-Delivery.

They are obviously very different. The former refers to learning pure science knowledge, and thereby creating a wide and thorough foundation of understanding. This can then be applied to a multitude of situations. As we discussed earlier, this has fallen out of favour. The amount of work needed to achieve this is now considered to be too onerous - both by the educators, and by the educated:

Across most of higher-education, educators are experiencing a changed relationship with their student. Exactly like the changed relationship of *clients to veterinary services*, students now regard themselves as "consumers" of their university education. This means that they are more critical of their education and how it is delivered. They are now empowered to having choices. And they are vociferous in their demands to have more control over their education.

This state has arisen partly because of high university fees. Students pay for their university courses directly. They take on huge student-loans to cover education and subsistence. Thus, modern consumer logic means that they will *expect* to negotiate the conditions of their training in return for paying their money. As Universities are run as businesses too and in order to receive fees, they have *had* to allow this change of power within the relationship. As long as the student pays the money, then universities will accommodate their wishes. So students now have a significant impact on both course content and on design. If the students don't want to learn about slaughter-house meat inspection, then the university drops it from the course.

This all obviously results in a change of teaching emphasis. As we discovered in the last chapter, pure science education is being replaced by a more *interesting* and practical approach. Our students are driven by the desire to *be vets,* not scientists - so,

" Let's crack-on mate. Teach me some vetty stuff - now!"

Responding to their student's wishes, universities are dropping many of the pure science aspects of vet training. Students are now taught the absolute minimum necessary to enable them to perform as vets.

This produces vets who are actually pretty good at being vets. They become 'better vets' sooner than their predecessors did. But they lack the broader education and the critical-thinking skills needed to progress beyond performing routine vet work. Their skills (and so their clinical careers) plateau sooner. The universities' formulaic approach towards a vocational qualification therefore obviously risks creating vets who are less flexible in their clinical approaches to patients. They have not been taught the skills necessary to cope when they are presented with situations outside their immediate training and experience. Because vets are experiencing surprises and challenges every day, this deskilling can contribute to a lessening of a *new-vet's* self-confidence. More on this elsewhere.

Box Tickers

Taken to its logical conclusion, one can imagine vet students, and *new-vets*, will become somewhat over-qualified "box-tickers" - trained only in how to follow guidelines and algorithms for diagnosing illness and treatments. In a few years time, most *new-vets* may be spending much more of their time monitoring the work of technicians and computers. They will have less animal-contact themselves. It is likely a vet will be employed mainly as a quality and accuracy check. (Visit any high-street chain optician for an eye-test these days and see how they use unqualified personnel to do many of the tests using machines and technology. It's not too much of a leap to imagine this happening in the vet surgery too.) We call this *de-professionalization:*

> A definition: *Where the work of a professional (often autonomous) is increasingly carried out by unqualified personnel.*

This results in the systematic deskilling of the professional role. The early signs of this are made clear by the increasing number of vets who are choosing to take *Advanced Practitioner* qualifications (a collaboration between the universities and the RCVS). These are qualifications that increase and improve practitioners' skills and knowledge to an MA level (the next level up from a university graduate).

Universities are not stupid

Universities are beginning to realise that by training vets capable *only* of practising in a commercial setting, the other parts of the vet market are becoming empty of talent: namely scientific-research; industrialised concerns such as farming and food production; and non-commercial (governmental) roles. To counteract this potential vacuum, some universities are now offering different tiers of vet education. The *University of Surrey's* new Veterinary course has a distinct bias towards training non-clinical vets (correct at time of writing). The University of Keele has gone into partnership with CVS (one of the biggest commercial-owners of independent vet practices in the UK) to create a new Vet School focusing more on agricultural practice. Soon there may be universities offering tiers for research and inventions; tiers for training vets to work with dogs and cats in a high street business. A tier for government / pharmaceutical vets maybe.

My brilliant plan:

This is where my ground-breaking, unique and also brilliant *new vet education plan* may be realised:

> *For the first 3 years at university, students are trained in a generalist veterinary degree.*
>
> *Then they elect to follow a 2-4 year add-on in a specialist subject.*

Simple huh?

This way, at the 3 year point, vet students would have the opportunity to get off their 'escalator of excellence' for a moment. They would be given guidance and counselling on which direction to go next. My amazing plan offers a *hiatus*. It *forces* our high-achievers to step aside from the academic 'escalator of excellence' and makes them look at a new set of career and education options. No doubt, many vet students at the 3-year *hiatus* stage would still opt to follow one of the commercial routes. But that then becomes a *positive* and *informed* decision - rather than simply the next stage in a formulated automatic course. The strength of my plan is that for most students, this may well be the first time they have truly stopped and thought about their futures. Some will opt out altogether and become policewomen.

Universities don't like my idea much. They worry too many students would drop out after 3 years and do something else (where the university can't earn as much money from them).

The University Veterinary "Associates"

Associates are the organisations and businesses that universities forge relationships with on behalf of their students. The "associates" provide the bulk of a student's practical experience (Extra Mural Studies or EMS) whilst at university.

These are commercial relationships formed between universities and private business. This relationship has arisen because of a dearth of private practices prepared to host trainee students. Back-in-the-day, students gained much of their practical experience by way of a voluntary arrangement between the student and her chosen independent vet practice - normally the 'local vets'. This relationship has now almost collapsed: Vet businesses fear their clients - as we have touched upon already. They fear taking a wrong step and then being sued by an angry owner. Vet practices are run as businesses and they see little to gain by having students getting in the way of their doing decent work.

The huge numbers of students enrolled onto vet courses means that there just aren't enough of the remaining few willing 'local practices' to go around anymore. So universities have built commercial and semi commercial relationships with veterinary businesses in their area. These businesses (known as associates) are paid by the university to 'take' students.

***

Nottingham University Clinical Associates as of 2016.

Defence Animal Centre (DAC)

Dick White Referrals

Dogs Trust Minster Veterinary Practice

Oakham Veterinary Hospital

PDSA

Scarsdale Veterinary Group (Farm and Equine)

Scarsdale Veterinary Group (Pride Veterinary Centre)

Twycross Zoo

Animal and Plant Health Agency (AHVLA)

***

Most of the "associates" are not general or normal practices. Most are focused on their own specialized referral practice. The vets who work there are mostly *Certificate* or *Diploma*-holding vets who drive to work in shiny German cars and wear crisp dark blue suits. Pretty well all the work they do is paid for by insurance companies. Some of the *associates* are Zoos, or Animal Charities. Government departments perhaps, or laboratories. This is a huge problem because students in their final years *need* experience in bog-standard vet work. They need experience that will help them on their first day at work.

As we saw in the chapter on *How to make a Vet*, the more clinical experience a student gets *before* graduation, the less transition stress they suffer on becoming qualified and working their first job (Brennan, 2010). It is only when a vet qualifies, and takes their first job that they will start learning *real skills*. More scary still, is that newly qualified vets are paid so little, and are working such onerous hours, that they are effectively working as "interns on expenses". Vets are driven individuals and so many will convince themselves that they are still *achieving - by gaining experience*. Some newly qualified vets who can't land a proper vet job will even accept work as vet nurses in order to get some animal experience. Others work as out-of-hours vets. Some take 'internships' in referral practices and in middle-tier general practices (better than high-street franchises, not as good as referral practices). Many newly qualified vets are looking at a further 2-3 years of 'in-work training' before they become experienced enough to be employable in their own right and on their own professional merits.

If my 'brilliant idea' (the generalised degree followed by specialism options) was taken up by the RCVS and the universities, then vet students would be able to choose *where* they obtain their experience more effectively. A student who had chosen to specialise in business could sit in directors' meetings, or work as a receptionist. A student who had chosen to specialise in *GP* practice could work in a pharmacy, or shadow a *GP* vet in their consults. These experiences would give them a much better understanding of the nature of their chosen specialism, and in particular would inform their expectations of what work will really be like. This way, they would realize early on in their training that *care, compassion and animal welfare* are charged out at £215 per hour. Surgery is 3 times that. Plus tax.

'Freshly squeezed'

Every July, the universities in the UK squeeze out well over 900 new vets into the world of professional vetting. These lucky folks have earned themselves a *career identity* which will most likely stay with them until they die (Page-Jones, 2015). The title of "vet" will shape them - it will bind them together with their peers. It will inform their life and their interactions with the world.

"What do you do?" They will be asked at a party. *"I'm a vet."* They will reply.

The reality for these 'freshly squeezed' vets is one of employment. Employment into any one of the various vet-shaped-holes shown below in Fig.4:

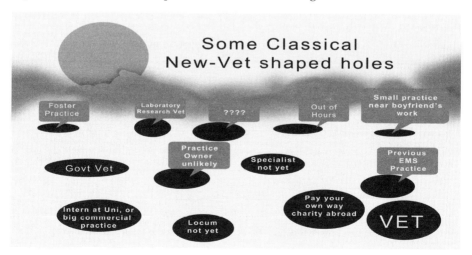

Fig.4 Some Vet-Shaped Holes

And these holes all have one thing in common. They are ALL businesses. Corporate businesses - which include franchises; consolidators; universities; charities; labs; Government agencies; pharmaceutical firms. Business is life. And life is now business.

Being a Vet

But until someone asks them to do something Vetty, and rewards them for it, then most *new-vets* won't really believe it themselves: "Becoming a vet" has been the sole purpose of the last 5 to 8 years of their young lives. And to become a vet now, they really need to get a vet job. And fast.

But competition for decent first-vet-jobs is fierce. With over 900 graduates coming from UK universities every year, and similar numbers coming from abroad, finding decent jobs as a *new-vet* is difficult. Many 'freshly squeezed' vet graduates will wait 6 to 9 months to land a job.

Hair Kiri. Women vets

As we have discussed, psychologists have identified that women are more conscientious than men. And that they are less interested in *status* than men (status includes money, career progression, size of your car, etc.). The vast majority of *new-vets* are women. So it makes sense that after chasing this dream for so many years they would probably rather have *any job* than none at all. Psychologists confirm that a woman's needs tend towards the social and nurturing aspects of their vet-ness. And not mundane things like money, status and job-conditions (Rubinstein, 2004. Ganai, 2013).

The demographic changes in the veterinary profession over the last 25 years (more women, less men *(sic)*) have thus inevitably led to lower wages and worsening working conditions. Despite a job's wage and conditions being poor, many more women than men will still pursue their 'need' or 'desire' *to vet*. They take the job nevertheless.

Here's a challenging statement: Women *new-vets* seem to be prepared to take jobs that pay less than being a refuse collector in Birmingham. Less than a medical nurse. Or a teacher. Wage deflation is purely due to market-economics: if a manager can find someone to do the same job cheaper, then they'll employ them. Unfortunately, in the commercial *dog-eat-dog* world of modern vet business, if vets are willing to work for less money, then it's only a small step for managers to compound the misery by also increasing their working hours; and decreasing their working-conditions. There can be no doubt that women's personality and motivational characteristics are being taken advantage of.

Vet jobs don't come with flats or houses any more. They did once upon a time. Vets don't get a car either. Taxation changes and competition have put paid to that.

You can't really blame the employers. The world we live in is designed to allow *'the market'* to dictate the shape of people's lives and work. If *'the market'* can squeeze more profit out of every human transaction, then it will do so. And that profit will always end up in the pockets of the owners and managers. Remember that it is the vets in the consulting rooms who generate the money for a vet business. It's the managers who seem to benefit most from that effort. If you own or run a business, why wouldn't you want to employ highly motivated, highly educated, loyal professionals for less than what that nice Eastern European car-wash woman gets for cleaning your car? This is what all businesses do when we live in a *Keynesian* world: They pay low, and sell high.

Get your own business - you know it makes sense

Why doesn't everyone own their own practice then? That's where the money is. The answer lies in the changed veterinary demographic. Women on the whole - talking generally with a broad brush - all things being equal - no-offence-mate - are less interested in the business side of life. This is especially true in their first few years after graduation from university. It's a fact. Honest. Don't shoot the messenger! Women are more interested in Being a Vet, and less interested in the framework that surrounds and facilitates the act of being a vet. And this is why salaries have dropped. And why working conditions are poor. And why more women don't own more vet businesses.

Compounding this focus on clinical vetting is the universities' training for life after graduation. Vet students are all about learning how to vet. Apart from the odd session on working *within* business, students are never introduced to the idea that they could actually own their own business - let alone encouraged in the idea. Or manage a business. And so it doesn't form part of their life-aspirations or expectations.

Pet Insurance - driving peoples' dreams (and vets' BMWs)

Pet Insurance has become a major driver of the UK vet business. Because *new-vets* use EBVM techniques extensively, it is an unfortunate truth that many animals are being 'over-treated'. Possibly nicer to say they are receiving everything possible to help answer their owner's questions. Remember that we suggested earlier that EBVM leads to more tests and procedures? Why make intuitive guesses at what's wrong when you can do another battery of tests at £35 each? Thus, charges for the majority of animal visits at middle-tier practices are rising fast:

Blood machines; X-rays; MRI; Ultrasound; tomography; GA monitoring; Anaesthetic machines; Health & Safety legislation adherence; extraction; air conditioning; waste protocols; etc. These are all very capital intensive and they require expensive equipment and services. In the UK, insurance take-up by owners (attending vet businesses) is currently claimed to be as high as 25%.

The average cost of a visit to the vet is increasing rapidly, and insurance premiums have naturally followed suit: Many owners now spend more on their pet insurance than all their other household insurances put together. Which is why some commentators are suggesting that there is a ceiling on how high premiums can go before clients begin to rebel. And rebellion may ultimately mean lower incomes for vet businesses.

Some insurance companies have created lists of 'preferred vets' in order to keep their costs down. These are those vet businesses who are prepared to commit to lower costs of treatment. These vet businesses effectively enter into contracts with the insurance companies. Sounds good, but the vet has been placed in to a position of conflict as a result of their relationship with the insurance companies. Should they offer the client the cheaper treatment or the more expensive? The insurance company will pay the charges which ever they choose. So vets are under pressure to charge the more expensive option. It's much better for their business' profit.

A Dog Diarrhoea Examination - 'Now'

Consultation fee; Blood sampling fee (vet); Blood sampling fee (nurse); Blood sampling disposables - needle syringe sample pots; Blood tests; Blood and lab reporting fee; Faecal sample lab fee; Sample disposables; Lab handling and packing fee; Injection fee x2; Injection disposables x2; Injection Drug 1. 0.5m;l Injection Drug 2. 1.25ml; Tablets x10; Dispensing fee; Medicine x50ml; Dispensing fee; Special Diet 5kg Bag;

Dog Diarrhoea - 'Then'

Consultation fee - plus some kaolin.

A comparison of a common treatment protocol - 15 years apart

Where's the beef-cake?

So... Why are men disappearing from the vet profession?

As we discovered earlier, *money, reward and status* are the most important features of work for men. Men generally respect status more than women do (*on the whole; notwithstanding; no offence mate*). Men thus measure 'Being a Vet' differently than women do. And inevitably, men are recognising that the poor career and salary opportunities available in the vet profession don't offer much status - so they bugger off to some other better job.

Those men that still want to be vets often move into industry, government jobs, or para-veterinary roles soon after graduation. These are roles that offer clearer progression and salary growth than within clinical practice. These are the people who are hoping to use their vet training as a stepping stone to higher-value and inevitably *non-clinical* roles.

Many men have left the profession altogether. Young high-achieving men, who would have given vet training a go in the past, now no longer even apply for vet school as their first step in a career plan. Instead, they apply their high achieving, science-focused, self-disciplined and conscientious abilities to other careers. With universities now offering a much wider range of academic courses, many super-bright school students no longer automatically become a vet simply because it's the most difficult thing available. (Honest. It used to happen A LOT. I had at least 5 fellow students who told me this was their motivation. It probably still does occur to an extent - but less so with the men.) (The usual politically-correct apologies for generalizing and lacking full inclusivity Terms and Conditions apply. ©*HonestBobResearch2017*.)

Men no longer remain so readily on the narrow and un-self-critical 'academic escalator' that takes 15 year olds at one end and dumps out vets at the other. The increasingly low-status of veterinary work gives men a clear nudge to look around for more appropriate training or better roles. Men now choose a *first* degree that more closely suits their long term needs and desires:- They take degrees in *Biodynamic IT Engineering*; Or *Sports and Exercise Science* at Loughborough; Or *PPE* at Exeter.

Vet school courses have become very narrow - from a life-skill point of view - as we have discussed already. "Just being a clinical vet" doesn't promise an exciting future: Courses being restricted to the "necessary clinical applications of vet medicine" means Vet Medicine courses at university have also lost their attraction as foundation degrees: Degrees that would once have provided a basis for further research and skill development.

Those men that are still in the profession have set up para-veterinary businesses. Such as Emergency Care (OOH) Clinics; Surgical Instrument manufacturers; Drug and Service Buying Groups; Corporate Practice consolidators and franchise companies. Men have set up probiotics companies; management consultancies; animal-food companies. Some become media tycoons. Increasingly few men are solely occupied with clinical work. Those that are, are invariably heading towards being specialists in their field; or owners of their own practices.

Of course there are women who have done great stuff as well. We are after all, talking about a group of very high-achieving and driven people. People who have a strong sense of themselves and what they want to do. But we have to recognise that there are simply fewer women vets in leading roles *because* women know what they want. They want to be vets, not managers. And there are not many leaders' roles that include being a clinical vet: The women vets who are in leading roles have usually left clinical vetting far behind.

An EasyNote® for employers

How to use your cheap *new-vets* - A guide for employers

Don't mess about. Get two of them. They can look after each other that way. Like puppies. Make sure their contract is probationary for 3 months and terminates in 13 months. Make sure they have to work 3 months notice if they resign. Start looking for the next batch around Easter.

Plan to use them as nurses initially - your own veterinary nurses can train them. Then after a few weeks, they can nurse for each other as they begin to do vetting work - keep costs down. Maybe use them in your daily vaccination or cat neuter clinic at the branch surgery. Or they can do the home visits and taxi the difficult cases in for further workup. If you *do* keep one beyond the first year, renew the contract for a further 13 months (4 months notice) and they can mentor the fresh batch of new graduates for you.

Some new graduate vets are so desperate to have a job that they'll work for free. Do not do this. It is more work for you - they'll let you down when they *do* find a job, and the working relationship is all wrong. Free nurses and vets can upset the rest of your workforce as well, so be careful and remember they still need a vet's indemnity insurance.

How about using them to run your new Out Of Hours (OOH) service? The first 3 months can be a bit hairy, but after that, especially if you manage to retain one into a second year, then it's all hunky dory. And they'll clean the premises at the end of evening surgery, and feed and walk the animals in the evening and early morning.

You won't need a nurse because the vets will nurse for each other - there's a saving of £25,000 right there. You'll probably need three of them to make this work - which'll cost you about £70,000. You've saved £25,000 on the nurse. You've saved on cleaning and feeding. £10,000. They answer the phone at night - and so the client / practice relationship is in *good* shape. You lose fewer clients to the independent OOH provider: Say you retain 50 clients a year by providing this service - an expected usual service spend of £200 each, you've saved £10,000 on not losing clients. Not to mention what you earn for the OOH work actually done. There's no capital set-up costs (an IKEA bed and Billy book-case perhaps). Essentially, it's a free service for you.

The Eternal *New-Vets'* charging issue.

The introduction of computers changed veterinary pricing forever. Before computers, pricing for services was either guesswork, or simple fixed pricing: a calving cost £13.50, a dog with diarrhoea £5.65. If the client smiled a lot and touched your elbow, they often got it at half-price. When clinical records and work pricing transferred to computers, then detailed sequential costing of services, and drugs and disposables was possible.

Practice owners and managers have been *going on* at their vet assistants to CHARGE PROPERLY since Adam vaccinated his first kitten. *New-vets* have huge problems with pricing their work correctly. Explanations for this recurring 'problem' vary from laziness

all the way through to deliberate sabotage. But in reality, *most new-vet* pricing issues are down to self-esteem and confidence: *New-vets* just haven't developed the necessary resilience to be able to charge £50 for bandaging a dog's foot when they know it will probably fall off before the dog gets home.

They stress about charging £24 for an injection their boss has told them they *have* to give to every case of kennel-cough. An injection they have been taught at University is scientifically-unnecessary (EBVM). They find it hard to charge a 'late consult fee' (after the clinic should be closed), when in fact,

"the client phoned up 10 minutes after surgery ended, and I was doing a stitch-up anyway".

Employers. How to treat your new-vets so they charge-right:

You have two options when it comes to **paying** your vet a salary:

1) Pay them the same you'd charge for two cat vaccinations. And be a bit nicer too - give them some positive feedback and support. That'll help them to charge properly.

2) Or be an ogre: "Shout at them: Charge; Charge; Do bloods. Do x-rays. *Push* wormers. Don't just mention fleas, sell product. Do blood tests every 3 months. Use *CopyDrugh* instead of *BrilliantDrug* - yes the tablets are bigger and harder to give - just tell clients to cut them in half. And sedate more animals for minor procedures. And charge a sedation fee *and* the drugs."

Remember the 50% of new-vets who change jobs within a few years

New-vets soon stop working for practices run by ogres. Hopefully. They cite their main problem being a difficulty to be true to their *ethics*. And they also point to *control* as the biggest influence on their decision to leave the job. After only a few weeks working in an ogre's practice, our *new-vet* will be showing signs of wilting. Her skin will be grey, and slightly lumpy. Let's not forget she is still a driven high-achiever - just a very tired one who would kill for some respect from her colleagues. Oh, and some 'space' and support. She's finally realized there's nothing to be learnt in this particular practice. She knows she's a vet, but just not the one she wants to be. With luck, she finds the confidence to leave her first job and try elsewhere (Robinson, 2013).

Ethics

Not a county north of the Thames near London. It is the framework within which vets practice. It is how vets put into action their principles and morals. Vets deal with ethical problems every day. When new-graduate vets are forced to do clinical work that doesn't make sense to them they struggle. If a vet is prevented from following the ethical principles they have been taught and that they believe in, then they will begin to question their own professional status. Which leads to self-esteem issues...

Millennials

All those folk born after the mid 80s. Marketing companies view them as being the most significant demographic to lean towards individualism. Sinek (2016) stereotypes them as 'kids' who are very hard to manage. He accuses them of being 'entitled' and narcissistic, self-interested, unfocused and lazy. He suggests many are the product of 'failed parenting' - namely that their parents have *failed to show them how to fail.* Their parents applauded absolutely everything they did through their childhood, and gave them medals for coming in last.

Parents then passed the responsibility for good parenting onto the teachers. Who added to this failure by giving the kids good exam marks because they didn't want to be confronted by the parents.

Why is this important? ...It is because Millennial vets are thrown very suddenly into the real world of vetting when they land their first job. Here, mum can't get them a promotion, and they suddenly discover that they get nothing for coming last. Failing is not rewarded. So their self-image is shattered and their self-esteem plummets very quickly. Simon Sinek insists this is not their fault. He says employers of Millennials now have to change what they are doing. They have to find ways to build the confidence of their new employees. To reverse the huge confidence issues that Millennials are hiding behind their bravado. It is now the employers' turn to provide the support the parents and teachers have not.

Really? How does a business make money with new graduates then?

You would assume that with poor support, no mentoring or shadowing, long hours of demoralizing work, the *new-vets* would be killing animals left, right, and centre. But *new-vets* possess a special tool that they discovered all by themselves in their final years at university: cooperation. *Competition,* which had got them through the previous 3-4 years is now replaced by *cooperation.* Students are drowning in work during their final university years and to survive, they learn that competition with their friends is too brutal and too tiring. By using *team-working* instead, they find their life is easier. And safer.

In their last 2 years of training, they experience an awakening realization of the value of mutual support - the weak are supported by the strong. And vice versa. Because of their cooperative experiences at university, newly qualified vets try to hang together after graduation too. They network constantly. Invariably on the phone every evening and weekend - seeking and giving advice to their vet friends. They share their concerns. They become mentors for each other. How do they find the energy to work all day and think about work all night? They are high-achievers remember! These people never stop.

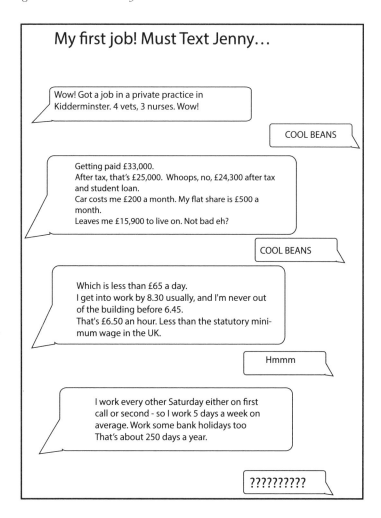

Because *new-vets* have this support network animals don't die. And clients don't sue (quite so often).

Mr Employer, if you are going to get a new-graduate, then as we recommended earlier, get 2 or 3. They are much better in packs because they are able to *cooperate and support each other*.

Remember the more experienced vets (who usually work more independently than *new-vets*) may have little time to offer support or encouragement to the *new-vets*. So if there are 2 or 3 of them, they just look after each other. Good for the manager. Not good for the *new-vets* as this is just another form of professional isolation.

If management is really bad, the *experienced vets* may be so appalled at their employer's attitude towards the *new-vets* that they themselves lose any compassion and interest in them to. A succession of new faces arrives and leaves every few months:

"The boss is away on holiday again which means more work for me looking after the new-grads"

The experienced vets *have a job to do* too, and they need to protect themselves and their own well-being. This can result in the *new-vets* feeling they are unworthy of their colleagues' time and effort. Which can leads to feelings of *isolation* for the *new-vets* (a bit like the new-recruits who arrived on the front lines in the Vietnam War. They were largely ignored by more experienced soldiers - until they began to show some skill and initiative or 'cracked-up' - or died.)

Mentoring & Support

The business owner's perspective:

- He had to pay for the premises and its design.

- He had to pay for the business in the first place.

- He had to work 14 hour days for the first 4 years.

- He had to pay for all the equipment.

- He had to pay for all the licences, Health & Safety protocols, lawyers, etc.

- He has to pay the staff - their wages; taxes; pensions; clothing; holiday pay; sickness pay; maternity pay; Jury duty; CPD allowance; training; support; mentoring.

- He has to pay for the drugs and disposables.

- He has to pay for marketing and online stuff.

The employee vet's perspective:

- She made over £1200 today with consults, drugs and ops.

- That's at least £300,000 per year she's making for the boss.

- She gets a tiny fraction of that back.

- She doesn't even get the mentoring he promised at the interview. Or the CPD allowance. And he never says anything good about her work…

Employer and employee - Poles apart

The Vet Times newspaper ran a job special edition that was published during Christmas 2017. Let's take a flying guess and assume the two smiling and happy people on the front cover are from a model agency and don't reflect reality. Let's turn the page: to Page 3. "*Meet the recruiters*".

The page features 3 Employers:

i) An innovative Private Practice;

ii) a large Referral Practice; and

iii), the main UK Out of Hours emergency provider.

Each employer has been asked to put 5 job priorities in the order they think is most important.

The Vet Times page also features 3 "job-seekers".

A) A 4 year-qualified vet looking to leave clinical work;

B) a final year student looking for clinical work; and

C), a 37 year old specialist veterinary nurse pharmacy manager who wants to improve on their £35,000 salary.

These 3 were asked to arrange the same 5 priorities in order of importance for them.

See the results below (Fig.6). These two young female vets state they mainly are looking for *supportive colleagues*. They list **salary** and **career prospects** as the least important factor when looking for a job. On the other hand, the employers are prioritizing the opposite: The two corporate practices think **careers and salary** are more important than supportive colleagues. The private practice recognises the value of support; but misses "*a perfect 10*" by thinking career opportunities are more important than a vet's control of their working environment.

When employers finally sit up and recognise that the jobs they are offering do not fulfil their *new-vets'* needs, then, and only then, will life begin to improve for the young profession. As Simon Sinek suggests in his treatise on "*Millennials in the Workplace*" (2016), these young people have mostly grown up in a positive reaffirming environment. Everything they have done so far in life has been applauded and rewarded by their parents and teachers. As a result, they don't know *how* to fail. When these young people do leave home and get a job and then fail - as we all do sometimes - then they will blame themselves. But we now know - you and me - that this is actually the employers' fault. It is actually the employers who are failing:

Employer and employee - Poles apart

Private Practice Priorities	Referral Practice	Emergency Vet Service	Vet 4 years out	Final Yr Student	Specialist Nurse
Most imp: Supportive colleagues	Most Imp. Working environment	Most imp: Career Progression	Most imp: Supportive colleagues	Most imp: Supportive colleagues	Working environment
2nd most imp Working environment	2nd Salary	Working Environment	Working environment	Working environment	Career Progression
3rd - Flexible working	3rd Career Progression	Salary	Flexible Working	Flexible Working	Salary
4th Career Progression	Flexible Working	Supportive Colleagues	Career Progression	Salary	Supportive colleagues
Least important: Salary	Supportive Colleagues	Least imp: Flexible working	Least important: Salary	Least Career Progression	Flexible Working

Fig.6 Comparing employee and employer aspirations

They are failing to recognise that this generation is different. They are failing to recognise that Millennials (as a group) have a need to be supported and cared for. It is what they have been given all their lives and they have no experience of a life without it. Millennials need to have their self-esteem bolstered within a safe environment. The gritty truth is this: *employers have to give their employees what their parents failed to.*

Other ways to be a good employer

We touched on this in the personality chapter when talking about the drift (downwards) in a vet's *conscientiousness* over the years. This decrease can be due to accrued 'experience' - as a vet becomes better at what they do, they become more selective about the parts of their job they need to be conscientious *about*. This results in an *overall* reduction in their Conscientiousness trait score. Other pressures on a vet's conscientiousness are more insidious and damaging - most often these are due to the vet's working environment. Namely working hours, holidays, recovery time, salary, clinical support, availability of valuable CPD, etc. Let's remember that we are talking about a group of people who *want* (or need) to be conscientious. When they are unable to be as conscientious as their innate trait-preference indicates they *need to be,* then *emotional exhaustion, stress, and disengagement* (from the job/the day/the world) are more likely. These mental pressures are the precursors of *burnout* (see the Chapter on Personality).

Employers, you need to support your vets so they can *be conscientious* if they need to be.

Rigid edicts and micro-managing

In this chapter, we are looking at the business of vetting, and these days, management is all-powerful when formulating a vet's day. The reality of the modern vet practice day is one of strict routines - consultation slots; surgical slots; duties; visits; paperwork; insurance claims; etc.

Vets (and nurses) are expected to fit into pre-determined roles at scheduled times of the day. And managements are increasingly dictatorial on *how* a vet should complete their role. Many vet managers now provide strict advice on *which* drugs to use and on what types of case. They create guidelines on what surgery to perform and how. They even list what tests a vet should offer in particular disease situations. Because

of the increased power of management within veterinary businesses combined with time-restrictions imposed on vets, these clinical guidelines tend to dictate rather than advise. Which we now know our stereotypical *Millennial vet* may well embrace initially. They quite like the idea of rules - makes them feel safer perhaps.

But the result of working within such a system of diktats over time will be the *new-vet* will feel dis-empowered within their role. This powerlessness is aggravated by the *new-vets'* inability to "shape their own day". Such dis-empowerment and lack of control are further precursors of *burnout* (see Chapter 1:).

Burnout is a product of an imbalance between

1) The *demands* of the job (sustained mental demands, emotional and physical effort), and

2) The Job *resources* available: this refers to the availability of help and support to enable the vet to achieve their goals.

Vets need to deal with the *high demands of the day,* and also less obviously, they need help for *personal development and growth*. Particularly important for our high-achievers is the provision of situations which facilitate a vet's *autonomy* (which is the ability to decide *your own course* through your life/job/relationship), *social support* and *career opportunities* (Mastenbroek, 2013).

When talking about Millennials working within the caring professions, *Simon Sinek* points out that their managers nearly always tell them every day that they must

> **Care for their customers; Care for their patients; Care for the organization.**

They are expected to make the customer and patient the centre of all they do. Then he asks,

> *But why do the managers not care for the carers?*
>
> *Carers have a need to be looked after too, and if they are not, they become exhausted, less interested in connecting with people, less caring.*

How to be a good employer - a list

Here are some ideas for employers (management) to consider - especially those who want to maintain the health of their employees:

- Help younger vets retain higher levels of conscientiousness with the simple act of supporting them: By reducing their workload; reducing their working-hours; and especially by giving them "recovery time".

- Help them by *avoiding work conflicts* (an example of such a conflict is asking a vet to *be their best* whilst not providing the *means* for them to be their best. A common example of this is to insist that a vet complete 15 specific actions during each consultation, and yet not provide them with the time to do it).

- Employers can help by allowing employee vets to be more autonomous

- By giving them positive feedback on their work
- By supporting their home demands (giving them time to pick up the kids from school; supporting an ill relative; etc.)
- By discussing their professional development with them.

These are just a few simple ways to keep our particular (and special) group of vet-people healthy, productive and happy. Management must remember that vets are not like normal employees - they are special, and they have a set of needs which are peculiar to them.

Where do old practices go when their parents retire?

Back-in-the-day, owners of practices would offer their more experienced 'vet assistants' a *partnership* in the business. The assistant would pay some money to the business, and they would then own a part of it. They would have more 'say' in the business, and would collect their share of the profits. When a partner decided to retire, he would sell his share back to the business for money. Easy.

This rarely happens now and this is why:

- Partnerships are actually a very cumbersome way to invest your money. If you are in a partnership, and want to sell your share, the only persons who can really buy it off you are the remaining partners. If you have fallen out with the other partners, then it can take years for you all to agree. And young people no longer want to tie themselves down for two decades. The world is a big and exciting place. Where's my passport?

- Men are generally more willing than women to invest capital (money) into a business for the longer term. But there are fewer men-vets these days…

- Tax changes have now made partnerships redundant. The majority of vet businesses are now Limited Companies with Boards of Directors. The owners of the business are the directors. They own *shares* in the business (a bit like the stock market). But to sell your shares, you have to sell them back to the other directors. So still a bit like partnership then! And it is hard to get *new-vets* to buy your shares because of their long-term *commitment issues*. Young vets already have large student debts from their university years. Not many want to build on those debts. Most clinical veterinary businesses keep the number of directors to a minimum so that when they do decide to sell, then there are fewer share-holders to please.

So who buys a practice when the owner's had enough?

Currently, the main buyers of private practices are the 'consolidators'. These large companies buy private veterinary practices. They all have their own particular business models on how they manage their practices, but most will continue to run them as standalone practices with their original names and branding. The 'business advantage' of consolidation is that all the individual practices can *share* 'back-room' resources (accountancy; legal services; human resources; drug supply, etc.).

The established and once loyal staff of these practices often drift away to other jobs after the purchase by big-business. New faces begin to appear and working practices inevitably change. Big-business brings big-business management ideas to replace the original - maybe somewhat amateurish - approach. The customers and clients invariably notice a gradual change in attitude, friendliness, service quality, etc.

Consolidator businesses will often try to retain the previous owners as employees after the purchase event. This is an attempt to stabilise the staffing of the business. They are often given the title of *'Supreme Clinical Director'* and will have responsibility to shape the clinical offering whilst passing administration and strategy onto the new owners - the consolidator company. If the original owners don't wish to stay, the consolidator company will appoint a new clinical director externally. They will guide and support the new clinical framework.

What if I want to buy a vet practice?

Men and women now have a wider range of options available to them if they wish to own or run their own clinical practice:

- **Buying an established practice** is not really a possibility. They are just too expensive and too tying. A large part of the sale cost of these private practices are the buildings and land. And we know how expensive property is these days! Incidentally, most consolidators do not buy the building when they purchase a private practice. They usually buy the 'business', but will usually just rent the building off the previous owner(s). The odd private practice still comes to market, but if the consolidators don't want it, then you probably shouldn't either.

- Buying (or renting) some premises and setting up a basic practice on your own is perfectly feasible, and is a relatively cheap entry route. Be aware though that there is increasing competition at this lower tier of vet-work :-notably from the 'high-street' franchise-practices (read on for more information). There is an ongoing 'land-grab' and there are very few sites (geographic areas) not already occupied by these franchises. But if you think you could be better than the practices already there, then set up next door and knock their socks off... You need to be brave, resourceful, and fairly well funded so that you can weather the inevitably slow start. You'll face sophisticated marketing and retail competition from the franchises as they are backed by highly funded businesses: Be aware that new franchise practices will usually sell their services very cheaply for the first 6-12 months to get customers through the doors. Do consider the methods of the large international coffee chains and American-style fast-food stores who entered the UK markets by setting up next door to the competition, and then wearing them down by offering falsely-cheap and sparkly products. They create a strong brand - which they advertise extensively on TV, internet and all the other media outlets. They can afford to do this. You can't. And by undercutting the prices of existing 'local' independent coffee shops and cafes, they force them out of business. You probably can't afford to fight these large American businesses head-on...

- Franchises. This is the increasingly popular route for experienced vets (6-10 years graduated) to obtain some kind of control over their professional lives.

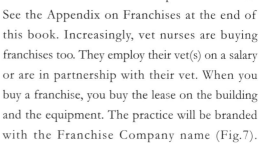

See the Appendix on Franchises at the end of this book. Increasingly, vet nurses are buying franchises too. They employ their vet(s) on a salary or are in partnership with their vet. When you buy a franchise, you buy the lease on the building and the equipment. The practice will be branded with the Franchise Company name (Fig.7).

Becoming a franchisee means there are rules that you have to follow. These will include:- How much to charge; how much to pay your employees; how many employees to have; they dictate your opening hours; etc. More contentious is some franchise companies will 'suggest' you follow their guidelines regarding your own clinical choices. This particularly relates to 'elective work' such as vaccinations, dentistry and neutering. The franchise company will provide your accountancy and legal services. You will usually have to use the drugs they supply to you through their own wholesalers.

Franchise owners are usually paid a minimum monthly retainer (salary).

Additionally, they receive a share of the practice profits. (It is important to note here that the accountants who control the money are in the employ of the franchise company - not the franchisee. This is an obvious conflict of interest - the vet generates the turnover and the franchise company's accountants decide how much of that money is returned to the vet as profit. Remember that accountants are clever folk and profit is a very flexible idea. I need you to know that your profits won't be as high as you think they should be!

Predatory lending. This is a term that Niall Ferguson introduces to us in his book The Great Degeneration. Quoting from Kennedy and Stiglitz' book on Law and Economics (2013)… he uses the term to describe the situation where large companies loan money to purchasers so they can buy goods and services from that same large company. Rather than a vet having to borrow the franchise purchase price from their bank to buy a vet franchise, the franchise companies will now offer to 'lend' them the money (that they then use to buy the franchise).

Ferguson quotes their work thus: *Current laws allowing financial firms to engage in predatory lending, combined with bankruptcy laws, have created a new class of partially indentured servants - people who might have to give as much as 25 per cent of what they earn for the rest of their lives to the banks* [or franchise companies - my words].

Predatory Lending

I have an apple.

You want an apple but you have no money.

So I lend you the money to buy the apple from me.

You now owe me money.

I will charge you interest on it until you pay it back.

Franchises have one big attraction for *Millennial* vets who are looking for a change: Namely, **'Security of income'**. Take a look at *Chapter 1. on Personality Traits* for the discussion of vets' generally low Openness to Experience traits. Low O reminds us that many vets aren't great personal risk-takers. And for women, increased *security* is one of the major attractions of owning a franchise practice. There are a few corporate alternatives to the Franchise offer, but they essentially add up to the same thing under a different name.

More on Franchises and all that.

You're 10 years out of vet school. You've 'lucked-out' - you've only had two jobs; both of which were supportive and encouraging. You've paid off half of your student debt. You recognise there's not much change on your career horizon. Your salary hasn't improved much in the last 6 years; you still have very little control over your 'working day' and this makes your social life very difficult to organize. You're tired of nagging your boss to upgrade the *Progressograph* machine. You've studied hard over the last 5 years and finally been awarded your *Advanced Practitioner (AP)(FU-RCVS) Certificate* of excellence. You have a *gorgeous* baby boy with your equally *gorgeous* man. Tolerance of your boss' meagre and self-interested ideas and methods has slipped of late. Morale at work is rather stretched; and at a low ebb. Your friends suggest you've reached *the* time - the time to be your own boss.

You want to be a vet. You always have… But business isn't very interesting. You *do* want to be part of a tight-knit small team that you choose yourself. You need enough money to live, but what the hell, you've never earned that much. You certainly don't want the debt and commitment that buying a directorship would entail. Franchises sound interesting. And they are very sparkly and new: Guaranteed income. Help with 'business stuff'. Don't have to think about equipment, premises, drugs. Franchises can feel like an exciting step away from the stifling atmosphere of employment.

The disadvantages of franchise ownership:

You don't have control of practice opening hours or of the structure of the day.

The franchise company 'do your books' for you - so you have to trust that they tell you what your *real* profit is - remember part of your income is a share of your practice's *profit*.

You don't have a full choice of drugs.

You have to do what the franchise company's marketing department tell you - even when it affects clinical decisions and your profits.

You have to follow rigorous sets of rules regarding employment, Health and Safety etc. There is still a lot of paperwork to be done despite your first impressions. You have taken out large loans through the franchise company. They are in a very powerful position should they disagree with your methods.

Advantages of franchise ownership:	Franchise description:
• Perceived- less risk to your capital (money). • You decide your personal hours of work (as long as you employ another vet). The practice will usually need to be staffed by vets 7 days a week - all day every day. • Predictable minimum salary. • Always-available advice from the franchise company. • The franchise company will hold your hand early on. • The franchise company has lots of experience. • They will do *some* staff training for you. • If you need to sell the business, it is easier to sell your franchise than a directorship /partnership. (You may get some of your original franchise fee back if you are lucky. The truth is many franchise holders who want to stop working don't even get their initial purchase fee back . They have to just walk away.)	• Small(ish) up front franchise purchase price which the company will lend to you. Bank loans to build the practice and purchase equipment which are organised through the franchise company as guarantor[i]. • The franchisee (the buyer) is essentially buying a commercial *brand* and paying for the building / equipment. • The franchisee does the vet work. • The franchisee chooses their nurses and support staff. The franchise company do the paper-work; legal and accountancy work; They do the marketing. Some *special offers* have to be offered to the clients; there is a (restricted) range of drugs available; they pay the staff and the franchisee out of the business' turnover.

_____

[i] Thinking of owning your own practice: which path to choose? 2014. Anonymous. Vet Times.

Fig.7 Some tabulated franchise pros & cons

Happy smiles after 5 or 6 years as a franchise owner when you realise how easy it all was. Maybe you should have taken the risk of just setting up a business from scratch? Maybe you should have not bought the franchise at all. Maybe taken out your own loans and retained more control of your finances. Taken a risk - and set it up yourself. Then you'd have more autonomy (total in fact), and accountants don't really cost that much.

You've discovered that you actually enjoy the training and staff thing... Hmmm. But high street brands are becoming very important for the consumer, and you can't just buy that. Hmmm.

Why are franchises so popular with the public?

Franchise practices seem to be popular with clients. There are very few that don't get very busy soon after opening. Why is that?

Most of these new customers come from other practices: Some to see what it's like, some to get the opening offers. These aren't new users of vet services, they are simply other practices' clients who live close by; are coming for a look; or fancy the opening cut-price deals.

Some of the new customers would never think of going to a 'normal' old-fashioned private-practice any more - many perceive them as elitist; expensive; unfriendly; etc.

The franchise model is so successful because it offers the customer all the usual *visual and shopping cues* that they understand. Customers are now savvy consumers, and they know what to look for when they buy stuff. Their consumer *language* has been developed by visits to other 'medical' professionals like opticians and dentists. Clever vet-franchise-designers have recognised that they need to use these cues in order to appeal to a modern-consumer. So they have plate-glass frontages with bright red and green posters featuring dogs, cats, rabbits, happy children and money-off-offers. The colours are primary, and the staff are pro-active and smiley. These consumers know what they want, and a converted Victorian semi with a cold draughty and badly painted waiting room just won't do any more. Not only does the franchise offer 'bright and cheerful', but it often seems cheaper too. At least for the simple stuff. Bit of a no-brainer really.

New business models coming our way

They are coming… Business is always innovating and there will be yet another way to be a vet soon.

For example, *drug buying groups* which were originally set up to negotiate better drug prices for independent practices, are now expanding their business models. They now provide equipment and services to practices. They supply employment and accountancy support. They arrange CPD - professional further education for vets. They do sound very much like the franchise offering don't they? Which is why drug buying groups are currently being bought up by *Big Business* as part of their UK expansion plans…

A recent development are the co-operative groups. Privately owned practices come together in an attempt to ape the efficiencies of the *conglomerate* model whilst retaining full clinical and business independence. Rather than the practices being owned by a large organization, the co-op is owned by the private practices themselves. The practices use the buying power of the co-op to obtain discounts on drugs; they have access to improved management and support networks. Many services (e.g. laboratory services) are cheaper. This is a relatively new model of practice support, and we don't know how stable it will be. Its success will depend largely on whether the constituent practices all get on together and have similar ambitions.

The over-arching aim of the co-ops is to provide practice owners with more business management options than they currently have. One of their ambitions is to provide their constituent practice owners with options when it comes to selling their business too. *What would be really great would be if the co-ops* could somehow encourage women leaders into some form of ownership model.

Distance diagnosis and treatment : Telemedicine

This is where a vet does vetty stuff from a distance. Either on the phone, or more commonly now, on the internet. Currently this model is not *customer-facing*. Distance medicine is currently only offered to GPs (General Practitioners) who may require qualified *advice* on their cases. Many GPs (normal vets) will telephone *specialist* vets at their preferred referral practices and discuss cases with them. Up until now, this has always been a free service. If professional second-opinions are required on X-Rays, blood results, etc., then a charge may be made.

VetCT is a new company in Cambridge who offer advice and guidance to GPs (normal vets) for a fee. The company sells the expertise of its specialists who offer interpretations of the data sent to them by GPs in practice. They offer interpretations of CT Scans, X-Rays, MRI, etc. They also offer unlimited access for GPs to talk to specialists about cases.

Which is all rather significant for our story: We have already discussed the drift towards de-professionalization and what it will mean for *new-vets*. We have predicted a gradual slide from vets being fully fledged professionals towards becoming 'advising and monitoring technicians'.

Therefore it is easy to see that a normal vet's clinical duty will be to follow (increasingly simplistic) EBVM algorithms which are designed to reduce vets' mistakes during diagnosis and treatment. VetCT are part of this drift: By supplying freely available access to "state-of-the-art" data, information, advice and veterinary protocols there is a risk of creating a new lower tier of vets. These would be vets who don't need great skills and knowledge to do the job day to day - they just need a phone or the Internet. VetCT's service, and services like them, will inevitably lead to GPs needing to be less good in their work.

These services risk giving them (or their employers) permission to acknowledge there is 'someone who knows more than I do'. Employers will love it because it will mean they can still get the job done, but will be able to pay less for their vets.

Another interesting aspect of VetCT's service is that they claim it will reduce the stress of being a GP. I can see that. But it will also reduce a vet's self-esteem; it will lessen the sense of their professional status; and their autonomy. Being a Vet will become less attractive - certainly to those self-actualized people currently thinking of it as a career.

Augmented Intelligence and Artificial Intelligence

A futuristic vision of *Telemedicine* includes remote vets *actually interacting* with the patient in real time. Advising the GP on tests to complete, treatments to give. It isn't a huge leap to imagine vets actually manipulating machines remotely: Using the internet and some *clever 'kit'* will be great for the highly skilled and highly paid vets who are sat at home holding their joysticks. Particularly good for those vets with low Extraversion who dislike dealing with people directly. It will be a less fulfilling life for Svetlana, the actual referring vet who spends her every day in a stuffy veterinary practice at the back of the Penge Branch of *Uncle Sam's Doggy Everything*.

A relatively small step from the vision of our remote vets sitting at home is AI: *Artificial Intelligence*. This, put simply, is the use of *algorithms* working alongside other technologies to *replace* the entire complex scaffold of the *"Veterinary Process"*. The more *AI*, the less work and responsibility for Svetlana at *Uncle Sam's Doggy Everything*. But as Vivienne Ming (2017) is keen to remind us, Artificial Intelligence is a *block* between people and their lives. *AI* removes the need for people *to do*. And so Vivienne Ming prefers the idea of *Augmented Intelligence*. This is where tech *helps* a person. To do their job better; to be healthier; to be more fulfilled.

And Svetlana in the Penge branch of *Uncle Sam's Doggy Everything* will prefer Augmented Intelligence too. She wants to be a vet. She wants the opportunity to care for animals. She doesn't just want to watch someone else do it for her. Artificial Intelligence would take her job *away*. Augmented Intelligence could make *her better*.

But we are not in San Francisco...

Vivienne Ming and Google are having a ball thinking of great ways to change lives, but 5 thousand miles away, gritty commercial reality will be with us here in the UK for a while yet:

I would guess that once the majority of private vet practices have gone, then the *Big-Money* owners of the high-street chains of vets will accelerate their simplification of the 'veterinary service':

Further evidence of the gradual de-professionalization of vets is seen with the traditional vets' roles which are being nibbled at by nurses, referral services and by augmentative technologies (*smart-phones*, *'Google'*, *Telemedicine*). The Federation of Veterinarians in Europe (FVE) recently commented about this insidious process:

> *"...the constant threat from highly-qualified non-veterinary individuals who are able to carry out tasks and functions previously the sole domain of the veterinarian, will ensure employment opportunities for veterinarians will decrease..."*

As we have now learned, consequent upon this de-professionalization, *vet students* are now being trained in algorithmic process (diagnosis and treatment using tick-boxes, 'mind-maps' and 'flow-charts'). This inevitably will lead to a simplification of the processes of clinical work: The vet will no longer need to use their own skills of deduction and interpretation: The algorithm will provide it all for them.

In the future, the well-financed high-street vet chains will install machines that can be operated by nurses/technicians. These will generate health and disease data and the 'results' will then be analysed and *interpreted* by computer technology. The computer will provide a tentative diagnosis. The same technology will then suggest the next diagnostic and therapeutic steps. Human vets will be needed to monitor these processes and will be involved in affirming the next treatment steps. Vets will use their training to check the machines' suggestions. As the technology improves, these human interactions will naturally decline further. Humans working in the 'industry' will become polarised into button-pushing technicians - lowly trained - on one side, and a new tier of *less-well trained* 'vets' who will apply a simplified series of treatments.

Grim and dystopian that may be, but it is exactly what happens in the high-street optical industry now.

More about the future of women : leadership

The talk on the street is all about women as leaders. There are many organizations and forum groups devoted to this important subject. I've attended a bunch of lecture threads at vet conferences totally focused on developing the young female majority in the profession. The profession is increasingly female - particularly those members who are working within a customer-facing role. Go to any decent vet conference now and there's nearly always a series of lectures on 'Women as Leaders'. Women are recognising that the vet business was essentially created by men - and it has been run for men ever since. This situation has made it almost impossible for women to find complete personal and career fulfilment in the existing veterinary framework. Women vets have often felt like a square peg in a round hole.

Now that the men are disappearing from the profession, various enlightened women are considering changing the framework. They hope to redesign the entire working-vet profession. Their hope is that this will lead to careers and business structures more suited *for women*. Women, with their particular gender-related and personality needs, could find positions that fully correspond with those needs and desires. Vetting could be fun again. And hopefully women who wish to progress will no longer need to keep trying to be men…

It is implicit that in such a rapidly changing profession, women *have* to be the new leaders: The main career path for vets used to be: Qualify; Become an assistant; Buy a partnership; Sell their share of the partnership to one of the assistant vets after 20-30 years. This model never worked too well for women - 20-30 years as a partner without a break feels like too much of a tie. But if a woman did decide to make partner, then she would invariably put herself under a load of pressure in order to justify that partnership. Partly for this reason, many women make excellent leaders.

As we have discussed, franchises have become the default choice for younger female vets wanting to have more control over their careers. There are immensely more opportunities for women to practice leadership in this segment than anywhere else - including the old-style partner/owner model. And the bonus is that women can continue to do clinical vetting in their new role as 'clinical directors' within their own franchise practices. As a franchisee, they can have significant influence on clinical matters, some business matters, and can have marked influence on employing practice staff.

A word of caution - before we get too excited: Clinical directors are often leaders in name only. They are in fact operating deep within a tier of management beneath head-office, and just above their employees. To advance their career beyond clinical director, a woman has to join management. *Then* they will certainly begin to have more control over practice strategy and development. But they have entered into a *Faustian Pact*: The price of this increased control and power is that they will have to stop doing clinical vet work.

The features of a leader

Do you have some of them. Do you think you will ever have them?

Here's a list of leadership attributes referenced against the 5 *Big 5* Personality traits To remind you, they are, Agreeableness, Openness to Experience, Conscientiousness, Neuroticism and Extraversion (Chomorro, 2010):

- Determination and high self-responsibility - We have to agree that vets usually have this in buckets. They need this to qualify as vets in the first place...

- The ability to learn from adversity and to seize chances - You need a high Openness to Experience for this. Vets tend to have low O.

- They need to be innovative and not constrained by procedure - *you need high O here to succeed.*

- Positive and self-confident - Many vets will struggle here - high Neuroticism can get in the way of feeling good and as N goes up, E goes down.

- Risk management - risk takers - People with low Openness to Experience are not risk takers - which explains the popularity of the safer routes to practice ownership namely franchises and partnerships.

- Motivation - High Conscientiousness levels will help here. Women are less motivated by money than men.

- Good people skills - hmm. Vets have been criticized since Noah for being rubbish managers of people. I've heard it a million times.

- Leaders have to be resilient_- very important. This goes some way to explaining vets' poor upper management skills. The typical vet with high N and low E has reduced resilience. They want to be liked by their employees. A vet with high A and high E is better here.

- Open to criticism - It's all about self-esteem - high N ain't good here.

There's a load more, but you get the idea.

A note of caution here :

Remember that although the men are leaving the profession, they still rule the veterinary businesses. Men are still the managers and business-men who create the rules and guidelines. Male managers, and women-acting-like-men, focus on reducing costs, increasing productivity, getting more value from their workforce and from their equipment. Caring for the people doing the work will often come second to *business success.*

It is true that women-vets may be able to negotiate improved working conditions for themselves. But as a group, they are still struggling to make any impact on the broader picture of vets' employment and conditions. The vet industry is absolutely commercialised. It is dominated by chains of mini-businesses owned by overseas mega-corporations. And large business is invariably male. Both in its personnel and in its business practices. I worry that the time may have passed when women could have significantly influenced the shape of the vet profession in order to consider gender issues more thoroughly…

So how can women be more than leaders-in-name-only?

How much of a leader do you want to be? Logically, that seems to be the first question we should ask.

If all you want is to be *top-dog* in a vet practice on the high street; and you are happy to accept business and (some) veterinary guidance from head office; and you are happy to have a ceiling on your income; and your ambition stops at a single practice - then

buy into a franchise model. If you want to be a leader *and* control *all aspects* of the business - then *setup* a new practice or *buy* an existing practice.

If you want to be a leader within a team of like-minded vets and nurses, and you have areas of interest (marketing, or maybe something clinical) then consider one of the declining number of privately-owned practices. Join as a vet employee and then hope to be offered some kind of directorship / ownership. You'll need to stay a while before you'll be offered this. This is the old-school model of vet ownership and even this is being corrupted by modern business practices:

Large privately owned practices are increasingly offering *limited partnerships* - this is where *new partners* (usually an effective and useful vet 5-8 years post-graduation) buy limited partnerships with their own money or debt (bank loans/'predatory lending' by the practice itself). These *limited-partners* have less influence on important practice decisions. They receive lower bonuses or profit share than full-partners do. Various management roles like HR, or making rotas, or nurse training, etc. are often given to the *limited partners* whilst the *full partners* make the bigger and more important and exciting decisions. Leadership? Sure! - But make sure you'll be happy with the restrictions on your powers. Read the small print…

Employee Ownership. Owners of private practices who are looking forward to retirement are searching *for different ways* to sell their businesses. Perhaps they just don't want to sell to the consolidators; perhaps they have an elevated sense of responsibility toward their employees. 'Employee Ownership' is the model used by the John Lewis Partnership in the UK. Everyone who works in their business 'owns' a part of it. They all receive a portion of the profits. No one is quite sure if this model can be applied to private vet practices yet, but there can be little doubt that workers in the business will be attracted by the idea of profit share.

Leadership ...

To my mind, if you seek (true) leadership opportunities whilst still wanting to be a vet, then choosing one of the private-practice *adaptations* is probably the best way to go. Your clinical skills will be appreciated by your colleagues, as will your developing management skills. These innovative business groups have enlightened approaches and will hopefully encourage the development of further 'soft skills' that will benefit you and them equally. Just make sure you've read the small print so that if you *are* taking a leadership role and are not just being given a title and expected to do all the dirty work. Make sure you are secure *and* that you will be rewarded and recognised for your work.

A note on rewards. Women are less influenced by money than men as we have discussed before. Women tend to look for other kinds of reward for their contributions - often in the form of increased *control* over their work environment. They are more likely to prioritise part-time working over more money; or flexible hours over a shiny *progressograph* machine. They will want clinical autonomy most of all. They will seek specialist qualifications; or will want to be supported in their role as Chair of a favourite charity. We all have a price and it's important to know what yours is.

Oh yes...

And why would you want to be a female leader?

The answer is easy:-

Being a leader is protective of burnout. And so by definition, it is protective of the effects of stress, depression and suicide. So even if you don't want to boss people about, or make loads of money, or gain more clinical freedom, you probably still want to be healthy!

It's Very Summary (today)

In this chapter, we've talked about the new vet landscape. We've mentioned new-style employers and how our increasingly fragile and 'sensitive' *new-vets* are experiencing the rapidly changing work-dynamic. Big Business, in its highly-visible high-street USA/ Venture-Capital-style form, is here to stay. That is, at least until the *'Great Reckonin''* - at which point, all deals are off.

There is no doubt that multiple-outlet, *Branded* suppliers of veterinary services to the public have 'hit the spot' for the consumer. The Public is expert in buying stuff, and they understand this new landscape better than most vets working within it. From the Public's point of view, it is a system that is hard to criticize. If the Public were to suddenly (and surprisingly) develop a genuine ability for empathy, they would be very shocked at the fragility of the people working in the practices they visit: Modern veterinary practice, from the vets' point of view, has many features of 18th century colonial slavery: 10 to 12 hour days. No support. High expectations. Severe punishments for failure. Little reward. No escape...

Hey! Cheer up. It can't be that bad - surely.

What about all those lovely *fur-babies* a vet is lucky enough to help with every day. And all their lovely *parents*... Let's talk about the group of people for which this faux-sentimental, yet in reality industrial, veterinary landscape has been specifically designed:- *The Client*...

Chapter 4

The Client

"There's an ever increasing divide separating the past from the present. And the client from the vet..."

Here's a slightly odd question: What is a client? And how are they different from a customer? That is two questions in fact. Someone clever once said,

"the difference between a customer and a client is the patient".

Which is really very clever indeed. Hmmm…

OK. Less of the messing about. This is a better definition:

A customer buys services and goods for themselves. They buy a new TV at John Lewis; Or broadband from E-BT-Talk. Or they get their boiler mended by a plumber. These are all customers. A client on the other hand receives services and goods on behalf of their animal.

Individualism

You may be aware there's been major social change over the last 100 years. The world, and particularly the way people interact within it, has changed hugely: One of the most notable changes in western society has been the development of *individualism*. This describes the situation where a person's main priority becomes *his own* needs and desires:- Rather than considering his role and responsibilities within a (cooperative) society, he considers more what society can do for him.

"Think not of what you can do for your world. Think of what the world can do for you"

Individualism is what informs the daily outrage we read on the social-media: Outrage at reduced government support. Outrage at poor policing. Outrage at the colour of a neighbour's swimming costume. *Individualism* is what makes people shout about *their rights* rather than about their *responsibilities*. Individualism is what shapes a person's self-belief: Think about it - how rarely do we hear someone genuinely admitting to being wrong these days?

Consumerism

If you *combine* individualism with an improved consumer skill-set, then you end up with some very savvy buyers of goods and services. *Individualistic* people spend a lot of their daily effort on learning and refining the "art of buying". Many consumers may not be very well 'educated', but they certainly are well-informed. With the advent of the internet as an information channel, there is now a massive amount of information available to anyone who has fingers and a keypad. The more information - the less mystery there is in the world.

Freely available information leads to the slaughter of many a *sacred cow*. Once upon a time, our only buying option was the choice of shop, or which dentist to use? Our questions would have been,

> **"Can I afford it? Is there any car-parking? Do the shop-assistants know their stuff and are they helpful?"**

But now, shoppers self-educate about the product or service *before* buying. The guy in the local electrical store no longer offers advice. He just makes you feel good about your own choice and collects your money. The doctor in your local surgery doesn't tell you what should be done. He asks *you* what *you* want him to do.

Less and less people [*sic*] buy anything without doing 'research' first. People spend many hours searching for marginal savings on goods. Seeking out the 'latest fashion', and finding how to get it before anyone else.

Some consumers have taken on the role of crusader: They seem to regard their purchasing efforts as being the equivalent of being 'ordained by God'. Many feel their rights as purchasers are inviolate. They feel their cause is right, and that *'to buy'* is as close to godliness (or whatever the modern equivalent of godliness is) as *Ant is to Dec* (once popular double-act entertainers in UK).

Some philosophers suggest money has become a real alternative to God (Wariboko, 2008). We are told that religion allows people to connect to an *outer* reality (God). It is this connection that then informs and affects believers' social relationships on earth. When God is no longer around (or as important as in our secular world), then it seems that money can fulfil a similar role: Both money and religion are based on belief. Trust me. (You *believe* an apple is worth 50pence. You don't *know* it. In fact it may be 75p next week. And the apple hasn't changed...). Money and Religion give structure and meaning to life. They both offer routes toward aspiration; and they both offer dreams of fulfilment.

Cooperative medicine

Human patients in the UK now experience a very different form of medical health delivery than they did in the past. Medical practitioners - doctors - are now trained to practice something called cooperative medicine:-

A patient's health was once a matter for the doctor. The doctor made a diagnosis and then instituted treatment. With the advent of cooperative medicine, a patient's health has becomes a team effort - the patient's opinions and choices have become integral to the treatment process. The patient is now as important a team-member as the doctor.

Thus doctor / patient boundaries have changed: The modern doctor, having made his provisional diagnosis, offers a list of treatment options, and the patient expects to (and is expected to) make a choice. The patient feels involved, and paradoxically, the patient experiences the feeling that their doctor trusts them *and* their opinion in return! The patient has been empowered by making them part of the team.

Surely you've noticed that pretty well every adult acts like they're *now a doctor* - in all but name? Which is a turn-around from 20 years ago: Back-in-the-day, a patient would go to the doctor because *they didn't* know what was wrong. They expected the doctor to reach a diagnosis, and then tell them *what had to be done.* The doctor was expected to make choices on behalf of the patient. The change to *cooperative medicine* encourages patients to seek information *before* meeting with their doctor. In fact, the process *demands* that they do their research first! The patient is expected to have enough information so that they can understand the choices better. With guidance, they can then feel *they* are choosing the best, or most appropriate one.

Cooperative medicine works reasonably well for patients who are bright-young-things with access to the internet and medical search engines. It works less well with older patients, and those incapable of *demanding* quality health care. Or those incapable of questioning poor health outcomes.

Vets now recognise cooperative medicine playing out in their own practices too. Increasingly, clients enter the consult room with a list of provisional diagnoses on a sheet of A4, or on their iPhone. They often have reams of information; differential diagnoses; opinions from the "great unwashed" on forums or from 'online sages'. They have spent hours reading blogs on www.beyourownvet.kim. Consequently, many clients arrive at the vets with established and pre-formulated ideas on their pet's diagnosis and treatment plans. Which means that the visit to the vet is often seen primarily as a process of verification. Or as a source of drugs or investigatory tests depending what the client has decided.

More sinister, occasionally a visit to the vet becomes a game of testing and trapping the vet,

> *"Let's see if the vet knows as much as we do!"*

Society, and Millennials in particular, are rejecting experts of all kinds (Powys-White, 2010). As part of a generalised disengagement, people have developed a suspicion of people who profess a monopoly on knowledge. Driven both by TV and by *'Doctor Google'* (more later), many people are trying to take direct control of their own problems. There is a theory that this is driven by people's insecurity and fear. A modern distrust of the world overflows into a distrust of experts within it. The reality and accessibility of the information-&-opinion-rich-internet is that people now trust their own 'research' rather than the real-life expert's. Paradoxically, and somewhat ironically, this rejection of *real person* help can lead to a further increase in their own stress and insecurity. By rejecting expertise and support, people are simply adding to their problems.

The vet profession's response to the challenge of *the informed client* has been to teach 'cooperative medicine' to its vet students. This is reactive and reflects the changes in client relations we have already touched upon. The end result is that by giving the client choices, the vet feels they are *sharing responsibility* for the outcomes - perhaps a way for a vet with lower self-esteem to avoid taking so much responsibility for any adverse health outcomes.

Professionalism

20 years ago, a client would be unlikely to question a professional's opinion or advice. Almost by definition! This state of affairs was encompassed in the word 'professional' - there was an assumed trust in the professional's ability and their knowledge.

There is now a new sparkly *'digital information curtain'* hanging between advisor and the advised. And along with other changes in this relationship, there has been an inevitable and growing distrust of professionals of all kinds. Interestingly, professionals themselves are reporting a corresponding loss of trust in themselves: *Cooperative medicine* can lead to a vet (or doctor) questioning their own value within the relationship: Perhaps this is a feature of the *'Impostor Syndrome'* - the psychological problem that we talked about in the second part of Chapter 1.

The consumer too, although initially puffed up by being more closely involved within the medical machinery, is often confused and overwhelmed by their ever increasing responsibilities (to themselves). They must often feel out of their depth with no one to turn to as they are constantly encouraged to retain personal control: No longer do they go to the doctor to be treated. Increasingly they are expected to be both the patient *and* doctor.

The confusion caused by cooperative medicine means the consumer or client is no longer sure what a visit to the vet *is for*. Increasingly, vets are mentioning that clients don't seem to know what to do with the information and advice delivered to them in the consult room:

> *Recently, the boss of a practice received a letter of complaint from a client. The client had visited the surgery the previous week for a health check on their new puppy. The young vet had discovered a heart murmur and suggested they bring the puppy back for a second-opinion with the practice-owner in a few weeks.*

> *The letter of complaint referred to the second visit with the practice-owner:*

> *It transpired that the client was complaining that the practice-owner didn't fuss the puppy enough and had spent too much time talking about the heart murmur. They felt that their puppy's needs hadn't been respected…*

This story demonstrates the confusion clients are feeling. They increasingly misunderstand exactly why they are at the vets, and often don't know what it is they need or want from the vet.

Clients, especially the younger ones, are now looking to fulfil 3 things during their visits to the vet:

1.   Affirmation and congratulations on their puppy purchase (with approval of the huge sum of money spent on buying it).

2.   Affirmation of their own (internet derived) diagnostic skills. I've noticed increasing numbers of clients are intolerant of history-taking - a prerequisite of a valuable diagnosis. They seem to want the vet to simply listen to their own diagnosis, and then start treatment.

3.   Confirmation of their own treatment ideas.

Additionally, our consumer-savvy clients are looking for added value on top of the usual vet services: They are looking for a kind of vicarious love from the vet who must fuss their animal 'properly'; Or free stuff; Or membership of branded Practice 'Health Plans'.

Health Plans

The client joins the practice health-plan by paying money to the practice every month by direct-debit. The benefits of membership are usually "free" worming and 'free' flea control. Often discounts on certain procedures are included (dentistry, neutering, etc.). A large part of the success of this innovation seems to be that it reinforces the client's own sense of *their* 'professionalism' - about which we spoke above. Health-plan membership supports the client's conviction of their own veterinary knowledge and skills. Health Plans also can make a client feel part of the practice's brand. People love belonging to clubs. Even if they mistrust the profession as a whole, they still want the reassurance of being part of the brand.

> *To paraphrase Oscar Wilde, Clients are people who know the price of everything and the value of nothing.*

Relationships

Savvy clients consider themselves to be *empowered consumers of veterinary services*. The most obvious result of this is a loss of 'practice loyalty'. The term 'Practice Loyalty' refers to the situation when a client unquestioningly always visits the same practice for *all* their veterinary requirements. Having loyal clients is something that vets pride themselves in. It helps the business in times of economic recession and also makes vets feel good about themselves. But increasingly, clients are using their 'knowledge', and particularly their "understanding" of their pets' needs, to go to whichever practice best serves those needs: Clients may go to a small corporate practice for cheap vaccination and worming. They may join its Health Plan. They will chose to go to a 'middle tier' practice if their dog is ill. They may go straight to a referral practice if *they consider* the problem too complex for the middle tier practice. Clients are now self-referring their pets based on their own 'veterinary judgement'. This lack of loyalty is hurtful to many vets - partially because many vets, being high achiever types, want to be

'All things to all men'

They want to offer as many services as possible to their clients - which is partially the reason behind the 'Health Plans' we mentioned above. Many vets feel they are letting themselves down when a client drives past their door without stopping. Many older vets, who haven't got used to this phenomenon, can't understand why someone *wouldn't* always come to their surgery for all their needs. It seems odd to them. Paradoxically and somewhat patronisingly, these vets feel the client is losing out (on their skills). Sorrow then can turn to anger and annoyance with the 'public'. This further alienates the vet from the client. It's not really about the money - Vets, when they are wearing their vet hat, are all about what they feel is best for the animal…

The RCVS used to make it very difficult for clients to swap and change between practices. Whenever a client and their animal moved from one practice to another, the RCVS made it mandatory that *all the animal's clinical* history was transferred *before the animal was seen.* The RCVS even stated that the client couldn't carry the history across themselves - it had to be requested directly by the new vet from the old one. This procedure made visiting a new vet practice clunky and tedious for client and vet alike. But now, clients are refusing to fall in with this system. As we noted, many are not loyal to one practice anymore and so 'have' 2 or 3 practices that they call their own. This has made the transfer of clinical histories a bureaucratic nightmare.

The introduction of the GDPR (Regulation (EU) 2016/6791 of the General Data Protection Regulation privacy protocols) in 2018 has added further problems for vet practices attempting to obtain consent for such data transfer. The RCVS system has become cumbersome and effectively useless. Many generalist vet practices receiving a visit from a new client now rarely bother to ask about an animal's previous vets. High-level referral practices (universities and the like) are pretty well the only ones now seeking all previous clinical histories consistently. The chances are that this system will soon be replaced with a simpler *qualitative* one - probably sooner than later.

More about the RCVS

The *Royal College of Veterinary Surgeons* is the regulatory body for the vet profession. Their statutory (yes - legal) aims are to 'protect the public' and safeguard the 'welfare of animals' *from* veterinary surgeons. Notice that their aim is NOT to protect or help the vets themselves. The RCVS exists to ensure vet practice is carried out within a set of guidelines, and that the *public and animals are protected from any veterinary excesses.*

The RCVS performs its duties by interpreting Government Law (The Veterinary Surgeons Act 1966 - soon to be updated). The RCVS regulates its members by publishing 'Regulations' that vets have to follow in their daily work. These are enforced by a 'triage' system which feeds unlucky vets who have had complaints made against them into a *full-on* in-house legal court system (wigs and all!). These are the 'disciplinary committees' which have the ultimate power to remove a vet's name from 'the register'. Having your *'name removed from the register'* (aka. "struck off") means it is then criminally illegal to practice veterinary surgery. That is until such time as you are able to persuade the RCVS to put your name back onto the register.

There is a (somewhat paranoid) worry within the vet-profession that 'the public' are learning to use these published codes of conduct *against* vets for their self-benefit. Many clients complaining to the RCVS have not even informed the vet themselves that they have made a complaint. They are using the RCVS disciplinary system as a first resort. Which is further evidence of the loss of trust and greater moral distance between the public and their vets. The widespread emergence of online lawyers, generic advice and uninformed trolling on forums has led to a major rise in *speculative* complaints to the RCVS -

"Let's give it a stab, and see what we can get"

Interestingly and not surprising: many complaints made to the RCVS follow sharply on the heels of a large vet bill landing on the door-mat…

Complaining is being made easier for clients: The consumer organisation *Which?* even produce template complaint letters, and they offer advice on the best procedures to follow. Vets increasingly feel that they are a soft target.

To further add to vets' feelings of paranoia, a recent CEO (Chief Executive Officer) of the RCVS was previously the CEO of Australia's leading consumer advocacy group CHOICE. This fact has added fuel to the fire of vets seeming vulnerability to the public's wrath. They are correspondingly worried that this change of leadership has led to the RCVS encouraging the public to make even more complaints (now euphemistically called 'Concerns' by the RCVS). And additionally this public-facing agenda means many vets fear that they will not be 'heard' sympathetically by their judges at RCVS Towers in London. They fear that they will be steam-rollered by the diktat that *the customer is always right*.

Le Boureau.

Don't get me wrong, I have nothing against openness and honesty. If a client has cause for complaint, then they should have recourse to the law or to the RCVS. The problem is that the public's complaint threshold is obviously decreasing. And there is no risk for the client when they take a complaint to the RCVS. There are no costs involved for them.

Vets have little or no recourse to justice when they are unfairly accused, and certainly cannot demand recompense from the complainant if the complaint is subsequently dismissed by the RCVS. The disciplinary process usually takes many months, and the vet has to continue functioning throughout this time. They have to try and ignore the possibility they may be "struck off". They receive little support from the RCVS during this process. Some less resilient vets quite naturally suffer significant health-damaging mental strain whilst waiting for the process to complete. The complainants have nothing to lose. The vet has everything to lose:

Many vets (*VPP survey 2015*) cite their worry about complaints - particularly complaints that escalate to the RCVS Investigative Committees - as being one of their main stressors in practice. The younger, less resilient members are particularly vulnerable.

Defensive medicine - partially a response to clients' attitudes

As we have seen, clients are consumers, and they are increasingly well versed in their 'consumer rights'. They see little difference between buying a bitch spay, and buying a central-heating boiler.

A constant fear of complaint, and the imperative *to always be correct,* has led vets to perform 'defensive medicine'. We have discussed this in the previous chapter. But being a central response to the *confrontational nature* of veterinary practice, it is worth revisiting:

Defensive medicine describes how a vet approaches their work. The most tangible result is they do absolutely *everything* veterinary that they *should*. They can't afford to be seen to have missed a part of whatever the 'recommended' approach to a case is. Which sounds good, but is in fact causing animals to undergo far more tests and to receive many more drugs than is reasonable for their medical condition. These vets who are practising *defensively* will 'bend' their practice protocols. By doing everything possible, they are protecting themselves from an accusation of professional negligence. The end-result often unfortunately disadvantages the animal either through 'over-treatment', or no treatment at all because the client feels the costs are too high: The *ethical and morally balanced treatment* of the animal is being forced into second place to the vet's need for *safety from complaint and litigation*.

A quick look at the current *Code of Professional Conduct* (the written veterinary code of ethics) confirms this shift. Constant (almost weekly) updates to the code now reveal that the RCVS is giving specific advice to vets on *how* to practice - an area of regulation they previously eschewed (*smaller than a hide-bone; tastier than a tin of tuna*).

An example: The RCVS Code Of Professional Conduct (April 2018) - on the provision of first aid and pain relief:-

"Veterinary surgeons and veterinary nurses should ensure that support staff for whom they are responsible are competent, courteous and properly trained."

The definition of the word 'professional' has changed.

Back-in-the-day, professionals were people who performed specific roles within a set of strict rules and regulations. These rules were set out by government in the form of laws. These rules were then applied by the specific professional bodies to their members - say The Law Society, The British Medical Association, The Royal College of Veterinary Surgeons.

'Professional' is defined as "A paid occupation, especially one that involves prolonged training and a formal qualification." (Oxforddictionaries.com)

In the 1970s and 1980s, the government turned its focus on to public-sector jobs. Jobs such as social work and teaching. These roles were based (and still are) within a regulatory framework, but it is a framework focused on the end-user rather than the 'person' doing the work . These are the laws and regulations that apply to children, or to the homeless. Because they are working in a regulated area, people in teaching and social work have begun to call themselves professionals - obviously encouraged by their employers (the government) in the hope that a change in status would make up for a reduction in working conditions. (Cynicism alert.)

There is now significant slippage in the term professional . Managers now call themselves professionals. *Footballers do too - even people working behind bars.* Consequently, there is a change of relationship: Professionals were once regarded as being skilled, adept and moral in their work. It was assumed they followed a code of ethics. With the change of meaning explained above, the word professional no longer carries such weight. A professional no longer is seen to be 'above' the rest. This definition slippage has a significant effect on the relationship between vet and client. It informs how clients view vets.

I'm not sure why the word *courteous* is in that sentence on the previous page. It has little to do with protecting the public or animal welfare. The RCVS are telling vets to smile more!

The Code Of Professional Conduct - on the transfer of animals to emergency carers:-

"If the expectation is that the period of veterinary care might straddle a change of personnel: (e.g. staff duty Rota changeovers) or even a change of practice or premises (e.g. transfer to a dedicated out of hours provider or to a referral facility) it is imperative that a plan is developed to manage this and a contingency plan considered should circumstances change. Such a plan should encompass:

a) the transmission of relevant clinical information

b) the availability of the necessary staffing, equipment and medicines

c) the method of transportation and any necessary ancillary considerations (e.g. oxygen therapy, continuous fluid administration, pain relief, professional staff in attendance)

d) the likelihood that the period of care will exceed that available at the place of transfer, i.e. the animal should be subjected to the minimum of transfers appropriate to that animal and owner.

All of which suggests the code of conduct is becoming overly dogmatic, and is attempting to micro-manage the practice of vet medicine (through imposing rigid guidelines (however commendable these may be))... Another step in the de-professionalization of the modern vet.

Profit through fear

Defensive medicine can be good for the bottom line (business profit):

- Defensive medicine means everything has to be discussed, explained, and signatures obtained to show understanding. It all takes time - add £10 to consultation fee.

- Defensive medicine means that more tests (lo-tech or hi-tech) are used on all cases - add £35-£2500.

- Defensive medicine means referrals are offered to clients sooner - vets' perceptions of what constitutes *advanced treatments* is changing and they are becoming less willing to perform treatments they are not 'expert' in - add £1800-£15,000.

STOP PRESS: With clients increasingly using technology (smart-phones etc.) to *actually record or film* their interactions with the vet (usually secretly), there is little wonder we all practice defensively. Don't forget to try and smile for the camera...

Clients and their changing relationships with their animals

Take an average UK family in 1985: Two adults, 3 children, a dog, and a cat. Uncle Jim and his wife live 3 doors down. Grandparents live 2 streets away. The adults meet their friends in the pub, or the club. The children meet theirs in the park, or on the corner. Mum and Dad are the dog and cats' owners. They feed them. They walk them. They are fond of them, and they form an indispensable part of everyone's lives. The animals fit into what is known as a(n) *'hierarchy of concern'*. Meaning the 'two adults' care firstly for themselves, then their spouse, their children, their relatives and their friends - in that order of preference.

In 1985, the dog and cat were almost always at the bottom of this pile. Friends were favoured over the animals - relatives certainly were. If the decision was to help Uncle Jim get over his 'stroke', but it meant getting rid of the cat, then so be it. Bye-Bye Pussy-Cat.

Over the intervening years since 1985, society has changed - not least in wealth and 'mobility'. It can be argued that with increased wealth comes isolation. Although wealth is often regarded as a major life-aspiration, possessors of wealth will often view other people with increased suspicion. Wealth contributes to people building high walls around their houses; and also around themselves. In the pursuance of wealth, people are travelling further afield in search of jobs and leisure which are no longer available locally. The increasing refinement of industry, commerce and logistics has led to job specialization. Specialized jobs tend to concentrate in certain areas of the Country, and to participate, a worker has to move house. This has led to a fragmenting of the  family unit - grand-parents are less likely to live within a few minutes of their grand-children. When children leave home, they now move far away for a brighter and better life. Friends who live locally move away. Thus new-made friends are less likely to be life-long, and more often than not, are no more than close-acquaintances.

The modern family looks different: not least because our 'two adults' are now more *socially* isolated - as well as geographically. Grandparents live in Durham. Parents live in Milton Keynes. Kids go to school in North London and will probably work or study in the capital before moving to Bristol. Often the only constant in people's lives is their relationship with their animals. They naturally believe their animals are totally dependent on them. And this is inevitably (mis)interpreted as unquestioning trust. Animals are un-threatening and trusting - which looks very like "love".

Love is what many modern people now believe they are seeing in their pets' eyes. So they love their animals in return. In extreme cases, this can lead to adults developing all-consuming relationships with their animals: Some even imagine they are living within a loving monogamous relationship.

Another extreme is when some overly-pet-attached people become crusading serial 'rescuers' of dogs and cats from council and charity dog-pounds. Some people go the next step and 'rescue' dogs from Eastern European countries such as Romania and Belarus. Our model family's two adults now often favour their animals over their friends and relatives. Some will happily state that if it came to a choice between their animals or their children, then the dog would win every time. They devote huge amounts of time and money to their animal's care. They exhibit indignation when they suspect that someone else doesn't share their anthropomorphic attitudes.

Some anthropology:

I was staying at a Turkish holiday resort last year. There were plenty of kids and babies. Many of the inmates were newly affluent Russians. I noticed something happening I had never seen before: I saw a change in how people related to their children - notably they appeared to view them as possessions. These parents showed a constant desire for approval from other adults in the resort: A stranger would wander over, and begin to talk to the child. Its parents would positively glow as they basked in the child's reflected glory. The parents would beam, and smile. They would move closer to the child, maybe lay a hand on their shoulder. Maybe show an image from their phone. They seemed very pleased with themselves. It happened again and again.

Another manifestation of this 'possession phenomenon' will be recognizable to us all: Many of the parents seemed to relate with their children predominantly through the screens of their phones and 'Tablets'. I saw parents watching over their kids on the climbing frame whilst filming them. Often, a mother would direct their child to this climb, or to that slide - shaping them for the video. The kid would be nudged into smiling for the camera. Maybe the parents would buy a pomegranate from the beach vendor, and excitedly present it to the child whilst taking a 'Selfie' of their act of giving. It looked like these parents were making their children some kind of STAR in their own lives...

Why is this important? Well, the point is that not only do these actions further people's isolation from fleshy reality, but they reveal the lack of authenticity in people's lives. It shows their inability to experience and have 'normal' relations. People are increasingly living an individualistic life where friendships and co-affirmation are obtained by *purchases,* by *possession, and by telling the world about it through social media.* And as vets, we see this every day as clients walk into our clinics carrying hugely expensive puppies and kittens - about which they know nothing. They seem to know little about responsibility, and little about care. Their prime motivation for visiting our clinics is that they seek our approval.

Possession and relationships

It is no surprise that people apply these values to their animals - much like the Russian mothers who felt so rewarded by *being in possession* of their children. There is a psychological condition called *Pet Attachment Disorde*r which describes the intense emotional relationship people can build with animals (Brown, 2001. Krause-Parello, 2008). In parallel with the formation of human / human relationships - and probably as a substitute for them - these human / pet relationships can become extreme and essential:

Sometimes these relationships are so 'central' that the relationship warps - to a point where the psychological disorder *'Münchhausen's by Proxy'* may become apparent in a person's behaviour (Rosenberg, 1987. Meadow, 1995). In this social/mental disorder, which is more usually associated with mothers and their children, animal-owners become so intensely involved with their pet that they begin to imagine their pet is suffering an array of increasingly serious 'illnesses' for which they need to seek veterinary help. This is an extreme warping of the pet / human relationship admittedly, but there is no doubt that in parallel with the anxiety parents now feel for their children, there is an anxiety and fear growing in the hearts of many 'pet-parents'. And these maladjustments manifest themselves in a similar fashion to the faulty parent / child version of the disorder.

The opposite side of the *ownership* coin is seen when people use their dogs and cats to raise their own self esteem. Like their expensive leather handbags and shoes, some animal-owners now prioritise their responsibility for *the purchasing decision* and the resulting *ownership* of their pet - rather than the *having*. This can lead to a changed relationship with other aspects of pet ownership: Vets are recognising that many owners have a decreased sense of *responsibility* for the health of their animals. They rejoice in their *ownership*, but give away the job of caring to others - dog walkers, vets, groomers, etc. Vets see this manifesting as an unwillingness to apply treatments to their pets. Or the rejection of advice on 'correcting' their pet's behaviour. (Vets widely report that they see the behaviour of dogs worsening.) Etc.

This is partly why some clients *demand* that the vets fuss and pat their pet. It's a reaffirmation of the clients' purchase choices, and also the elevated position the pet now holds within the family structure. Pet owners don't want to hear didactic lectures on health and behaviour issues. When a vet suggests their dog's behaviour needs correcting, or that their new kitten has an unhealthy over-bite, clients' first reaction is to feel that their *purchasing decisions* are being questioned. Some feel *insulted*. Rather than consider the problem, they adopt a defensive and outraged stance - they *shoot the messenger* - the vet.

Which is not to say people don't have their pets cared for. They just don't take *personal* responsibility for their health. Paradoxically, as they take less responsibility themselves, many pass it (self-righteously) on to the vet, or their insurance company, or the RSPCA, or the PDSA, or the police etc:

√ "Why didn't you send me a (SMS) text to say Bella was due her worming?"

√ "I can't give her tablets. You have to do it."

√ "I just couldn't keep my sweetie downstairs all night. It wasn't fair. So you now need to re-stitch the surgical wound that popped open."

√ "How was I supposed to know grapes are poisonous?"

√ "I pay the insurance premiums every month. What else do you want?"

This consumerist relationship between owner and vet means that the vet's role, which should be to help a client care for the health of their animal, has become blurred and muddy. Vets don't (shouldn't) have responsibility for their clients' dogs. A vet's responsibility is to offer advice, guidance, and to perform surgery. But ever desperate to help, vet practices now offer non-clinical services to dog owners:- applying treatments, giving pills, boarding; grooming; food and shop supplies; dog walking; and so on. Which further contributes to the client's confusion over a vet's true professional purpose.

Disposable and short-term pets

The distancing of a pet owner from their responsibilities is evidenced in their changing attitude to ownership itself: If a pet owner admits to themselves that they have messed up their purchasing decision, they may return the animal to the shop, or the breeder. Some people, as Shona Sibary told us in the Daily Mail Newspaper (2015), give the dog away when they've had enough of it. And then they go out and buy another pretty fluff-ball of fun the next day. Then they do it again a few months later. And then again.

> " *Clients, increasingly, are people who know the price of everything and the value of nothing."*

The Good Client:

"Never remembered for long the good client. The bad client remains etched in the mind forever... It's regrettable."

Do you remember studying for your exams as a teenager? Imagine you're back in your mixed-ability class. You're studying geography: Do you remember the good students? The ones who answer all the questions. Those engaged students who point easily to Burkina Faso or Zanzibar on the map. Or do you in fact just remember the disruptive bullies, the slab-headed monsters who screwed it up for everyone? Probably the latter. It's the same with clients - the vast majority of the people a vet sees in a day are lovely people who care greatly for their animals' welfare. These are the level-headed normal folk who manage to keep the relationship with their vet healthy. These are the clients who understand the vet-client-animal relationship, and how to get the best from it. They invariably want what's best for their pet, not themselves. A consult with these good people is a joyous experience. It is, probably, the ONE MAJOR REASON WHY VETS CONTINUE TO DO WHAT THEY DO. Interactions with these normal clients make the vet feel confirmed and trusted. She feels she has made an impact and has shared a valuable part of herself willingly.

It's the bad clients who force vets to practice defensively. The clients who disbelieve everything. Who "know" more than the vet. Those clients who "know their rights" and who's prime aim is to "engage in order to condemn". When a vet calls one of these clients into their consultation room, they know they are about to be trapped. So a vet will defend themselves from any perceived danger: And that can make a vet appear unfriendly and aloof. Which leads to more client distrust. Which means the client is more likely to make a complaint. Which then leads to the vet practicing even more defensively and giving even less of themselves.

A viscous circle [*sic*].

Defensive medicine? A definition...

Medicine needs a process to work -

Obtaining a history; assessment of symptoms; assessment of patient; selection of treatment goals; selection of treatment options; treatment application.

Sounds clear doesn't it? Not much room for interpretation or manoeuvre. But the truth is, vets choose how much to commit themselves to each stage of this process: Some have a bias to various treatment types. Some prefer surgery. Others prefer medicine. Others have differing opinions on goal selection - what is treatment hoping to achieve?

Defensive medicine occurs when a vet applies a

modifier to ALL the stages of their process. It is a type of medicine built around "the avoidance of clinical mistakes, inaccuracies, or less than perfect expected outcomes". A defensive vet uses less intuition and fewer subjective experiences in their decisions. Instead they use *quantifiable* data (stuff you can see and count). In fact, they use statistics:

"If 30 dogs with diarrhoea are treated with PoopStop, then 90% get better within 3 days. If PoopHaltTasty is used instead, then 82% get better in 4 days". The defensive vet obviously uses PoopStop, even though they know it is more expensive and tastes horrible. It is hard to give to dogs, and the vet suspects (but has no proof) that PoopHaltTasty actually works better than PoopStop if you add Marmite®. But to avoid any contention, our defensive vet sticks with the foul-tasting PoopStop.

This formulaic use of "research data" is informed by EBVM (Evidence Based Veterinary Medicine) as we noted earlier. It is a construct that is now widely taught in universities, and most *new-vets* use EBVM in their vetting practice. It keeps them safe. By using the guidelines that EBVM represent, they are less likely to chose the 'wrong' treatment. Perhaps more importantly, if they receive a complaint against them, then by practicing EBVM, they can defend themselves to the RCVS by showing they are building their treatment choices upon the opinions of 'better' vets:

Client types:

We like to compartmentalize things don't we? Well I do anyway - it helps... In my mind, there are many 'types' of client, and it would be fun to write about them. But I am reminded by my softer-tongued critics that that would be fatuous and severely 'off thread'.

There *is* one type of client I would like to write about though - because it is this type that causes so much upset, hurt and distress to vets. This is the client that vets cite when they talk about their own feelings of professional inadequacy and failure. This is the client that contributes to vets failing. It is the client that breaks the camel's back. Vets leave the profession or quit clinical work because of this client. These clients are a major contributor to vets' ill health - mental and physical. How should I describe and classify this client? They're not all tall; they're not all men, and they are not all horse owners. No, this is a classification of attitude and behaviour. I'm going to call them "The Self-Righteous Client".

The Self-Righteous Client : And compassion fatigue

There follows a dreadful series of generalizations and no small amount of bigotry. Indeed, this should have been written in a small text box, shaded grey and with warnings of INSUBSTANTIATION.

The Self-Righteous Client is:

- Usually Female - or occasionally a male/female cooperative unit

- Low income

- Dys-educated [*sic*]

- 30-50 years old - the demographic is sliding younger

- They wear an aggressive posture

- More than 1 pet - usually dogs and they are usually inappropriate - Mastiffs, Newfoundlands, Great Danes, Rottweilers.

- They usually have little or no history with the practice. They are often 'practice vagrants'.

- Here's the typical 'situation':

    The dog is ill and the vet advises some investigations and treatments . The Self-

Righteous Client makes an attempt to sell themselves as worthy 'rescue saints'. "The dog would have been KILLED if it hadn't been for them rescuing it from the dog pound. Who else would have this dog? Aren't we good martyrs? Can you do it for free like - for charity like - like?

"Can't it be done CHEAPER? How about just doing one thing rather than both? This is so wrong - you *should* make my Monty better. You have a Hippocratic oath!

"VETS ARE ONLY IN IT FOR THE MONEY - *just looking after yourselves. YOU VETS ARE S'POSED TO LOVE ANIMALS*

The Self-Righteous Client is adopting a patently false moral position. This enables them to feel it is OK to try and bully the vet into moderating their own ethics so the client can benefit.

The Self-Righteous Client is surprisingly damaging because they make it all so *personal*. And the vet obviously *can't answer* these accusations. She is a professional. She doesn't have the space in her day, or in her confidence, to respond with:

"that's ridiculous; unbased; irrelevant; hurtful; ignorant; smelly; stupid and idiotic."

The vet sees her duty as caring for the health of the dog. What use exchanging insults with its owners? How would the dog benefit from that? Many vets cite hearing,

"you're only in it for the money" as a major contributor to their compassion fatigue.

Vets know they are *trying very hard* to be compassionate and caring (often outside of their personality trait - see Personality Chapter) - and this costs them a lot every day anyway. To then have a total stranger come up to them and (ignorantly) accuse them of a lack of compassion for animals, and rapacious financial gluttony is *the most* hurtful thing ever.

But vets are intelligent and socially adept. They realise there is little to be achieved by engaging the Self-Righteous Client in argument. There's often no point as the client isn't actually listening anyway. The Self-Righteous Client will leave the practice - to try the same thing at another vets. But they leave behind a surprisingly deep scar on that vet's day, or week. Their self-confidence and self-image takes a knock. Many vets (especially the young ones) would really prefer to do it all for free of course. They do actually feel some sympathy for the Self-Righteous Client's plight. Which makes the insults even more painful.

Slowly, over time, vets' sympathies and compassion are worn down. *Compassion fatigue* approaches slowly - taking small steps.

A post I saw on a vet forum (www.vetsurgeon.org 2015), published anonymously, gave one vet's experience of compassion fatigue:

> …I have been experiencing the feeling … that whilst I care deeply about individual animals and do everything I can to prevent suffering and ensure successful treatment outcomes, I feel that I no longer have what it takes to put on the "front" and give the compassionate and caring approach to all of the owners, at all hours of day and night. Maybe it's because I have become cynical to the sob stories about why they can't pay bills or afford more than the very basic treatment for their animals...

> I personally have reached the point at which I no longer hold any desire to do clinical work because it brings with it the pain of having to explain the same things, over and over again while all the time feeling that any attempt to educate the client about their pet's needs and welfare is useless…

> …a sweeping generalisation I know, but explaining over and over again to people the benefits of preventative healthcare when in many cases you know they will fail to heed your advice because it's not what their breeder/sister/ aunt/dog walker has told them, is just getting too demoralising.

The angry and aggressive client

It does seem odd why a person who is bringing their animal to be helped can so easily become angry and intolerant. But look at the safety/aggression statistics for the NHS (NHS Protect Tables, 2017). They do not make pretty reading. Physical and verbal assaults are common for those working in the 'caring professions'.

I don't know for sure, but this phenomenon may relate to patients' sense of powerlessness. People (patients or customers of vets) are increasingly placed in what may seem to be faceless-bureaucratic machines, where they are expected to fend for themselves. A sense of powerlessness is a prime mediator of aggression and violence in some people. To get something done in the NHS these days, one has to "play the game". And the easiest way to play the game is to demand *'my rights'*. Some people are unable to claim their rights properly (for whatever reason), and their demands then overflow into violence. Some clients arrive at the surgery, already angry because of their prior *expectations* of being frustrated and powerless (BVA, 2017).

I took my Dad to A&E (Accident and Emergency Ward) the other day. We were sitting and waiting with 5 or 6 others. I walked back to reception and stood behind a young mother with her 3 year-old who was sitting on the shelf of the reception desk. The mother's mother was there too, and she told the receptionist the child had a severe rash. She said it was probably Hand Foot and Mouth disease. The receptionist stood up and excused herself saying she would see if the child could be placed into isolation. Once she was gone, the mother's mother turned to her daughter,

"It's always a good idea to exaggerate the symptoms. We'll get seen quicker this way."

A case of cynical and self-interested manipulation. Showing how readily people are willing to play the system. Every man for himself…

A note here on Animal Charities and their clients

Having said in Chapter 3 that the practise of veterinary medicine is characterised by a commercial relationship with the client, there is one area that isn't.

That is the area of Animal Charity work. Charities such as the PDSA and the Blue Cross who offer to treat people's pets at no cost to them.

Vets working in these environments organisations experience a markedly different relationship with their clients than those working on the High Street. Most of the Charities' clients are not expected to pay for their animal's treatments and so clients experience a different form of exchange with the veterinary process. Because this is not a *consumer-driven* purchase, clients tend to be more sanguine about receiving 'perfect' customer service and clinical outcomes. They are invariably less critical of the process because they have a lower stake in it.

This is not to say it's an easy ride for vets working in these environments. Vets still get shouted at - but there is a lower risk of criticism or litigation. Therefore vets can be less concerned about 'being struck off'.

This is an environment where there is a generally reduced demand for the *'personal touch'* and *empathy* from the vets. These attributes are therefore less relevant to their working day. Thus vets working in charities may be able to avoid some of the well-being issues that vets are at risk of in normal commercial practice. Especially if they have lower levels of Agreeableness - which is protective of burnout and depression.

The real deep-down vet

In this chapter we have discussed the relationship between vet and client. Practising as a vet is in large part a *customer-facing* role. Yes it's *about* animals, but more than 50% of a vet's day is spent talking to, or thinking about, the client. And so it is vital that we consider the client when we consider the life and work of a vet. The client is what shapes the vet's day.

Many vets, and even more the vet nurses, prefer spending their time and effort with animals rather than on people. For whatever reason, they feel more comfortable around non-humans and so have chosen a career where they can prioritise animals' welfare and health. Unfortunately, and paradoxically, choosing to be a vet is not a good choice for these people. The best vets turn out to be those folks that actually *like* people. Good vets are those that genuinely want to help animals *and* people. Good vets like to explain things and they have infinite patience.

> *"It would be a fantastic job if it weren't for the owners".*

Chapter 5

Being a Vet Or "What are Vets doing?"

So… You are thinking of becoming a vet. Or your teenager has mentioned veterinary as an option. Or you are a vet already, and you are wondering if there is anything else to it. Did you miss something?

How do you find out what being a vet is like?

The obvious thing to do is to take a look at some opinion-makers:- Books, TV, Film, teachers, friends, social-media, etc. Perhaps you will find information on *The Only Way is VetSchool* - my favourite episode is the one where Bonnie, the new vet intern, gets her boots dirty with the woman who does her eyebrows. Or maybe it is Afternoon TV that gets your attention: the not-so-memorable episode of *RemarkableVet* in which *Professor Remarkable* sews a new credit card into the flank of a Sprockä puppy after performing liposuction on its ear flaps. If these are your influencers, then you *really do* need to read on…*Really*…

Here are your research options:- I'm going to list them - I like lists because I'm a scientist at heart. And I have the concentration span of a 4 week old squirrel - I *will* forget what I've just read if I can't tick things off a list.

How to find out "What's it like *Being a Vet*?"

a) Try asking someone who *wants you* to be a vet: There are many influential people and organisations who directly benefit from you becoming a vet. Obviously, they're only going to tell you the good bits:

i) Number one and possibly the most influential is: **Your Mum and Dad** - that well known manipulative and opinionated organisation known as "the parents". They'd love you to be a vet. Being a Vet is easy for them and their friends to understand. Remember that "the parents" will never really understand a desire to do "Pure Chemistry at Oxford", or "a BA in the lesser known poetic works of Vladimir Turkoman at Bangor". They *will* understand doing 'vet'.

Who else wants YOU to be a vet?

ii) **Universities do definitely**… Their adverts and prospectuses are plastered with glossy images of smiling students and seriously-focused and reassuring professors. They show pictures of happy farmers and grateful cat owners. They'd love you to sign up.

Universities make a bunch of money from you: They collect money directly from your course fees and student accommodation. They collect money from various financial commissions, and On-Campus rents from cafés, bookshops, supermarkets; and etc. They *indirectly* benefit from keeping student numbers high too: Student numbers directly boost course desirability and academic kudos which then enables them to collect more money from the government.

Once you have graduated, then universities try to 'sell you' Post-Graduate education (MAs, PhDs, etc.) at £15 - £30,000 a year. An added bonus for the university is if you're a good student and you begin to *publish* written research then that means even more Kudos which means more income for them. And universities run on £udos. It is how they measure themselves against other universities.

iii) RCVS - The Royal College of Veterinary Surgeons wants you to be a vet too. The RCVS is the regulating body of the Vet Profession. It exists to protect the public from wayward veterinary surgeons, and it maintains standards.

The RCVS collect fees from Members and from Veterinary Specialists. The RCVS collects money from registered Vet businesses. It charges to register a vet. And to register a vet's hard-won post-graduate qualifications. And so on. More vets *means* more money.

The RCVS and the Universities are in bed together

The RCVS has a very close relationship with the universities. Some say too close (and sticky). And together, the universities and the RCVS have jumped onto the *Qualificationism* bandwagon:

Qualificationism is a university inspired process where a normal degree is deemed 'not enough'. As graduate degrees have been gradually devalued (for a bunch of reasons), so universities have encouraged graduates to complete further advanced qualifications after finishing their main degree. They offer a ladder of qualifications from MAs and PhDs through to a series of RCVS approved and promoted *Certification Schemes*. Their aim is to create an advanced tier of "more qualified" vets.

b) Q. What is it like to be a vet? Try asking practicing vets - the people doing the job:

> i) "It's the best thing I ever did. I love my job. If you work hard you can be as happy as me" or

ii) "It's a very hard job. Long hours - very long hours. Training is hard. It's all very rewarding though - despite the owners! I get to improve the welfare of animals and I relieve suffering. Work hard and you can be a vet too!" or

iii) "Sorry. I have no time now. I'll try and catch you later. Why not ask Tina Ay-Star who's our current student observing practice - she's in her final university year."

iv) Tina Ay-Star says " It's a great course. The teachers are amazing and I'm surrounded by other vet students. We all help each other. The campus is great. 'pretty busy at nights... You know... I've not had much time to actually think about actually Being a Vet. Too busy revising and lectures. It's gonna be amazing though eh!? Ask John, he graduated last year and is in his PSP year."

v) John shrugs, "It's too soon to tell. I can't help you. I'm off into industry as soon as I can. Always fancied Global International Soft Commodity Economics at A level, but messed up my Oxbridge exams - so talked my way into vet 'cos it was the next hardest thing to get into - 'thought it would look good on my CV"

If you ask 100 vets, you'll get 100 answers. Every answer is different. Obviously everyone has an opinion and remember *Being a Vet* is an incredibly complex idea.

Where do vets work now? A list - look out for this symbol →

Where do vets work now? **→ Vets for companion animals (dogs, cats, fluffy bunnies)**

During the 60s and 70s, what we now euphemistically call Companion Animal Practice began to lose its frivolous image. Skilled and respected practitioners began to concentrate on dogs and cats and pets. Others followed where these pioneers led. And over the last 40 years, the fruiting of our own *consumer society*; the increasing isolation of people from rural society; and increasing financial wealth; have all encouraged the creation of this sophisticated commercial veterinary offering to pet owners.

Where do vets work now? **→ Vets in Large Animal practice**

These are the guys treating sheep, cattle, goats and horses. Horses are now a leisure industry, and so working in this sector looks rather like the Companion Animal sector mentioned above. Farm animal practice has changed as we have discussed elsewhere. Increasingly, vets practice their surgical and medical skills on animals that are brought by their owners to the Vet Surgery premises. Occasionally a vet will visit a farm to treat a single animal, but only when it is very valuable, or possibly a pet to a wealthy owner.

Most large animal vets have adopted a consultant role. They spend the bulk of their time advising on herd care - focused on herd management, nutritional design and disease prevention. They often do routine health visits to farms every few weeks.

Where do vets work now? → **Vets in Industry:**

Callum Blair in an article in the Vet Times (2014) points out there are many roles for vets in industry. But he has a word of caution,

> *"If you don't like people, then don't come into industry, because we have to deal with people a lot..."*

Some vets work in industry in order to do *Research* - not many. Most *clinical* vets in industry spend their time looking after the animals that are bred and grown for *experiments* - investigating various human surgical procedures and the safety of chemicals and compounds. Some vets run technical teams and contribute to the training of drug-sales people (no clinical work). Some deliver technical 'lectures' about their company's products to practicing vets and nurses (no clinical work). Some become managers. Some enter marketing, some deal with drug licensing and some pharmaco-vigilance (no clinical work). Some become self-employed 'consultants' and sell their skills to industry (no clinical work). Some return to clinical practice.

Where do vets work now? → **Vets in Government:**

Almost 4% of working vets work within the UK Government. Most work in one of the spin-off agencies characteristic of the current government practice of decentralisation. Our main one is currently called the *Animal and Plant Health Agency* (2017) (the name and management structure of this organisation has been changing every 6 or 7 years for the last 3 decades- depending on government whim). These are the front-line vets who check and monitor for notifiable (horrible) disease outbreaks - mainly in food production animals. Some vets work in government-funded laboratories checking samples, and the rest are scattered across numerous other departments. There are surprisingly low numbers of vets working at the Food Standards Agency (less than 50). In European countries and the USA, vets are much more involved in this area.

Where do vets work now? → **Vets in One Health:**

This a designer label created by universities in an attempt to broaden the appeal of *becoming a* vet (see the beginning of this chapter where we speak of universities looking for income). One Health is an attempt to create a new role for qualified vets within the arena of health and health prevention. It encompasses human health, animal health, disease, environment, etc. The hope of One health is that vets, who have a sufficiently wide skill set, could become consultants and advisors for global disease security and environmental issues. The hope is that vets may join those specialists who already sit at "the long table" - the medics, epidemiologists, environmentalists, security experts, disease experts, etc. Unfortunately One Health doesn't appear to be happening much. Currently there are only a couple of short One Health courses at universities, and a few academics head up proto-departments labelled with overly long titles. There are not many vets directly involved in the actual processes of One Health - most get to the "long table" from industry or from government roles. Or they are academics in their 50s who are developing their careers through committee work.

Where do vets work now? **→ Vets in Academia:**

This is the upper tier of Amazingness - especially if you fancy yourself a bit:

Professors lead the veterinary departments. Under them, they have associate Professors or Readers. There are Senior and other Lecturers. Research fellows and other such sundry ranks. This is all pretty standard.

It is in the lower tiers of University staffing where things are more challenging. This is where it gets a bit grubby: A recent innovation is the Teaching Internship. A Teaching Internship is now the main route for recently-graduated vets who wish to work in academia. Their role is to teach students. Many Teaching Internships are called *"PhD studentships"* - they promise a qualification in a few years. Whilst PhD students have always contributed to teaching through *demonstrating* or by leading seminars, their contribution has become an *essential part* of a veterinary course rather than just a bit of extra interest. These young teachers are especially used in teaching peripheral (soft or non-clinical) subjects e.g. client interactions; empathy and emotional intelligence; litigation avoidance; business; finance; etc. They deliver pre-scripted lessons to the under-graduates.

The HR department use them because Interns are cheap and relatively easy to fire. The Professors and Lecturers like them because it means *they* don't have to teach soft subjects. There's not much academic glory to be had by teaching the techniques of angry-client management!

Obviously, both the under-graduate students *and* the PhD interns are being short-changed by this system. The under-graduate vet students are not being taught by a teacher; and the PhD Interns are being used.

Why do PhD interns do it?

The answer is, if they succeed in obtaining their Doctorate, then they can join the queue for a lectureship. This is the *real* doorway into academia. But unfortunately the queues get longer every day and competition to get into academia is fierce. Which is why so many *normal* vets are now publishing 'papers' in veterinary magazines - a probably futile attempt to pad out their CVs.

(Proper) lecturers work very hard on the Vet course. Unlike lecturers in *French Studies*, or the *Mathematics of Fractal Banana Republics*, they don't have 4 hours off each day to do their research. The truth is that Vet Lecturers are too busy guiding students through the 8-hours-a-day maze that is the Vet Course to do much original research. So they often also use their PhD interns to help them with their own research areas…

Where do vets work now? → **Academics going private:**

See Chapter 3 : The Busyness of Business: A significant income stream for those amazing vets who work in academia is lecturing to normal practicing vets. There is a RCVS requirement for vets to fulfil their *Continuing Professional Development (CPD)* commitment annually. As we touched upon in our Chapter on business, CPD is becoming a significant business in its own right. There are several large private companies devoted to providing CPD opportunities to vets. Some celebrity vets are even creating 'fun and facts' events which also can be *claimed* by attendees for their CPD hours. This ever expanding CPD business needs suitably qualified vets to do the teaching. When the organisers run out of university academics to employ, they will call upon the more highly qualified private vets. These practising vets - who operate outside the academic world - have pursued Higher Qualifications. They supplement their income with CPD teaching.

Where do vets work now? → **Vets hanging out of helicopters:**

A few - a very few - vets get to hang out of helicopters darting marauding elephants whilst shouting over their shoulders into the film-camera. A few - a very few - vets get to treat big cats in Zoos and Safari Parks. [And that is a welfare paradox in itself - right there.]

Where do vets work now? →

Holiday Vets

There are some Western trained horse-vets in faraway lands: Lands where horses and other Equids remain a vital part of subsistence living. Usually (stereotypically), Western ideas of welfare are not practiced there

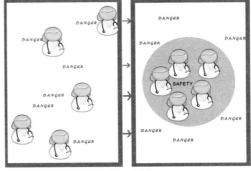

The Circle of Safety

- much. Indigenous peoples will often regard horses as tools only, and certainly not as pets - or member of the family. In these faraway lands, their horses are given just enough food and care to ensure they continue to work. It's a bit like my chain-saw. I'm pleased to have it. It works well and I maintain it. It does the job.

Western-trained vets choose to work in these countries with the prime aim of advising and cajoling horse owners into improving welfare. These vets don't just medicate, they also educate. Their hope is that 'life' gets better for both horse and owner alike.

As the locals hopefully adopt these new practices the foreign vets are ultimately replaced by locally trained vets.

Many of the visiting (Western) vets will stay a year or two at most. Whilst it initially feels good to help neglected animals in neglected societies, vets are usually driven and ambitious types - so career progression; finding a home-life; a need for a less alien environment; increasing boredom; all contribute to the decision to move on.

Very occasionally a few vets stay. They have made life-style and principled decisions to stay. They have experienced western life and now seek a kind of alternative fulfilment. Or perhaps they are looking for the 'exotic'. Maybe searching for a way "to give something back". If these worthy folk fully and permanently subsume into the indigenous society, then they can make a sustainable difference to local animal welfare over the long term.

Idealistic new-graduates on the other hand are hungry to make a(n) *heroic and worthy* contribution. They don *head-scarves, or stop shaving*. They slip on some crispy desert boots and a beige jacket with baggy pockets. Being fresh out of university, they are slightly attracted by the idea that they can make their newbie mistakes where it doesn't matter too much (Any complaints to My@email.com !! Haha). They return home in 6-12 months - all their youthful veterinary and personal mistakes left lying in a corner of some foreign field somewhere - probably under a few feet of dust.

A sub-division of vets working abroad is the **One Week Holiday Vet.** These worthy people's motivations are to offer themselves into various pro-bono / self-indulgent / vanity project / leisure motivation categories. They are usually older affluent vets (rich in money or rich in time). They may take a vet-nurse-friend with them. They neuter some dogs and cats on Rabidos - a Greek island with a 'stray' problem. Fabulous beaches and lots of local wine help with their decision. These worthies often write articles for the Veterinary free-papers - detailing their travails in an alien land - cementing their feel-goodness by summing up with some pocket-philosophy on how good the world could be if only...

That was a list of areas of work where vets find themselves - so...

?????? What do you fancy doing out of that list?

MY advice would be find a vet doing a bit of what you fancy. Find them on Google. Give'em a call. Ask them,

> "What's it like being a **** ing vet?"
> "Do you enjoy it?"
> "Would you do it again if you started over?"

What's it really like Being a Vet?

Question: What's common to all the people in the roles listed above?

Answers:

1)They all hold a vet degree from one of the world universities. Some are good. Some bad. 2)They are all vet graduates - and that is something rare and special. It is what marks them out as different. Most vets possess a painfully won accumulation of skills, knowledge and most importantly, a specific set of ethics. They have a particular set of specialized concerns that are hard to find in any other type of person.

Question: Is being a vet like being in a club?

Answer: Vets are all so different in their motivation and their outlook, that the answer is probably no. Clubs usually have a narrow focus - scuba diving; fitness drumming; cycling. Vets certainly are all coming from the same place - namely a Veterinary Degree - but they are using that degree to fly in multiple directions, and they have many differing motivations. No, not a club. More like a fraternity. Or crew…

"Hangin" like Celebs

And having said they are all different, rather like Doctors, celebrities and film stars, vets do tend to hang out together - a lot. Why do they do this?

→ Firstly, because it's easy. They have a shared language and a shared set of ethics. So they choose to spend time with people who can share their concerns and their joys. → Secondly, when spending time with other vets, they don't have to be guarded in their speech or their attitudes: I watched a *Simon Sinek* talk on *Ted*® the other day. He describes how stone-age man congregated in groups because of the dangers surrounding them. The danger of starvation; the danger of bad weather; the dangers from sabre-toothed tigers. He describes the *"Circle of Safety"* which is when people come together to support and protect each other. This mutually beneficial arrangement applies to our vets too - on a smaller scale. Vets perceive many dangers in the world which are specific to them and to other vets. To protect themselves, they create their own "Circle of Safety" in which only vets are welcome - because only vets perceive those specific dangers. As Simon reminds us, safety and trust is a mutual arrangement.

Additionally, all vets eventually despair of the 2D nature of their relations with the public. They will seek deeper friendships with people who can see past their *vetness*. They want to have a normal laugh with normal people without having to worry about "damaging the reputation of the profession". (Believe it or not, maintaining the reputation of the Veterinary Profession is an RCVS requirement of all members at all times - Membership cannot be turned off at dinner parties! So vets can only get drunk (high/stoned/wasted) with other vets - who hopefully will not tell the RCVS.) Vets like to hang out with vets.

"I'm an Air Crash Investigator"

Yes, that's what I answer to anyone who asks me what I do for a living. It works a treat because no-one asks me boring questions about their pet's itchy skin. I avoid being told about BillyPug's toilet habits / or Cassie's amazing intelligence / or how Benji loves to play in puddles.

But there *is* danger lurking when vets choose to spurn the company of lay (normal) people. They risk exaggerating their social isolation. In fact not only isolation, but also - perhaps more dangerously - some can develop a feeling of *elevation* over lay people. This can lead to vets being judgemental.

> *"Gawd. Mrs Bloggins was in again today and she still hasn't changed her dog's diet. It's no wonder the dog is so sick."* Or,

> *"...No, Mrs Bloggins. I'm obligated to tell you what is best for Bonzo, and the only way Bonzo is going to get better is by feeding WondoMix. He will not get better if you keep doing what you are doing. Trust me."*

Social isolation can thus lead to many vets appearing distant and aloof. Many vets find making friends outside the profession difficult.

Nineties television - where it all started to go wrong

Like neurosurgeons, vets have been traditionally regarded as being semi-mystical beings with innate magical powers of understanding and god-like healing all wrapped up in a mysterious yet caring *superhero cloak of excellence* . Or at least that's how it used to be:

In 1996, a TV series called *Vet School* aired on the BBC. It was a *fly-on-the-wall* docusoap and it followed a group of vet students through their training at university. It sounds grim, but the truth was it was fun to watch them struggle. We watched as they were viciously derided by their professors; and we winced / grinned when they were bitten by a nervous cat. We laughed as they screwed up yet another examination... *Schadenfreude* was the order of the day as we watched their incomprehension when a lecturer asked them a difficult question. We tuned in each week to see what other hilarious mistakes they were going to make: *Trude Mostue's* inability to inject a cat - whilst at the same time being a blonde Norwegian - has become part of veterinary folklore.

What we didn't realize at the time was that the public were watching too. And as more and more similar TV programs aired, so the mystique of the profession inevitably became eroded: Like the *Wizard of Oz* who the viewer initially imagines is superhuman is revealed as a wheezy old gent pulling on levers and puffing out smoke. In this story, we are encouraged to not only question the Wizard's veracity, but in fact to question the whole construct of the Land of Oz.

Vet-TV revealed to the public that vet students - and later on, practicing vets - make mistakes and get it wrong. The public began to see that vet students were just like any other student. Hard working certainly, but still fallible. And often drunk. We saw that some of the students were knackered, and had low self-confidence. Many seemed to possess very low self-esteem; (unhealthy) perfectionism; and we saw several experience extreme despair during their courses. The viewing public began to suspect their own (qualified) vet may actually be a *normal person* - hiding behind a façade. Perhaps metaphorically pulling on levers, puffing out smoke and waving flags.

Winning a *back-stage pass* is not always what it promises. It is sometimes better to dream than to experience the reality.

The Gods are falling off Mount Olympus

Partly as a result of this great media reveal, the public look at our profession differently now. They now know vets are not infallible. They have discovered that vets often get it wrong; or are in fact simply guessing.

TV gave them an insight into the truth behind the professional dignity. A knowledge-empowered public now questions their vet's pedigree. Especially the younger vets - the ones that have no fairy dust at all under their fingernails yet. As a result, vets no longer expect unquestioning and automatic trust - a feature of pre-TV days where trust was automatic and based upon the vets' training and qualifications. The public now ask vets to re-confirm their honesty, their ability to cure, and their trustworthiness - almost every time they meet. Vets are no longer regarded as omnipotent healers but perhaps as skilled technicians who should be questioned: Taking temperatures, collecting samples,

looking things up on the internet. The magic and mystery of being a professional has slipped away - hidden and significantly devalued by the public's newly acquired 'knowledge'.

Special vets

These are the Veterinary 'Diplomats' and Veterinary 'Specialists': Once an achievable dream of many young vets, these roles are increasingly the jealously guarded preserve of those vets who have been able to remain working in, or with, universities after graduation. They start their careers as teachers and slowly climb the academic ladder. The majority of specialists are now trained directly by the universities. Most specialists, when they qualify, move out into specialist vet centres as consultants. Some remain at the university and combine student teaching with their own personal private consultancy businesses.

Many university-employed academics now also have 'specialist businesses' which they run in parallel with their teaching. Acquiring advanced 'specialist' qualifications whilst still working in general practice as a normal vet has become almost impossible - as much anything because there isn't enough time or 'interesting' cases available.

Celebrity Vets - Venture Capitalists are trying to purchase the practices previously developed by celebrity vets (these are those vets who have achieved public success - usually on TV, Forums, etc.). Their businesses are increasingly valuable because clients are willing to uncritically bond with famous people. They confuse fame with worthiness. Celebrity branding is something they can accept. Clients of these practices will forgive much, and are less critical of the service they receive - especially when the cameras are running! It will not be long before The Venture Capitalists are developing Celebrity Brand pharmaceuticals and Branded surgical techniques.

New-Vets becoming old ones - a view/list/

New-Vets becoming old ones → **Yay! Post University: The first 3 years working.**

♦ **Vets who want to be horse vets:** After graduation, most will enter paid work as interns in one of the thirty or so major independent equine practices across the country. Depending on their abilities, most will take a PA (personal-assistant / intern) role to one of the practice's specialist vets. Their duties will be the equivalent of junior doctor or nurse technician roles - taking histories, holding animals, collecting samples, chasing results, phoning owners, etc. These internships will usually last a few years, and candidates will probably hold at least two separate internships before landing a proper vet clinician role.

Most of the interns will leave their mentor practices and will find better paid (albeit promising more restricted career opportunities) employment within the equine or mixed practice private sector. Here they will be working alongside other *new-vets* from UK and foreign universities, and they will be focused on routine and Out of Hours (Emergency) work. Salaries will remain low due to the competition for these roles from overseas applicants. Some interns will turn away from specialising in horse work - maybe to companion animal work, as there remains a strong demand for *new-vets* in this area.

♦ **Vets who want to be Companion Animal vets:** There are many more options in this sector than for Equine or Large Animal graduates - if only because the Companion Animal (pets) industry is larger and better developed. Most *new-vets* currently graduate with generalist degrees. On graduation, they will try to join practices employing one or more experienced vets in the hope that the practice will be able to offer mentoring and support. Most will join corporate practices. Pay will be low, and hours will be long and inflexible.

There are very few signs that this will change much in the next 10 years or so. Some *new-vets* will land jobs in a *private practice* - perhaps where they completed their EMS (Extra Mural Studies) as a student. The latter is probably the best of all their other choices for *new-vets*. Hopefully they will be more likely to flourish in these less management-rigorous businesses. Part of the support available to *new-vets* is the recognition of a their future potential. Salaries and conditions are still poor, but conditions go some way to counteract that deficiency. Often these practices are run and owned by vets and so they hopefully know how to bring the best out of their *new-vets*. Vets in these practices develop so rapidly and reliably that they are soon working with higher levels of clinical freedom than their contemporaries who are working in more management-regulated practices.

There is an argument that the large corporate chains should now be the best place for *new-vets* to start work. In theory, their management and training structures should enable them to effectively set up protocols across the business that enable support and guidance for every *new-vet* they employ. It should be simple for corporate management to find a few hours a week to help a *new-vet* to recover and de-stress. Should be easy to find a mentor, and to offer improved work-environment control (working hours; choices of work area; holidays; etc.). In theory this could be best delivered in a corporate environment. Unfortunately, it all costs money, and *new-vets* don't complain to management enough. Some of the larger companies are developing support procedures for *new-vets* which we have talked about in Chapter 2. I hope that this recognition of need is more than just a politically-correct means of making more money for the businesses...

New-Vets becoming old ones ➔ **Post Graduation life: 3 Years plus...**

Livestock Vets: By this point, those vets remaining in their chosen sector will be considering working towards practice-directorship. This is the old tried and tested model. As we have discussed earlier, this route is particularly suited to male vets who have an increased readiness to accept the responsibilities and ties associated with directorship. Some livestock vets will leave their first practice to try their luck elsewhere - another mixed practice perhaps or a teaching PhD post at a university. Some will enter industry at this point, and some will cross over to Companion Animal work. Equine vet options will be much as they were at graduation.

Companion animal vets may well be in their third job at this stage. Some will already have left to work in academia or industry. Upwards of 25% will have left the profession altogether - possibly due to a loss of confidence and disillusionment. Of those who remain, many will be trying to curtail their working hours in the hope of working part-time.

New-Vets becoming old ones ➔ **Post Graduation life: 8 years in**

♦ **Large animal and horse vets** are in the groove by now. They have found their niche, and they are enjoying every minute of every day. Their Jack Russell companion *"Mr Russel"* accompanies them everywhere; they have windblown hair, and early wrinkles around their eyes. They love their job and their clients. Every day they awake knowing they are highly respected. Many of the female practitioners are still trying to change working conditions: Notably, more time off from work and less Out of Hours (OOH) cover.

A surprising number of equine vets (male and female) have left their foster practices, and have set up their own practices which they run from the boot of their car. After 10-15 years, they feel they have not only achieved sufficient knowledge, but they have some sense of their client's loyalty. The (unfortunately common) lack of career and business progression opportunities allied with a lack of control over their working hours has forced them to leave their cosy employment. They're going to try it alone: Many stay in the same geographic region - effectively in competition with their previous employers. A scary fact about equine vets: they are at the highest risk of physical injury of all civilian occupations. Over 7% of injuries result in unconsciousness (BEVA, 2018). Many will record up to 8 life-time injury events. Many of which can be expected to impede their career.

♦ **Companion Animal vets** are in their early 30s. If they are lucky, they are in a loving relationship - recognised as being a notable factor in a person's sense of *well-being*. Up to this point, they have worked long and demanding hours - upwards of 10 hours a day, and at least 5 to 5½ days a week on average. Their salary has increased slowly since graduation and now stands at just above average for the working population. It is worth noting that their salary will be about 30% less than the equivalent Junior Doctor grade, and maybe 40% less than an equivalently experienced medical GP.

Because these vets are mostly female, salary is not all that important - as we have already discussed. More important to these vets are their working conditions; aspects of clinical work (clinical freedom); and the respect of their colleagues and clients. Related to this is the emergence of the term 'clinical director'. Initially created to indicate the most senior vet in a corporate practice (and the person who has the say on clinical guidelines within the practice), the term is increasingly applied to senior *employed* vets - formerly known as senior assistants. This change is a nod towards creating more visible career opportunities for a vet - something that has been missing up to now.

These vets will be good at their jobs and will have developed some resilience to the pressures and stresses of work. They enjoy their clinical successes, but non-clinical aspects of their work are beginning to weigh heavily: Dropout into academic roles is still *just* possible at this age - they retain the necessary free-time and drive, especially if they haven't begun a family yet. Many vets will elect to remain in the same role, but will be considering going part-time. Increasing numbers of these vets have left employed work altogether. Many have become self-employed locums.

Locum vets

Self employed locums are fully qualified vets who are willing to step in and take over a variety of clinical roles in a wide range of vet practices. The majority of locum work is holiday, sickness, or maternity leave cover. Locums are generally well qualified - either through experience or study. They are flexible workers - they are adept at fitting into pre-existing practice teams and work patterns.

The great attraction of locum work is that it gives the vet a sense of increased control over their work-hours. The pay received is generally upwards of 5-10% more than an equivalent employee vet - thus enabling a locum to work fewer weeks in the year for the same money.

The down-sides of being a locum are the lack of clinical continuity (e.g. seeing a long or chronic case to its conclusion), and the missing sense of being a permanent part of a team. Additionally, locums have even less opportunity to develop natural personal relationships with colleagues and clients. Which over a period of time can contribute to compassion fatigue and burnout. The greatest drawback is that locums have no employee 'rights'. They receive no holiday pay, sickness pay, etc. They pay their own income tax. They have no rights of continued employment - the practice can turn around at any moment and ask them to leave.

The best and most effective locums find they are in great demand - they'll often have a core group of 5 or 6 practices that they regularly 'service'. Some locums are able to develop more 'healthy' professional relationships with clients and co-workers despite not being there all the time.

Careers & Cheers

Most female vets more than 8 years qualified have spent a significant portion of their career in part-time work. A few have purchased franchise ownerships and now head up small 2 or 3-vet practices on high streets and in out-of-town shopping malls. Some vets have managed to support themselves through further qualifications, and now hold *Advance Practitioner* (AP) certificate status. This is an advanced qualification offered by the universities and is awarded by the RCVS. It usually forms part of a vet's continuing professional development. These qualifications sometimes lead to improved working conditions. What qualifications *do* supply is tangible evidence of a vet's development - which can help with the vet's self-confidence, and may also help with landing a new job in another business.

These more advanced vets are likely to remain in a second tier practice where they will perform about 80 - 90% first-opinion work (as opposed to work referred from other vets - known as second-opinion work). They are able to perform more specialized work supplied from within the practice by less-qualified vets. Very few of these vets would want to return to a *Tier 1* practice. (*Tier 1* practices are the lowest level high-street type practices. *Tier 2* are the middle level - better equipped and more highly qualified staff. *Tier 3* practices are the referral and university businesses)

Career progression is limited within *Tier 2* practices. Academic progression above their 'AP' status is almost impossible from within the private-practice situation. Higher qualifications can only be earned from within the academic world itself. Business-progression within the practice, on the other hand, is possible. These opportunities don't arrive very often - owners jealously guard their profits. But owners are beginning to realise that retention of good vets within the business is a good idea for the stability of their businesses. Many vets need a good sense of career progression to keep them engaged, and so some owners are introducing a tiered system of business 'membership': Progression to 'associate director' usually involves a payment of around a year's salary which gives a nominal stake in the business in the form of a profit share. Associate directorship doesn't confer part-ownership or voting rights, but does come with additional day-to-day administrative responsibilities such as doing the rotas, monitoring drugs, managing lay-staff, etc. Some businesses make this even easier by loaning the *buy-in* money to the 'associate' who then pays back the loan from their profit share over a few years (we already talked about 'predatory lending' earlier when we talked about franchise companies). Unlike 'partnership' which creates a rigid and inflexible 'prison' for the partners, the associate system is more flexible - associates can more easily leave the business if they need to - at short notice. The associate-director system, when refined correctly can be a very powerful motivator for middle-career vets. It certainly improves the retention of good vets for clinical businesses.

Those vets who have developed a specialist skill set are working part or full time as referral vets. They are generally working in academia or within the burgeoning number of Referral Practices (*Tier 3*).

In the same way that 'normal' vets are leaving the formalised and restrictive structure of modern vet businesses to work alone as franchise owners / practice owners / locums, some of these specialist referral vets are leaving larger established referral business too. Following a similar pattern, they aim to 'set up' on their own. With the advent of smaller and lighter technology, these specialists can become 'mobile vets'. Many develop relationships with established *'Tier 2'* practices and perhaps work one day a week in each of their favoured practices. They continue to perform their specialist work on referred cases whilst using their own 'mobile' equipment. Some use the practices' own staff. Some employ their own nurse technicians. This model works well with many veterinary specialisms including ophthalmology, orthopaedic surgery, ultrasonography, dermatology, advanced elective surgery, etc.

♦ **Industry Vets:** At this stage, many vets who have spent most of their career in 'industry' begin to feel increasingly distant from 'their profession' (see Career Identity). Some may consider returning to practice, to reignite their clinical skills - often complimented by their industry acquired management skills.

Disclaimer: These stages of a vet's post-graduate life have been assembled from personal experience, and from the comments in the *VPP survey 2015*. They remain generalisations and should not be used as a personal career model. This section exists solely to demonstrate the current and foreseeable condition of career progression available to *new-vets*.

What is it like being a vet? Ask a vet...

It is vital to go to a vet and ask them straight.

Yes you !

You! Ask them… Now!

You *must* remember that some of the answers you receive will be coloured by the person's unwillingness to admit that they did in fact make some career mistakes along the way. In fact you may notice many vets getting quite defensive when you challenge them...

Whoops

The major mistake that most young people make when they decide on a future as a vet is to assume they will be spending their time with animals.

Whatever a vet's role is, be it clinical, academic, or commercial, the truth of the matter is they spend the bulk of their time working with PEOPLE.

Vets spend a huge part of everyday talking; explaining; planning; empathizing and sympathizing (ha! - and you thought they were the same thing!); planning; teaching, demonstrating; arranging; facilitating. Most vets will have 2 vocabularies: A scientific one to think in and talk to colleagues in. They have a second vocabulary they use to explain to clients and the public: Stomachs become tummies. Vulvas become front-bottoms.

Freedom of choice

A lesser mistake young people make is to assume that a vet works as an autonomous and free professional. Possibly with a blue cloak and an uncanny ability to fly. They imagine they are free to do and practice what *they* think is in the best interests of animals. But No! Remember what we said earlier about the RCVS guidelines and what happens if a vet doesn't follow them?

Tick boxes…

Chapter 6

The Future of Life within the Vet Profession

Who knows what will happen in the future? I am pretty sure 15 years ago most vets wouldn't have foreseen the current state of affairs.

It is a fact that vets exist within an invidious relationship: Clients and users of their services are required to pay the full price for what is now a highly sophisticated medical service. A client's only other experience of such an advanced medical service is within the Medical and Dental Health services, and very few people pay the full (market) cost of those services directly.

Money is now the major pressure on the profession. It has also increasingly become the main driver for its progression. Private and family businesses have been sold off to 'consolidators' - for money. These Consolidators measure the success of a business by measuring financial profit. They are not vets, so we can't really expect anything else of them! What else can they do? And they know that profit is always 'better' if there is more of it.

Business recognises that *profit* is increased by

- Increasing client numbers visiting the business. This can be achieved by reducing prices, or by creating some added value: e.g. increasing the quality of their offerings and services.

- Client numbers can be increased by putting more smaller businesses on the high street rather than fewer large ones.

- Reducing costs - using cheaper drugs; paying lower wages; reducing staff numbers; using free or 'volunteer' staff who will work for non-monetary benefits (kudos / to be with animals / etc.).

- Consolidation: By buying lots of small businesses, overall costs can be reduced by sharing 'back-office' services - accountancy, marketing, drugs provision, etc.

- Profits can be increased by charging more for drugs and services. This increases profits significantly, but note that this may cause fewer clients to visit: So fewer people visit the practice, but spend more money.

There is a lot of pressure to economise. To reduce costs and to increase profitability. This has led to the profession being shaped more by business strategy and less by medical (veterinary) aspirations and dreams. 15 years ago veterinary wages were beginning to shrink: employers of vets were reducing the 'offer' to their employees. The vets' car, and the vets' subsidised accommodation - once a mainstay of veterinary employment - had been destroyed by changes in tax-law.

As we read earlier, the "Client" was changing too. They had begun to seek 'maximum value at minimum cost'. They were learning to be a sophisticated consumer. The recognition that vet practices were becoming financially-driven businesses led to a change in clients' expectations and altered their relationship with vet practices. They learned that they could apply "their rights" to their interactions with the vet. They discovered they could *appeal* to the vets' regulators and to the law courts in order to get *something back*. This has led to vets practicing defensively.

At the time of writing, the customer-facing parts of the veterinary profession are sliding toward a crisis of self-image. People working within vet practices are increasingly unclear what their daily motivation should be - to cure, to heal, to make money, or to please clients?

As a result of all these changes, vet practices and businesses tend to be chronically underfunded. That's not to say some vets haven't done pretty well out of their business. Some have successfully squeezed a decent profit, but that is invariably at the cost of investment in the business.

Say Hello to Big Business and their Marketing Strategies

Historic and chronically poor investment is what has attracted the large corporate businesses to enter the veterinary area. Correcting these investment deficiencies promise huge profits. They have the experience to refine costs whilst having the big-bucks to boost capital investment. Managers with a financial focus will refine the *veterinary offering* to within an "inch of its life":

When big-businesses move in, their first move is to start creating guidelines and policies for their employees to follow; Managers create reams of instructions; Receptionists and Nurses are given scripts they must use when talking to clients; Vets are given lists of drugs they must use in particular diseases; They are expected to deliver veterinary medicine of a specific quality, and that quality is decided by the managers - not the vet. Managers are removing their employees' autonomy by creating simplistic and therefore more affordable services. These refined structures are *just about* good enough for what the customer thinks they need:

Last century, the father of Public Relations, *Edward Bernays*, wrote an essay called *The Engineering of Consent* (1947). In this essay, he discussed his approach to *persuasion* - notably persuading people to buy themes and ideas:

To be successful, the themes and ideas must appeal to the motives of the public. Motives are the activation of both conscious and subconscious pressures created by the force of desires.

My *précis* of this rather wordy statement is:

First create a need. And then fulfil it

Bernays called this: *The Engineering of Consent* - he used the term to describe the manipulation of people's desires by business:

A company offering a service (we will call it XXX) employs a marketing person. That marketing person persuades the public that they have a particular need for XXX. The business then fulfills the public's new need by selling them some XXX. Until the marketing person told them, the public had never heard of XXX - let alone known they needed it!

A vet example: The public, who visit veterinary practices, have been persuaded by the marketeers that they have a need for good value (cheap) veterinary services delivered from shiny branded practices. They have been persuaded by

marketing departments that vet medicine is simple and uncomplicated, and that it should be valued by how cheap and how shiny it is. Now that the public think they have a need for sparkly cheap vet medicine, the large vet companies have 'obligingly' built bright and shiny high-street practices. They make them cheap and easy to understand by offering a simplified service. And complying with Bernays' theories, the Public then choose those practices subconsciously. The shiny and simple vet practices fulfil their needs - the needs they have been persuaded to have.

Pay, salaries, wages: Future Tiers of excellence.

In the future we will see much more of this marketing manipulation. This will be due to the size of the businesses involved, and the huge amount of money available to spend on marketing. Lower-tier practices (our *Tier 1*) are the easiest to brand and are an easy 'sell' to the public. Their service is simplistic. These are the practices that are easy to find, easy to visit, and easy to understand. They do health-checks on your new puppy, and they offer all the routine procedures like hysterectomies and castrations.

When things get more complex, say an animal becomes ill or needs more sophisticated care than *Tier 1* practices can offer, then other 'higher-up practices' (*Tier 2 / 3*) are referred to if the client can afford it. The result of this process is the delineation of vet practice into the layers we have discussed already:

Future Tier 1: The lowest tier of practice will be bright, shiny and Branded. They will offer a restricted service - limited to vaccinations, simple disease, and routine surgery. They will refer more complex cases to the *Tier 2* practices (or more likely the clients themselves will 'self-refer'). The *Tier 1* practices may be profitable for the owners, especially if they are in groups or owned by corporate entities. Vets and nurses will usually be poorly paid, because these businesses rely on throughput (numbers of animals seen per hour) rather than the idea of *adding value* to a visit. They will be under paid because they have to follow management's strict guidelines and so perform most of their work by rote. The trend to de-professionalize means that most of the work done in these practices will be performed by technicians rather than clinicians. And technicians are cheaper.

Future Tier 2: The vets working in the mid-tier practices will not be much better off. Vaccinations, routine surgeries are all relatively high profit procedures and the managers will want to grab some of that market share too. They will sell it to the public as a 'quality service' that basks in the reflected glory of the rest of their more sophisticated clinical offering.

> *"If you are willing to pay a little more, then you can have your new puppy vaccinated by a proper 'specialist' vet!"*

An alternative approach many vet practices will take is to offer routine work (vaccines, spays, etc.) more cheaply than they actually cost the practice. This is the 'loss-leader' approach to business which relies on building a relationship with a client, in order that they come back for more expensive vet work. So there are many offers - Vaccines for £10; elective neutering for less than the price of a *KFC Bargain Bucket*…

These *Tier 2* practices will have particular business problems: Notably they have higher capital and employment costs. They have more sophisticated equipment and employ more highly qualified personnel who cost more. They may also be providing 24 hour cover - another service that is costly to provide. Managers of *Tier 2* practices are under a lot of pressure to reduce costs in order to build profit for the business owners: As we have discussed, managers invariably first attack the "soft targets" when they need to reduce costs. Meaning those areas of the business that won't fight back. So when managers want to reduce costs, they invariably think about their employees first. This results in squeezed wages and increased working hours. As we saw in the Personality chapter, most vets aren't driven by money and consequently few complain. They are the 'soft target' of first choice.

Future Tier 3: The upper tiers - the referral practices and university practices - will be paying more for their well-qualified personnel. That said, there will be a lot of demand for these jobs from the vets in the lower tiers who want to improve themselves. And so conditions and pay will be under constant downward pressure from management. Most of *Tier 3* practices' income comes from Pet Insurance.

Mobile Vets

In just the last 12-24 months (Time of writing = 2018), we have seen a rapid emergence of Mobile Vets. These are fully qualified vets who have chosen to abandon traditional 'bricks and mortar' practices in favour of taking a veterinary service *into the client's home*. Most have purchased a vehicle, and some employ a 'nurse' to help handle the animals.

Benefits to the vet are that 'they are their own boss'. They do not have to follow a manager's guidelines. They gain control over their day - many have children at school, or other commitments.

Benefits to the client - they don't have all the bother of taking their pets to the vets.

These home-visit-vets (aka. mobile / community vets) can only handle very basic veterinary services - vaccination, fleas, worming, some simple medical conditions. The setup costs for the vet tend to be fairly low. Their major capital investment is their vehicle.

Their charges seem to vary enormously. I'll give you an example: Near to where I live, we have two new mobile vets. One charges £65 for a home visit to vaccinate a cat. (A franchise type bricks'n'mortar practice would normally charge anything from £35-50 unless they are running a (subsidised) offer when it could be as little at £20). To the south of where I live, we have another new mobile vet who charges £15 for a cat vaccination! And remember that a mobile vet has to drive to the house, enter the house, meet the owner and the pet, examine it, vaccinate it, take payment, leave the house in preparation to drive to the next house. It's hard to imagine the £15 guy will do it for long…

Mobile vets are a sub-tier of the *Tier 1* practices mentioned above. They can't do x-rays or ultra-sound examination. Many can't take bloods. Those without a nurse will struggle to do most examinations properly.

….the profession continues to morph…

24 Hour Cover

Currently the RCVS insists that all vets who diagnose and treat animals must also provide 24 hour emergency support for their registered clients. Large multi-vet practices are able to provide the workforce to comply with these demands. Small and medium practices struggle to provide this care themselves. This is because even though vets are pretty amazing folk, they can't work 24 hours a day! And there isn't enough money to pay for a vet to sleep at the practice on the off chance the telephone rings.

So most practices in this category now fulfil their 24Hour responsibility by paying dedicated emergency vet practices to answer their phone-calls and take their emergency Out of Hours (OOH) cases: From the end of evening surgery at 7pm to the following morning at 8.30am, any emergencies are seen by these OOH practices. The OOH practices will also look after hospitalised animals (from the day-practice) that need overnight care.

You can see from this description that this model of 24 Hour Care is a compromise. Especially for a sick dog or cat. As a result, there is pressure within an increasingly resentful profession for things to change. We have already shown that clients can now bounce between practices. So vets ask themselves why they should incur the huge costs of providing emergency care to clients who are not remotely loyal to the practice. If clients have no loyalty to them, then why should vets *ruin their private lives* by providing emergency treatment just because the RCVS says so.

The compromise I mentioned above is little talked about in the profession, but it should be: I'll give you an example:

> Mitzi, a female dog turns up to the surgery at midday and is diagnosed with pyometra. She's been vomiting for days and is dehydrated and weak. She receives emergency surgery which is finished by 5pm. The building closes at 6.30 and the vets and nurses usually go home shortly afterwards. At 6.30, Mitzi still can't stand properly, and is still weak. What to do?

> The owner is given two options. Either Mitzi stays in the practice overnight, on a drip, but with no supervision or care. Or she is transferred to the Emergency Clinic which is 6 miles away across the city. The owners usually opt for the latter. Mitzi, who has barely woken up from the anaesthetic is feeling nauseous and is still very weak. She is carried out to the owner's car on a blanket 'stretcher'. They drive to the Emergency clinic, where Mitzi lays on the waiting room floor for ½ hour whilst the paperwork is filled out. The owners have to revisit the emergency clinic at 8am in the morning, to pick Mitzi back up and take her back

to the original Practice. (The Emergency Clinics can't keep animals through the day.) She is then carried back into the (day) surgery, and it's another half hour before she's settled back in the kennels.

Why is this bad? Mitzi has a life threatening illness. She has received major surgery. She has to be carried to a car only a few hours after the operation. It will be 2 hours before she is back on her fluid drip and comfy again in her new kennel at the OOH clinic. And she is being cared for by vets who have less direct understanding of the case and the animal - they don't know the client or the patient. They just have the clinical notes to go on. The next morning, her drip is stopped again and it's another 2 hours and a 6mile car ride before she's back in a warm kennel again.

It is very hard to see how this process is *the best* plan for Mitzi's welfare. The problem is this: Because of the structure of veterinary practice, there are no alternatives… Many vets are *Millennials* (and those that aren't are beginning to adopt their attitudes), and they increasingly want 'a life'. They want to finish work in good time, and have time to see their partners, see their kids, walk the dog. Very few vets want to work through the day - AND the night any more.

Having to provide 24 Hour care gets in the way of improving vets' working conditions. Vetting is a very stressful occupation (see Chapter 1. on Personality). It is becoming more so, especially for younger vets who are not necessarily particularly well suited to some of the job-demands. Adding the additional strain of providing emergency cover simply adds to their stress - notably sleep deprivation; and a reduction in the *vet's recovery* time, which is vital for well-being.

The RCVS is a regulatory body for the vet profession. Its aims are to 'protect the public' and 'safeguard the welfare of animals'. The RCVS needs to realise that the best way to achieve these aims could be to look after the vets better! The RCVS needs to come up with a better recommendation for 24Hour care provision. And soon.

How can veterinary employment be improved in the future?

This is the most difficult question - and it probably has the simplest of answers. Ask yourself this question,

> *"Why are vets so badly paid compared to other professionals like Doctors and Dentists?"*

The answer? Vet fees are artificially low.

This is because vets charge the public directly for their services. Clients naturally complain about bills however high they are. Many vets worry that the public will *not like them*, and so they don't charge properly. Vets do the job primarily in order to treat and care for animals - not collect money. And veterinary business is competitive - there is always another vet business down the road willing to charge less. As a result, vets make a fraction of what their medical counterparts do on an hourly basis.

Ask yourself another question,

> *"When corporate managers reduce a vet's wages, why does the vet just accept it?"*

It is hard not to generalise here, but most vets do the job so they can do the job. They don't do it for the money. Just look at the Mobile vet I was talking about earlier who is prepared to do a home visit for £15. (A plumber wouldn't dream of visiting a house for less than £80.)

Employers are managers, and they are financially cynical. They will always try to get away with paying as little as possible. They are not stupid *[sic]*. They realise that vets have this special work-ethic and that they have little or no interest in money. (See Chapter 1. on Personality (*Self-Actualizers*)).

Changing the Future: Demographic issues.

The conditions of working as a vet we discussed earlier means the largely female base will remain unchallenged. A few males will continue to apply, but most will choose to follow a different career. They will be aiming to make short-cuts to more elevated professional positions. Many will forego clinical work altogether. These men are being true to their personalities by seeking better salaries, improved career prospects and higher status roles.

Increasingly, female graduate vets will be doing the bulk of first line clinical work in the lower and middle tier practices.

In the same way that more unpopular roles within the UK vet industry are currently taken by overseas vets (particularly obvious in Food Hygiene work), less popular roles will be populated by non-indigenous vets (Brexit® immigration rules permitting): Vets from overseas will work the night shifts; they'll take the jobs in seedy neighbourhoods and in the large American retail 'sheds'. They'll work long hours in jobs with few career prospects. Like our Polish visitors in the first decade of the 21st Century who transformed the UK service sector by manning the coffee shops, cafés and fish shops, immigrants will soon take the jobs indigenous vets don't want (Okólski, 2014). And at a lower salary.

But with luck, over time, as with the coffee-shops, these hard-working immigrant vets will have a similarly positive effect on our industry. My worry though is their health. *Immigrant vets* are no different from any other vet. They all have personality traits - which means they have strengths and weaknesses - and they are similarly 'afflicted' by their jobs. If immigrant-vets take work here in the UK, I am concerned they will simply be sucked into, and effectively support, our defective employment structures. The *VPP survey 2015's* most *at-risk* respondent was such an immigrant from East Europe. She had an extremely low *well-being score*, and a dangerously high *Keppler score* (risk of suicide). In her notes, she complained of experiencing feelings of isolation and low self-esteem. In the UK, as a profession, we cannot be seen to be transferring our structural and employment deficiencies away from home-grown vets and onto a new 'foreign' workforce. Not cool.

The future? Who knows and to be honest, we shouldn't spend too much time on that because:-

If we make the present better, then the future might well take care of itself.

Epilogue

How to be a Happy Vet

The obligatory positive words found at the end of every warning.

So you ignored all the other chapters. Maybe you thought,

> *"I've always wanted to be a vet. I'm pretty clever. Why on earth should I re-visit the decision I made so long ago?"*

You thought,

> *'Why are you trying to stop my headlong dash toward vetting glory?'*

The truth is that you are heading towards probably one of the most rewarding careers anyone could possibly have. It's varied, it's challenging, it can be exciting.

So go on. Take 10 minutes out of the rest of your life and ask yourself this question. Go on. I dare you,

> *"Why do I want to be a vet?"*

Oh sorry. I forgot to remind you of the stuff we just read in the previous chapters which boils down to the following - I guess:- Being a vet is incredibly difficult and you won't get much help from other vets these days - just your contemporaries and your university vet-friends. And the money is poor, and the work-hours are very long - every day. Oh, and the 40 or so clients you have to talk to each day have become very demanding of late and many will automatically distrust you. And you may spend much of your working day, and certainly most of the following evening/night worrying about cases, your performance, and your security. Oh, and some of your vet-friends will become mentally-ill or worse. OK. Sorry about that lapse. That's better. Now ask yourself that question again,

> *Why do I want to be a vet?"*

So you are actually now a vet. Unfortunately you weren't given the opportunity - or encouragement - to review your original vet-decision at any point until you picked up this book. So for 8- 10 years you dug your way through A-Levels and Vet School. You found a job straight out of 'Uni'.

The least I can do is offer you congratulations. Great job! I'd like to help you by giving you some support in your first few years of work: Here are some books you'll need in your pocket at all times (Beeston, 2017). They are the written equivalent of that mentor you haven't got. (Jenny is busy again, this time repairing a perineal hernia. She won't be able to help you today.)

- *The BVA New Graduate Guide*
- *Various BSAVA Petsavers Guides*
- *The Mini Vet Guide to Companion Animal Medicine.*

Perceptions

Back-in-the day when vets imagined themselves performing their professional caring role, they would conjure up a series of very simplistic images: Vets tended to think that in order to be a good vet, they needed to be strong, clever, analytical, patient and good with animals (Mellanby, 2011). Being handy with a needle is good. Not being too bothered about piss and shit are obvious benefits. And that was it. If you could be all those things, then you'd probably do OK.

In the 1990s, clients were asked for their opinion on what they thought made the perfect vet. They came up with a *totally* different list! They felt a good vet should have empathy, compassion, love of animals and some medical skills - in that order! Which goes to show how far apart vets and client's perceptions of what being a vet is, were (dreadful sentence!!). How interesting that 25 years later, *Being a Vet* is now largely focused on fulfilling those client needs from the 90s.

A quick MBTI reminder

We have already discussed Thinking and Feeling are opposite ends of one of the 4 main MBTI traits bundles.

Another one is Sensing and Intuition.

If a person favours Sensing, they like to have all the data before making a decision. If they favour iNtuition instead, they rely less on having all the data and more on their intuition (internal evaluation processes).

Now that we have delved deeper into the psychological makeup of vets, we see that in order to fulfil these changing client-needs, vets themselves are a now different type of person from the vets of a few decades ago. We see that modern vet students and newly graduated vets have a higher quotient of *Feeling* in their personality makeup. This is as opposed to vets who in the past tended to have more *Thinking* (and therefore proportionately less *Feeling*): Where (*Thinking*) vets used to made decisions based on logical argument and discussion and then acted accordingly, *new-vets*, because they are generally a different kind of people, are more likely to follow their emotions and heart as they decide on the best way forward for the dying cat (and its owners). Vets who favour *Thinking* will keep their emotions in check and often hidden. They can appear distant and aloof. They find advising euthanasia for an animal much easier than those vets who favour *Feeling* traits. The latter are more likely to cry when a patient is put to sleep. Vets with higher *Feeling* traits seek out puppies to love and cuddle. And obviously, feelings are what many clients now expect to see in their vet.

Rejoicing in difference - an example is 'deciding on euthanasia'

In an ideal world we (somewhat patronising) vets would want to offer the modern client a bit of both: a vet who *obviously* loves their pet nearly as much as they do, but who appears to be *vigorous and steady* in their approach to the case. Don't get me wrong, it is absolutely possible for a vet to be both these things. Especially between breakfast and elevenses (a historical and now somewhat parochial chronological term used to describe the mid-morning process of slaking your thirst for glucose, caffeine and fat). But after two epic four-hour sessions in a hot consult room and a two-hour operation performed over a (non-existent) lunch, most vets will begin to struggle to be *"all things to all men"*. When they are exhausted, all vets will revert to their trait norms - be they distant and aloof; or cuddly and crying.

Despite the ridiculously pressured job that vets do every day, the Vet Profession today remains as good as it ever was - *at the point of delivery*. In fact, it is probably better - in terms of extending life, and in correcting disease. If you take your poorly rabbit to the vet these days, the chances are that it will recover. Take your dog who has chronic cardiac disease to the vet, it's a given that you'll receive tests, medications, and procedures which will extend your pet's (happy and healthy) life significantly.

This amazing state is mainly the result of the profession's *medicalisation*. The term 'medicalisation' describes vet medicine's slide towards the working practices of the human health services in terms of its aspirations, motivations, and hi-tech Doctory *(sic)*.

> I took my father to A&E the other day because he had fallen. He'd grazed his elbow and his temporal forehead. We eventually saw a doctor four hours after the fall. Dad was mobile and lucid. Yet the Doctor, quoting NICE (National

Institute for Care and Health Excellence) guidelines, insisted on a CT Scan of Dad's head. I could see in his attitude that like me, he could see little point in this procedure, but he felt he had to do it. The Doctor and I stood and shrugged our shoulders at each other. These are the of attitudes and approaches to medicine that the Vet profession are now adopting, and this is *medicalisation.*

Medicalisation hasn't changed a vet's motivation to make animals better. What has altered is how that feat is carried out - namely within a structured matrix of *received* medical advice and guidelines. Unfortunately medicalisation forces practitioners to turn their back on a central theme of the older profession - namely the assessment of *quality of life* and the consequent consideration of the value of euthanasia for an animal. *'Care'* in other words. And not just the quality of life of the animal itself, but also a recognition of the value and importance of the animals' partnership with its people.

Despite younger vets favouring *F*eeling traits (over *T*hinking), and *S*ensing (over i*N*tuition (See Chapter 1 and also the Appendices), paradoxically it appears that vets with high *F*eeling traits are less able to react to, or recognise situations where the pet/owner relationship is breaking down - a relationship that comes under a lot of pressure at times of illness or old age. It seems that vets with higher *T*hinking traits are more able to make a rational assessment of an animal's welfare needs, and then to act on that assessment. They also seem to be better placed to assess the owner's needs. Vets with higher *F*eeling traits appear to be less well-equipped to make non-emotional assessments. Perhaps they find themselves too close to the whole situation. Many will procrastinate in such situations by offering more tests. And they will use EBVM (Evidence Based Vet Medicine) as their justification for delaying confronting the animal's welfare balance.

> *How many times have I examined an old-lady's cat who is suffering with a chronic recurrent disease? The old-lady has already been given tablets and medicine to administer to the cat twice a day by another vet. The cat is no better, and he looks wary and scared. Reading the notes, I see that the cat is on its third set of different tablets. Each drug change introduced because of the failure of the previous choice.*

A vet who has embraced medicalisation and practices EBVM will offer this old-lady another set of tablets for her cat. Or maybe a referral to a specialist. Or surgery perhaps. A vet who is able to reject the medicalisation approach will look at the old-lady first. She looks jaded and desperate. Her arms are scratched and bruised. This Thinking trait vet will consider the health of the relationship between the old-lady and her cat. This Thinking vet may ask if the old-lady has considered the euthanasia option for her cat.

How to lose your vet audience - have a subtitle like this:

The Art of Veterinary Science

Many older vets talk about the *art* of veterinary practice: They are referring to their skill of watching a tired old Labrador wobble through the door and somehow knowing instantly what is the best treatment for it. And being able to communicate that to the owner. This perhaps reflects their iNtuition traits - the ability to make connections and to recognise patterns. They are relating what they see in the dog with their knowledge, their experience, and their wisdom. They read patterns (of disease or behaviour) and they trust in their impressions of the case.

Sensing vets on the other hand seek more physical information. Sensing means they need *facts* and *things* to record. A Sensing vet will always want to do more examinations. They will take more tests. They will ask for second opinions, and will share with friends and colleagues. Sensing vets are great with EBVM: the system and framework built entirely on facts that is now accepted as the absolute minimum for modern vet medicine: Intuition is out - EBVM is in.

Ask yourself these questions once every 12 months.
Keep doing it until you are very old (30 years old +)

1) Why do I want to be a vet ?

2) How am I doing?

BEING A VET IN THE 21ST CENTURY

So the vet profession - *at the point of delivery* - is as effective as it ever was in curing disease. But there is unfortunately more pain and suffering behind the smiles and the extra 6 months of life. There's pain for the vet who has to work long hours, unsupported and often unappreciated. There's pain for the client as they are drawn into a costly medicalised veterinary world - unsupported. There's pain for the animals who are at risk of being over-treated, or having consideration of their real needs delayed or misunderstood.

Disappointment

As many as 50% of all vets in their first 8 years after university feel,

'Let down by their career'

They are frustrated by unclear career prospects, a lack of support, poor conditions. *Proto-vets* have, almost by definition, huge expectations of their career choice. Unfortunately, it's often a bit like Christmas: People spend November and December building up the excitement. Come January 3rd, they wake up disappointed. They ask themselves

"What on earth was that even about...?"

Many realise it was all a sham. Consequently, January 8th is *the most favoured day* for filing for divorce. Our *proto-vets* become *new-vets* after 5 years at university. They are working like crazy and many risk waking up one morning to realise there is a disconnect between the expectations they had at 16 years old, and their new reality. It is no wonder so many vets are leaving the profession early. It's no wonder so many are unhappy, or worse still, ill.

How to be a happy vet- the most thumbed page of the book...

What do you *need* to be a happy vet? The obvious answer is you have to be healthy. Happiness will follow. That was a bit trite so let's break it *down* a bit:

→ You will need *Tenacity* in buckets

→ You will need low Neuroticism trait levels - that way you will have a 'thick skin'. You will need a medium and enjoyable Perfectionism

→ Medium or high Extraversion would be good - you're able to make solid relationships - friends to support you. You enjoy talking to people…

→ Resilience - a 'thick skin'. Rapid recovery from insults and injury.

→ Low Openness to Experience - This is good because it helps you to ignore stuff around you. To keep your concentration. Un-swayed by distractions.

→ *Tenacity*

→ Medium to low Conscientiousness. A high C will make you a great vet, but because the majority of jobs out there don't allow you to be as conscientious as you personally need to be, then you'll get ill and emotionally exhausted. So a lower C is the order of the day if you want to be happy.

→ Rich parents or private income

→ Resourcefulness and assertiveness.

→ *Tenacity*

I have my trait score. I still want to be a vet. Are there any particular types of vet I should be?

Up to you mate! I'm not your father!

To be serious, I would rather you cut out the label below and stuck it on your fridge. Or maybe take a photo and set it up on your phone-calender to pop-up every 12 months. Or you could ask your mum to get you to read this book + epilogue again - on the 26th of December every year.

Ask yourself those questions once every 12 months. Keep doing it until you are very old (30 years old +)

Why do I want to be a vet ?

How am I doing?

Having said that, there are a couple of points I'd like to make regarding personality traits. This list is not exhaustive, but it may help you when you read Chapter 1 again:

- If you have a high Conscientiousness Trait score - when you are in your last two years at university, start chatting up the academic staff. Ask them for help to get into academia as soon as possible.

- If you have a high Conscientiousness Trait score and have just qualified, get a job as an intern at one of the referral practices. You will be badly paid, you will be over-worked and taken advantage of - but you *will* be able to be true to your trait.

- If you have a high Conscientiousness Trait score and a possibly unhealthy form of perfectionism (Chapter 1), then get help. Seriously - Perfectionism can be adjusted (made liveable with) whereas Traits can't be adjusted much in the medium/long term.

- If you have a high Agreeableness score, low to medium Neuroticism, low to medium Conscientiousness you're probably going to do OK in general veterinary practice. Or industry. Or even a Government Department. Thank Goodness! Something positive at last.

A tiny bit more Epilogue

I am concerned:

As you should be after reading this book. I joined the vet profession originally because I had a clear idea of what it was and what it was trying to achieve. I'm not saying I was correct in all of my expectations, but it certainly turned out to be a job I could 'do business with'. One within which I could carve out some kind of Paul-Shaped niche.

I have written this book because I am concerned. I recognise that the profession has changed and is still changing as I write. And policemen are getting younger. And my *iPhone®* is sooo confusing... Our profession, which cleverly presents itself as a sparkly loving and smiley place to be, is in truth less of a 'Home' and more of a synthesised service framework. A highly marketed *idea* of what a perfect life looks like.

Similar to other industries across the rest of the western world, the vet-people are seeing their profession polarizing into the "Rich & Powerful", and the Poor. The rich and powerful are usually men, and they are in bed with *Big Business* (American Conglomerates and the UK universities). The poor are the *new-vets* who are dragging their tired legs through the swamp of yet another 11 hour day. They have little to look forward to and no energy left for tomorrow. Hopefully you will find yourself in the increasingly empty middle ground somewhere.

I am concerned that the expectations - that originally motivated *proto-vets* to make all those life-sacrifices - are never going to be met. I am concerned that there are not more voices like mine that are trying to challenge the rosy visions young teenagers are being sold.

I have written this book for all the *Rosies* out there. If you are lucky, you are still at school or haven't yet committed to your own personal 'escalator of excellence'. Yes, you have this burning desire to be a vet. It feels amazing to know what you want to do. Your friends just seem to wander aimlessly through their lives and you hate their lack of vision. *You* have already found an identity built on these few words,

> *"I want to be a vet"*

As the months pass by after your first utterance of those few words, you have continued to build images in your mind. Many of them influenced and informed by books, by TV programs and by your positive imagination. You have created this amazing all-encompassing life-goal. But time is ticking, so you now have put those images aside. You've been informed that you need to *work very hard* to get into vet school. No problem. Let's go...

You will spend the next 10 years excelling at your academic work. You probably won't ever again ask yourself why.

"Why do I want to be a vet?"

Here's your chance… Read this book again.

Appendices

Appendix I

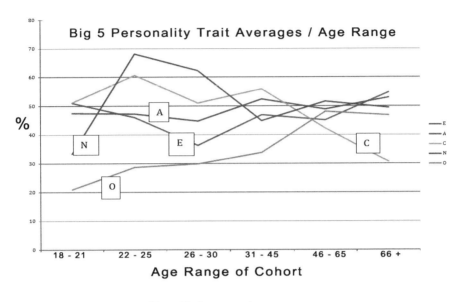

E = Extraversion
A = Agreeableness
C = Concientiousness
N = Neuroticism
O = Openess to Experience

The Veterinary Personality Project 2015 - A cautionary note on self-selection:

Surveys come in two forms. Those that you are selected to take (like the National Census) and self-selective surveys. The latter are those surveys that someone *chooses* to take…

There is always a bias with such surveys: The people completing the survey are not a random selection of the general (vet) population. It's hard to force a random selection of vets to answer the survey… Vets chose to complete the VPP. There was no force. No expectation. No pressure. The scientists (and statistics folk) amongst you will realise that the VPP is therefore not representative of all vets. But it gives an insight : The survey's

230 participants is slightly less than 1% of all registered working vets in the UK.

Critics and level headed types will suggest the participants may have had ulterior motives to do so. For example maybe they suspected they may be mentally ill and wanted to see just *how ill* they were; Or perhaps they were vets who already believed that personality traits were an important factor in veterinary work and they wanted to discover more... Or the opposite... etc.

So, when reading the VPP results, like all statistics and research papers, add lots of *salt* and practice some caution.

Appendix II

RESULTS of the VPP Survey 2015

This Appendix should be read in conjunction with the Chapter 1 : **Do you have the right personality to be a vet?**

These are the results of the Veterinary Personality Project Survey 2015. The survey was run online, and vets were invited to participate. There were no enticements or rewards for participation other than they could self-claim up to 1 hour of their annual requirement of CPD (Continuing Professional Development) .

The survey had 226 participants - 64 declared themselves as male, one didn't seem to know, and the rest were female - meaning 28% were male. The vet profession in 2014 had about a 43% male to 57% female ratio (RCVS, 2014). So we can conclude proportionately fewer males than females took the survey which might simply mean men couldn't be bothered. Or maybe females were more interested in the well-being aspects of the survey. As I (stupidly) didn't ask "Why did you choose to take the survey?" we'll never know for sure.

Age ranges of the survey filler-inners -

18-21 years old

22-25 years old

26-30 years old

31-45 years old

46-65 years old

65+ years old

This next bit is best in graph form. It will show the 5 Personality traits of each age range.

Remember that a trait result of 50% indicates the respondent has an average result (the average of all the people (anybody, not just vets) who have ever filled in a Big5 survey in an academic research situation globally. It is hoped that this large number (> 500,000) means an average figure equates to the general population (English-speaking countries). So if a person has a result of 63, then they are above the average. A result of 37 is below average. "Ah ha!" I hear you say - "you have highlighted Neuroticism and Conscientiousness on your chart!". Yes I have and you'll find out why later on.

Oh go on then, I'll give you a hint now. There is currently a discussion within the profession about the well-being and mental health of vets. In particular, younger vets. Some say there is a problem. Others say it's not the case. Ask two vets the same question and you'll get three answers. We'll talk about all this elsewhere, but just to note that raised Neuroticism and Conscientiousness levels can be associated with poor well-being, anxiety, stress, and mental ill-health (Chamorro-Premuzic, 2010). The chart above shows that vets in their 20s have higher levels of both. Personality trait scores change little during a lifetime as we discovered in Chapter 1. So this data suggests vets in their 20s are a different sort of personality group to those over 30. There's also some academic research work at an American University which shows exactly this (Johnson, 2009). The authors have written a paper that shows that the average type of person entering the profession as a student is measurably different in terms of their personality traits. Extrapolating these results suggests that students' moral and emotional priorities will have changed too. Which reflects not only on how they practice vet medicine, but on how they handle the stresses and strains of their lives. We'll talk about this elsewhere!!

OK. Back to the survey results:

By Age:

18-21 year olds

We weren't able to promote the survey to 18-21 year olds because the Universities' vet departments wouldn't pass on our information. Which is a shame as there is evidence that various health problems evident in working vets often have their seeds sown whilst at university. So we only had a few respondents which is too few to make any concrete conclusions. Suffice to say that one student respondent had the highest Kessler score of the entire survey (risk of mental health related suicide). They also had the *lowest* WEMWEBS score of the entire survey (a well-being score). They had a very high Neuroticism and Conscientiousness score. They had considered suicide. I hope they managed to find help.

22-25 year olds

These are students in their last year at university and those in their first year or so of work.

Personality traits:

The results for this group suggests average extraversion and agreeableness. Both

Neuroticism and Conscientiousness were well above average. Openness to experience results were low (less adventurous).

Extraversion - The results suggest that those with a lower extraversion score are less likely to have outside interests beyond vet work. Those that *did* have outside interests generally had higher Extraversion scores. They tended to participate in *solo* activities such as running, climbing, etc.

Notable stuff

Most thought they would move jobs within the next 18m. This is a huge number and supports our comments elsewhere on the presence of significant employment issues.

The biggest fear of the people in this cohort was making clinical mistakes. They were concerned with being sued, and more importantly being called to answer to the RCVS disciplinary body in London. Over 50% of this cohort listed *acknowledgement and the respect of their peers* (other vets and friends) as being the primary reward of being a vet.

Their comments on the future of the profession leaned toward the *bleak*. In particular there was concern for its corporatization and also for the ever decreasing rewards from clinical specialisation and academic advancement.

Notable concerns

There was reference to the difficult demands of vet practice - long hours worked, poor conditions of work, poor management, etc. There was almost unanimous fear of making mistakes and an acute awareness of the increasing pressure from client expectations.

Mental health

25% had received treatment for depression whilst at university. Nearly half were diagnosed with clinical depression whilst working as a vet and 2 had had treatment.

This cohort's WEMWEBS well-being measure was average (for the UK population). Their average Kessler (risk of depression and suicide ideation) score was high at 15. One respondent had a WEMWEBS of 36 (low), a Kessler of 24 (extremely high). Their Neuroticism score was equally high at 87% and their Extraversion was very low at 11. This respondent was showing signs of extreme stress and their trait scores agreed with their stated situation. The healthiest respondent (measured by WEMWEBS and Kessler) had a low Neuroticism score. But it would be a mistake to think that mental-health can be predicted by a person's N score alone. There was one respondent who had a N of 80, and yet scored reasonably well on their health. Their trait analysis was E48; A0; C48, N80, O0. They were doing OK because a higher Extraversion score can be *protective*, as can low *Agreeableness*. Common sense tells us that low Openness to experience is probably not helping the people with high N to remain healthy (e.g. combining *'not going out much'* (social isolation) with a tendency to *'over react to negative thoughts'*), but there is little formal research to confirm or deny this at this point.

26-30 Years

This age group have established careers in the profession, and one would assume are beginning to settle into the work.

Personality traits

Averages for this cohort were E 36, A44, C51, N62, O29. E is (surprisingly) low (average for the population is 50%). N is high and O is under the average as we would expect of vets in general. Those with high N and low E were the ones who revealed they had suffered with mental health problems and some had received treatment.

Notable stuff

Like their 22-25 year old colleagues, most consider *receiving* the *respect* of their peers, clients and friends as the primary reward of practice. Over 50% had no clear career plan or ideas, although around 25% of them felt they would be moving jobs within the next 18 months. Nearly 70% desired their conditions of work to improve.

The *average* working week was 46 hours. Some individuals were clocking up to 80 hours work in a week (this being a mixed practice. One companion animal practitioner was working 72 hours!)

Mental health

Over 35% of this cohort had experienced clinical (diagnosed) depression at some point - either whilst working or at university. Slightly less than 25% had received treatment.

The majority of respondents cited,

> **demands of practice (hours, work, career determination (which means how much control a person has over their job)),**

> **fear of making a mistake,**

> **client complaints,**

> **and client expectations**

as causing the most stress in their day to day work.

31-45 Years

This was the largest group of respondents. These are the vets who you would expect to be in positions of professional strength: In this age group, people have carved out a range of roles within the profession, but most are still working directly with animals, or just one step away (managing other vets, nurses, students, etc.).

Personality traits of the 31 to 45 year group

Averages for this cohort were E 36, A44, C51, N62, O29.

Neuroticism remains high - a similar figure to the younger vets. Extraversion remains low as does Openness to experience.

Notable stuff that this age group talked about

Interestingly, those vets who had a high Agreeableness score claimed they had a lower need for peer approval and respect. Being nice is obviously reward enough.

When talking about the future of the profession, this age group were more positive about the benefits of *corporatisation*. Many felt it would increase the overall quality of animal care, but they did recognise it would decrease working vet's welfare and conditions.

About 30% felt they had made the wrong choice in choosing vet medicine. Just over 60% felt they had a clear career view of the future - you would expect this age group to be working in stable jobs - partnerships / owners/ senior positions (clinical and non-clinical). But interestingly, over 25% expected to change their job within the next 18m. Job mobility remains surprisingly high even in this age group.

Average weekly hours worked was 44 hours a week which includes many who work reduced hours (part-time). Several vets were regularly working 100 hours a week (including emergency cover). The current UK Working Hours Directive suggests a maximum of 48 hours.

50% of the respondents reckoned the most stressful aspect of practice was the fear of making clinical mistakes. This was closely allied with worry about upsetting clients, and also about unfair expectations from clients.

Mental health and well-being

Slightly over 12% claimed to have experienced clinical depression at vet university and 80% of these had sought treatment. Over 30% of respondents had experienced depression at some point after graduating, and had sought treatment. I find these figures a bit scary - I don't know about you. I'll remind you (Dear Reader) that this survey was focused on obtaining information on personality types within the profession. The sections on well-being were not promoted at all and filler-inners only discovered they had been assessed for these elements afterwards. My interpretation of this observation is that the self-selecting participants were in fact a good broad range of vets - not just those having well-being problems. Therefore one could claim that although self-selecting, the VPP survey captured a representative portion of the profession.

Survey bias: Perhaps these high figures of mental stress and discontent are due to one or more of the following factors,

A huge proportion of vets interested in research on personality types have suffered from depression

Many vets suffer with depression - especially those between 31 and 45 years old.

Many vets who have the internet and complete surveys online have depression.

Many vets who are interested in their own personality type suffer from depression.

I hope you realise I'm being a bit flippant here. I am being tongue-in-cheek in response to the Vet Profession's "great and good" (the various professional organisations) who are currently getting very excited in denying the extent of mental health issues in the profession.

I'm going to go with number 2:

2) Many vets suffer with depression - especially those between 31 and 45 years old.

It's true that many people with mental health issues seek answers to why they are ill. This includes reading psychology books, learning about factors that may precipitate illness, finding one's own predisposing factors, etc. Filling in surveys... There is so little information on why someone is suffering - *Doctor Google* is sometimes the only source of help. Let's remember vets are high-achievers. This automatically means that many delay seeking professional help for their mental health issues. Many vets with health issues are low on the Extraversion scale - they keep their problems to themselves!

46-65 Years old

50% of respondents were *employed*. The rest were *self-employed* or *retired*. Average hours for all respondents was 44 per week. *Personality types*

Extraversion in this age group was averaging out at 45%, a similar figure to the previous age group. 48% Agreeableness, 42% Conscientiousness, 51% on the Neuroticism scale and 48% on the Openness to experience scale. Average well-being scale results were well in the normal ranges.

These results show a regularisation of personality types - this age group are the vets who came up through the old-school training systems. They experienced traditional educational structures; they were helped (mentored) in their first jobs. Excessive client expectations and a willingness to litigate were just a twinkle in Rupert Murdoch's eye. Yes, these people are very skilled scientists - their knowledge built on firm foundations - but they remain in control of their careers, and are generally pragmatic people with a common-sense and a *manual* approach to their world.

Interesting stuff from the 46-65 year olds

Fear of litigation (and RCVS disciplinary action) is lower than in the younger age groups at 31%. The spectre of clinical and professional stagnation is beginning to raise its head in this group. There is a fear of being left behind as the profession rushes forward both technologically and commercially. Interestingly, 50% cited gaining the respect of their peers as being the greatest reward of a life in the profession - a similar level to other age groups. This obviously remains a core value for many vets of any generation - See the section on *Self Actualisation* in the Personality Chapter.

Fewer of this age group were concerned about client complaints - 30%. Reported pressures were now more related to management issues and also increasing problems with coping with the day-to-day pressures of clinical work (which presumably come with age?

Mental health information 46-65 year olds

7% had received treatment for depression at university. Over 30% had received treatment for depression at some point in their subsequent career.

66 plus Years old

Personality types

E was 55%, A 53%, C30%, N 49% and O was 46%. Health and well-being measures were good and were an improvement over the previous age group.

Interesting comments

Over half claimed the respect of their peers was their most important reward - durr!

Comments from the General Survey:

Below, I have extracted some comments that the respondents left as *afterthoughts* at the end of the survey.

Comments from the whole survey - all age groups

Self Confidence :

> *A person can never know everything, but I was very hard on myself about doing things right and often over-thought my decisions. In the research (I now) do, mistakes may cost money, but seldom lives...*

Success:

> *I think we have the best job in the world. I think some other vets need to look outside their little bubble and realise quite how good we have it.*

Draining:

> *Often after being drained at work, I'm left with a lack of feeling in my personal life...*

The demanding public:

> *Public are too removed from the cost of healthcare (NHS). Ill informed and yet have high expectations and demands. Having a pet is seen as a right and vets are expected to solve their problems and bail animals out for free. We are emotionally blackmailed by society... for trying to make a living and accused of being in it for the money when (if) we are not willing and able to work for free.*

> *I would just like clients to stop thinking they own us*

Philosophy:

> *Just because we can doesn't mean we should - [there is an] increasing blind acceptance of 'gold standard' protocols.*

Demands :

> *I feel hung up behind the door*

Self deception:

> *It's not a mental health problem if it only occurs when bad things are happening. [several responders have said similar ideas: e.g. that the causes of their illness were nothing to do with the work - were relationships / external issues. Can this be true, or are they denying themselves the possibility they may be human and get ill like other normal people? Some research due here I think...PDS]*

Positive well being:-

> *...keep things in perspective - always remember if something does go wrong it is not because you intended it - generally it is despite your best efforts - not because you wanted to cause distress.*

> *What is a bad vet? Clients think one thing. Vets will think another.*

It's a small job:

...but what do I contribute to the bigger picture by dealing only with pets. In theory I am smart enough; educated enough; driven enough; to play a much bigger role in the world.

Busy busy :

What is it about being busy? Why does everyone have to be busy?

Perfectionism - Adaptive and mal-adaptive

Gossip in the practice leads to reduced self esteem. I feel commented upon. I don't worry about what clients say so much as what my colleagues <u>think</u> of me. I worry about peer opinion and comparisons with other vets. My unhealthy perfectionism... is built on my assumptions - in truth they don't say anything - it's all in my head.

Mentoring:

This assumes the mentor is in a healthy place / has time / interest / patience. Can't assume it.

Students:

Many current vet students are over sensitive and over caring.

Universities are selecting for high-achieving females- generally are hard working perfectionists....are not set up to cope with being belittled by clients, defend against 'you only care about money'. Why not insist on counselling students thru course?

Mental health - 1 in 4 of my female employees are under professional care for mental health disease.... Most of their stressors are external to work...

Time for evening surgery, but I'd like to revisit this section...

Expectation:

Management of expectation - in clients, and in graduates who are unprepared for the mundane emotionally challenging and financially disappointing realities.

Tears:

i....love my job. Sometimes I find tears coming to my eyes as I drive home thinking how lucky I am to be in a job I love.

Expectations:

I wanted to be a vet from 7 years old and it is how I define myself. The possibility of not being a vet, or admitting I cannot cope terrifies me as I would not know how to define myself.

Appendix III

Personality Traits - an apology on behalf of the Science of Psychology

It's worth noting at this point that many of my readers will be qualified vets - many of whom will be trained in *hard science*. These illustrious and highly skilled scientists are most comfortable with research results that can be measured in laboratories. They want results that can be tabulated, and then verified using various *statistical* and *ethical* academic tests. Part of the rigour of good science is that experimental results should be *repeatable*. I have read upwards of 100 *scientific peer-reviewed papers* on Personality Traits and their application as part of my research. Tedious it might be, but it is certainly rigorous. I have no doubt that it's as *hard* a science as any other - it's peer reviewed, statistically robust, reproducible, etc.

The history of personality research

Much of the science of Personality grew from the writings of an early 20th Century psychologist called *Carl Jung*. He was a some-time compadré of Sigmund Freud - whom you've all heard of. Together they hatched theories of how the mind works. Like most competitive scientists, after a while they fell out. Jung put a block on Sigmund's number and, alone, he began to develop his own complex set of theories on personality:

Jung suggested people can be broadly divided into two types,

Those that favour *extraversion* (where a person's primary interest is turned toward the 'outer world')

Or *introversion* (where a person's psychic energy (thoughts & feelings) is turned inwards into 'the self'). (Psychic as in psychological - not psychic as in stars and pointy hats.)

Jung then went a stage further and said people can be further sub-divided into other Types. He used descriptive terms for these sub-divisions of personality:- *Thinking and Feeling; Sensation and Intuition.*

These Types were assessed not by how a person appeared (rather subjective), but more objectively by identifying a person's own *preferences.*

By putting all these descriptors together, a person may be described through their preferences: 1) For example, a person may favour Introversion (or Extraversion) in their interactions with the world; 2) They may make decisions about their world using a process of Thinking (as opposed to Feeling (emotion)); 3) They may perceive the world using Sensation (rather than iNtuition).

This lead to Jung to place people in one of eight categories - do the Math!

ETS   ITS   ETN   ITN   EFS   IFS   EFN   IFN

E= Extraverted; *I*= Introverted; *T*= Thinking; *F*= Feeling; *S*= Sensing; *N*= Intuition

Since Jung's time, psychologists ("psychologists study cognitive, emotional, and social processes and behaviour by observing, interpreting, and recording how people relate to one another and their environments." www.bls.gov) have improved on these ideas by adding to and refining them. Each step forward has invariably made the 'science' more believable:

Early in the 20th Century, Katherine Briggs and her daughter Isabel Myers made some adjustments to Jung's personality theories, and they created the Myers-Briggs Type Indicator (MBTI). They added a fourth measure of personality that measured how a person *considers and acts.*

They used the terms *J*udging and *P*erception as either end of a trait scale. So a person was either *J* or *P*. Those that favour *judging* like to have matters closed, they are decisive, organised and industrious. At the other end of this scale is *perceiving* - these people favour curiosity, are happy to leave things unresolved, are flexible and tolerant. (I bet you can guess which end of this scale most practising vets favour!!)

With the addition of these two new traits (*J* & *P*), Jung's eight categories of personality became 16. (Keep doing *the math!*):

So these are the 16 MBTI trait types: ETSJ / ETSP // ITSJ / ITSP // ETNJ / ETNP // ITNJ / ITNP / and so on - oh well, you get the idea.

These 16 traits form the Myers Briggs Trait Index (MBTI), and it categorizes people into one of 16 types. Katherine Briggs and her daughter Isabel Myers produced a working indicator in the Second World War - a time when women were required to perform jobs formerly done by men. The working indicator was specifically designed to help those women find jobs most appropriate to their strengths. Since then, the MBTI has been widely adopted by "business" to match jobs with job-applicants. The categorization of people into types such as ENFJ (the teacher - Extraversion/iNtuition/Feeling/Judging), or INFP (the healer) is an easy formula for employers and HR departments to understand. Its ease of use, and categorical unambiguous results are the main reason why it has been so widely accepted and remains in use to this day. But… The MBTI measure has many detractors and critics:- They feel such categorization is an insult to individuality. They suggest labelling a person as either extraverted or introverted is too blunt and maybe a bit rude: The MBTI says a person is either *Feeling Or Thinking*. It doesn't allow for variation in the amounts of a trait someone may favour. (For example, what if someone is only slightly more extraverted than introverted. Is it fair to simply call them extraverted and ignore their introverted bits?) Another note on self-evaluation tests:

The MBTI measure is *self-evaluated*. In fact, this applies to *all* personality trait assessments. This is a major stumbling block for our hard-wired scientists who are reading this book. Many will struggle to believe in a science that cannot measure personality traits with a machine or a tape-measure. Ideally, in a perfect *scientific world*, an *evaluator person or machine* would test and observe the *subject* person. Then the evaluator person would *work out* a measure of personality for the subject. Nice idea but there is a risk of subjectivity (opinion) bias. The evaluator has a personality too and that might influence their opinion. So the only way (currently) to measure a person's personality traits is to ask THEM a series of questions to determine what they 'favour' in their interactions with the world. These are some example questions,

Question: *It is difficult to get you excited.* Choose an Answer : *Yes / No / Something in between.*

Or here's another one,

Question: *You are inclined to rely more on improvisation than on prior planning.* Choose an Answer : *Yes / No / Something in between.*

There are upward of 300 questions asked during a test and accuracy and reproducibility are improved through cross-referencing.

The person being measured during these tests chooses to answer truthfully. Or they can lie. In research situations, there tends to be little to gain by lying other than maybe to "save face". So in research, the results from self-declaring tests are pretty reliable and stable. If on the other hand you were applying for a job, it might be worth lying when answering the test questions. If you knew what *type of person* they were looking for, and you were as clever as you think you are, then it would be fairly easy to lie. You could corrupt the results by presenting yourself with a false set of 'preferences'. In fact, this happens a lot - there are plenty of books and websites written specifically to help people cheat the MBTI test.

The Big5 Personality Trait Indicator

As a result of the MBTI's weaknesses, another test has been developed. This is the so-called *"Big5"*. Like the MBTI, the *'Big5'* test uses a person's *preferences*, but the questions are different. More importantly, the results are represented on a scale. So rather than being either Extraverted or Introverted, a person will be given a *score* of Extraversion. 0 to 100. A person may have an E score of 35. A second person may have a score of 75. The second person has a *higher level of extraversion.*

The questions asked in the *'Big5'* are different too. Whereas the MBTI measures people's *behaviour* (in the many situations that life throws at them), the *Big5* measures people's *relationship to* their world.

The *Big5* is the system adopted by most academics who research personality. The *Big5*, like the MBTI is a self-reporting test, but it doesn't categorise. Instead of being given a simple label, people are given a series of numerical scores.

One of the 5 personality traits used in the *Big5* is Extraversion. It measures and reports a simple score of *Extraversion.* So each person has their own score: 65% extraversion, or 32%, or 89%. Or even zero is possible. 50 is taken as the average of all the people who have ever taken the test so far. Someone with low Extraversion could be regarded as

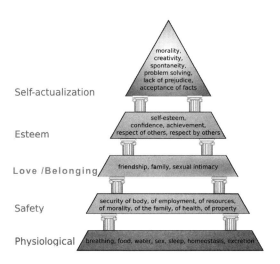

Maslow's Hierarchy of Needs

being introverted, but this term is no longer used much and it's not really that simple.

The *Big5* sliding scales enable traits to be viewed as *biases one way or another* - particularly important for those people who's tendencies lie towards the middle of the scales - which in truth, most peoples' do. Say for example Bob's *Big5* result was 49%. The MBTI would call Bob an Introvert which would clearly be inaccurate at best.

The *Big5's* trait descriptions are these: Remember this test measures a person's *relationship* with the world-

Extraversion 0%-100% (The Big5 avoids the term introversion - it just measures how extraverted you are. 50% is the population average for all 5 traits.

Agreeableness - measures trust, morality, cooperation, empathy etc. - again from 0% to 100% and again the average is 50.

Conscientiousness - high scores suggest a person has an efficient and organised approach to the world - people with very high scores could be called perfectionists.

Neuroticism - the most "loaded" term of them all. No one wants a high score here because in common parlance, the term neurotic has become a very negative term - almost abusive. In the 'Big5', the term neuroticism is the tendency to experience negative feelings. Minor events can be felt as being hopeless. Things are made out to be more important than they should be. People with high Neuroticism scores are 'sensitive' or 'nervous'.

Openness to experience - Higher scores suggest a person is inventive and curious, creative and empathic. They are "up for it". These are the people always looking for the next thrill, the next buzz. People with lower scores tend towards caution and are often more consistent in their activities.

So that's the *Big5*. It is now considered to be the best approach to personality trait testing - particularly in academic and research circles. It's also good because the results are numbers. This means averages and other statistical evaluations can be applied - and scientists like that!

It's also good because it doesn't force labels on people. It's also bad because it doesn't force labels on people. *Tee-hee*. Which is hard for business managers and HR departments which are peopled by very nice, but somewhat simple, folk. Which is why *they* use the MBTI.

Easy Box:

Just remember, the MBTI tries to ascertain how a person *would behave* in their world. The Big5 tries to measure the ways in which a person *does relate* to their world.

Can personality traits change over time?

Yes, absolutely they can change. Researchers have determined that if personality traits *do* change, it is on average only by a factor of up to 10% over a lifetime (Costa & McCrae, 1992). Additionally, personalities are pretty well set by the age of 30. So if Rosie has a neuroticism score of 65% at 14 years old, by the age of thirty it may have moved down to 59% or up to 72%. It's very unlikely to move any more than that.

Agreeableness tends to *increase* as people get older - (nice old grannies). *Neuroticism* slowly decreases over time - (thicker skin). *Openness to experience* ("base-jumping" & learning to ski) tends to decrease. *Conscientiousness* decreases over time too - people learn to recognise that it just doesn't matter if the cat's incision heals in 3 days or in 4: "It's healed! Enough already!" (In childhood and early adolescence *conscientiousness and agreeableness* tend to decrease temporarily over time. Quite rapidly. Durrr. What-ever)

(Cobb-Clarke, 2012. Costa & McCrae, 2003. Soto, 2011. Srivastava, 2003)

Appendix IV

Self-Actualizers (SA)

This is the description for a *state of being* that was developed by the psychologist Abraham Maslow. He explained that this term depicts the *absolute pinnacle of human personal achievement*. The state of *self-actualisation* is one that should be possible for all people to achieve if they try hard enough. It is the realization of a person's potential.

Psychologists in the 1970s used the concept of self-actualization as a means to *improve, develop* and *grow* one's own self (spirituality). Maslow didn't envisage it being used as a tool so much as being a recognition of the *achievements* of a person: - a subtle difference:

Read this diagram from the base.

Maslow created his theory of the *Hierarchy of Needs*. This hierarchy applies to all people through their life and tries to explain a person's needs from basic needs necessary for life, all the way to their highest intellectual / spiritual needs:

- A person's lowest need is physiological - air to breath, food to eat, etc. the base of the pyramid above.

- Next is the need for safety - a person needs not to be eaten by a sabre-toothed tiger, or hit over the head by the guy from next door.

- Next is the need to belong to a group or society.

- Next are a person's esteem needs - the need to be "recognised" or "loved".

- At the top of the hierarchy is self-actualization which occurs when all the other (lower) needs are satisfied.

It is accepted that different people aspire to different levels of Maslow's hierarchy: Some people (and I'm sure we all know some like this) are just happy just to eat, drink; shit and piss. There are many more that need that and also want to be part of a group - they want to stand on a crowded terrace with their mates and watch a group of footballers run around on a field - whilst eating, drinking, shitting and pissing. Or maybe they join the army; or a heavy-metal band . The need to be recognised:- This depicts a recognition of the power of love, a force from above... Or to be less flippant, it is the need to have one's presence and reality in the world acknowledged by others. Self-esteem - that's evident in many ambitious folk. The pinnacle of being - Self-actualization: it's a bit like being Azlan or Mr Spock. Maybe even Albus Dumbledor.

Below are some of the characteristics of a self-actualized person:

- They *know themselves* and therefore can see fakeness in someone else. This can mean they appear to be disdainful of others' achievements.

- They are less affected by desire, wish, fear or the idea of optimism. They *live in the real world*. They are less interested in abstraction or stereotypes. They accept nature as it is. So they are not bothered by pus or faeces - useful for vets.

- They feel *guilt at their own laziness*, thoughtlessness, temper, mental or physical ill-health, jealousy etc. And so they are intolerant of it in others.

- They can be *unconventional* - they may accept an award for excellence, but will ridicule it afterwards.

- They are *ethical* by using fundamental principles. They don't follow the herd. In fact they regard the herd as weak and possibly slightly ill.

- They *focus on external problems*, not their internal ones. (They tend to ignore their own illnesses.)

- This can all lead to them appearing steady, *aloof, calm, reserved*.

Appendix V

Overwhelmed : Stressed : PTSD

What is that?

We all talk about being stressed. When a friend asks how we are doing, we *always* say "yes we're OK, but very *very busy*". People are always busy. Always rushing somewhere. Many of us live in a world of competitive busyness. By declaring themselves anything less than very successful and totally occupied often risks feelings of failure - which can lead to shame, embarrassment and lower self-esteem. And with the changing social roles of women and men in society, women appear to be affected the most. And as we learned in Chapter 1. on Personality, women are generally more susceptible to stress than men.

What is stress?

A state of mental or emotional strain or tension resulting from adverse or demanding circumstances (courtesy of https://en.oxforddictionaries.com).

Why is stress so damaging?

→ Firstly, stress alters your physiology: Causing your body to work differently:

When stressed, hormones that in normal amounts help balance *life* are released in higher levels than normal - stuff like adrenalin, glucocorticoids (steroids), dopamines, etc.

→ Secondly, these hormones nibble away at normality:

Glucocorticoids in excess can contribute to renal and liver disease. They can contribute to diabetes. There is risk of heart disease and other organ dysfunction. They contribute to diseases like IBS and many other physical symptoms of anxiety. Dopamines have marked effects on mental function - chronic excesses will contribute to paranoia and psychosis. Psychological dependencies may include misuse of alcohol and drugs. Over-eating and obesity.

→ Effects on the brain: Dopamine and stress suppresses the brain's frontal cortex which normally helps calm the amygdala. (The amygdala is part of the *limbic area* of the brain. It is concerned with emotions, motivation and is part of the memory complex. Thus it is the seat of *fear, aggression and anxiety*). So stress can lead to increased amygdala activity which can subsequently lead to addictions, overeating and cognitive impairment.

Brigid Schulte (2014) tells us that stress actually DECREASES the amount of grey matter in the brain. Grey matter is the clever stuff. White matter is less clever. So chronic stress leads to smaller brains. Thus *function* is affected - which leads to impaired decisions and reduced attention. This leads to less effective *control* of normal emotions, appetite, anxiety and sleep patterns. A person may appear to be doing OK in their stressful life - but are in fact more vulnerable to extraordinary events because their stressed brains have been quietly establishing (as yet unused) pathways to depression and anxiety.

The power of perception

The *way people feel* about the stress in their lives is a powerful predictor of their general health. If people *feel stressed*, there is an increased incidence of depression; anxiety; smoking; overeating. Perception of being stressed leads directly to physical change and disorder. Thus if you are stressed, it's better not to *know*.

PTSD - Post Traumatic Stress Syndrome

PTSD is partly defined as the evidence of pathological fear and anxiety. It has been partly attributed to the same dysfunctional Frontal Cortex - Amygdala pathway we just talked about. Sufferers re-experience their traumas and practice active avoidance measures to associated situations and thoughts. Their amygdala has become hypersensitive to fear stimuli. Because of reduced frontal cortex inhibition (due to stressors) the symptoms of PTSD become evident. Use of the term PTSD has been hijacked recently by folks who have too much time on their hands. Many are self-diagnosing PTSD after a bit of cursory research on Dr Google. PTSD remains a serious condition despite these misguided folk stealing the term for their own self-pitying ends. Science (Akirav, 2006) has revealed that chronic stress leads to impaired Frontal Cortex activity. And along with high dopamine this leads to over-activity in the amygdala. This high amygdala activity reveals itself as emotional dysfunction, deficiencies of memory and over-reactions to fear-stimuli.

Why do vets accept the stresses of everyday?

If you place a frog in a beaker of hot water, it will instantly jump out again.

If you place a frog in a beaker of cold water, and slowly heat it up, then the frog stays and is eventually cooked.

Hmmmm....

Appendix VI

Burnout and why it is so important:

Burnout is a thing. It's not just something people moan about on the pages of self-help books. These days, people will use the term to simply describe a bad day. The truth is burnout is extremely serious. It is a form of mental illness. It can be measured. It's onset can be predicted by psychologists. Most people will recognise that a functioning relationship with one's life comes from a balance between the demands of life on the one hand, and the *resources* available to fulfil those demands on the other. (For example, the demands of your job are that you have to work 10 hours a day. You have a young family. 'Resources' would be someone you could do a job-share with. Or maybe flexible hours. Etc.) When resources run low, then exhaustion and burnout can follow. The demands of life can no longer be fulfilled - which leads ultimately to a sense of "failure".

Burnout is evaluated through assessing 3 features of a person - their emotional exhaustion; their cynicism; and their engagement. - High emotional exhaustion, high cynicism and low engagement (with job or other aspects of life) are all danger signals.

There are some interesting gender differences here. When a vet experiences burnout, women vets tend to show more *emotional exhaustion*. Men vets tend to exhibit *cynicism* more. Both genders become *disengaged* - with the job, the role, the clients, the profession etc. Or in extreme cases they become disengaged with life! To add insult to injury, it has been also been established that women vets are possibly twice as susceptible to stress than their male counterparts Van der Velde, 2010).

Things that can contribute to professional burnout include:

A lack of control over ones environment. Vets are by definition "self-starters". Give them a job, and they will get it done. Vets are expected to be leaders in getting things done. But if they feel constrained. Or if they feel they can't influence their hours of work; or how their nurses work with them; or what drugs they have available; or if their boss won't allow them to treat an animal how they'd like; etc. etc., then the vet is at risk of burnout.

A perceived lack of support from their managers, their colleagues, the nurses, their personal relationships, their boss, or even from their animal-owning clients can lead to burnout. For 'support' you could possibly read 'recognition' - a part of the definition of a self-actualized person (See Appendix).

A lack of personal professional progression is a precursor of burnout. Vets are very driven people, and they have a need for, and they expect the opportunity to, advance and improve their skills. They are not the sort of people to accept the status quo. Vets usually fulfill this need for improvement by attending lectures about new techniques, drugs, etc. They will expect to discuss difficult and interesting cases with colleagues and experts. Many seek formal advanced academic qualifications. If these opportunities for professional advancement are missing, then their clinical and therefore their personal self-esteem can fail. Related to this sense of one's professional status, burnout can be precipitated by something as seemingly vague as being unable to offer proper care to patients!

Other features of Burnout that I need to tell you about:

> *Burnout may be an "enduring quality of the person affected". This means that some people are more susceptible than others (below, I'm going to talk about the Neuroticism Trait which points to or can measure that susceptibility to burnout.)*

> *Women are more prone to "exhaustion" and "stress" than men. And are therefore more prone to burnout.*

Research on vets in crisis reports that vets are generally very unwilling to reveal that they are ill. Many vets experiencing burnout continue to work. Their family often doesn't realise they are in trouble. Most vets are cognitively self-aware, and many will try to self-cure, or at the very least will try to keep their illness under control. Vets often report they are unwilling to share because they feel ashamed - they feel less than perfect.

As people get older and the longer they spend in one job, the less stress, less anxiety and less depression overall. So that's good then (Mastenbroek, 2013).

Another note here on BURNOUT.

Burnout is the term we use for someone "who's just about had enough". They've worked too hard. They're tired. Some psychologists call burnout a *situationally induced stress reaction*. Which is a bit wordy and probably of little value to us normal folk.

> *Burnout - Affected people are in a dysphoric state - unable to deal with new stresses. They become panicky, dependent and despondent.*

A psychologist called Christina Maslach (1982) decided to explain and quantify burnout. "Burnout" is now an accepted scientific term. It can be measured and quantified:

There are 3 *outcomes* of burnout according to Maslach:

1) Emotional exhaustion 2) Depersonalization of others (cynicism) - resulting in a loss of interest and emotional bonds with other people including patients) (engagement and cynicism). 3) Feelings of reduced personal accomplishment.

Burnout is usually associated with ones work - job satisfaction, desire for change, issues affecting combining work and home demands.

McCrae and Costa (the creators of The Big5 test) in 1985 determined that some types of people have more resistance (or resilience) to burnout than others. Those that remain distressed after stressful events are those more likely to burnout. Remember that Neuroticism is described as "the tendency to experience negative feelings". So it follows that someone with a higher N will experience a more profound event (greater stress, greater negative feelings, longer recovery times, etc.) than someone with a low N score.

People with high Neuroticism scores showed more associations with the first two elements of burnout - *emotional exhaustion* and *depersonalization.* The statistical correlation was over 50% - which translates into our language as being "pretty well true and spot-on"! McCrae and Costa found that affected people tended to take these feelings home - which makes non-work relationships similarly at risk.

Burnout is aggravated by "personal dysfunction" - alcohol abuse; drugs; compulsive behaviours; poor physical health.

The third outcome of burnout - *Feelings of reduced personal accomplishment* - are associated with Conscientiousness: The higher one's C score, the more susceptible one is to burnout.

A high Agreeableness score is protective. So if a person has a high A score, they are *less* likely to experience burnout. They are more pro-person and helping-orientated - this gives them better stress-coping strategies (Maslach, 1982).

Appendix VII

A short discussion of Suicide in the Vet Profession

A USA study in 2013 found upwards of 22% of high school students had *seriously* considered suicide. The World Health Organisation found the number of UK teenagers self-harming *rose by 300%* over the previous 10 years. Suicide is a major problem and it is particularly prevalent in the group of younger people we call the *Millennials*. We have spoken about *Millennials* elsewhere - suffice to say here that they are at risk for a combination of reasons: from flawed parenting through to altered social status and interactivity. This is important because the vast majority of our *new-vets* are Millennials - and so they are at risk.

Are vets more at risk of suicide than other people?

Firstly let's talk about THE FACTS of veterinary suicide: The facts are that there are no convincing facts. Unfortunately, the official statistics that *are* available are extrapolations of other professions. For a sense of the scale of the specific veterinary problem, we have to rely upon a few research papers - many of which come from other countries. So there are elements of urban myth about the whole subject which unfortunately gives ammunition to those who deny there is a vet suicide problem *at all*. To our aid comes a fairly recent review of all the available literature (Platt, 2010). This has arrived at the conclusion that suicide, and suicide *ideation* (thinking about or creating mental images of suicide) *are* significantly higher in the vet profession than in the general population. So there you have it. No figures, but vets are up there with the other suicide high-flyers - farmers, doctors and nurses. Did you note that those who are most likely to commit suicide are *all* in the caring professions? We are back to Personality Traits again!

The same review suggests females working in companion (small) animal practice are more likely to ideate about suicide than other vets. We don't know why suicide happens. We don't really even know *'what it is'*. We do know some of the factors that lead to suicide. And we know that poor mental health is the main cause of people taking their life. Which is a bit obvious I know, but it needs to be said. So we need to think about what the term 'poor mental-health' means. And also the BIGGEST question for us is, *"What are the causes of mental ill-health in vets?"*

First let's briefly discuss where suicide comes from:

Clinical Depression and Burnout

These are two much bandied-about terms. Many of the 'great unwashed' use them as liberally as they use sweet-ketchup on their chips. The word 'depression' is a psychological medical term and it is used to describe a *collection of symptoms*. Here's a list from Lily Tran et al (2014):

♦ Feelings of dysphoria (a state of dissatisfaction, anxiety, restlessness, fidgeting)

♦ A sense of hopelessness

♦ The sense of devaluation of one's life

♦ Self-deprecation

♦ Apathy

♦ Anhedonia - the inability to experience normal pleasures.

There have to be hundreds of ways a person can become depressed. Each a combination specific to that person. What we *do* know though is that people who score high in the Neuroticism trait are at significantly higher risk of developing depression. We know that people with a high Agreeableness trait score are *protected* from depression and suicide: We also know that depression arises from an imbalance between life's demands and the 'resources' available (like burnout - see Burnout Appendix V.). Burnout is a term we tend to keep for work-related illness. But usually, work-stress is just a manifestation of a more general distress. *Depression is part of, and can lead to, Burnout. Maladapted perfectionism* (see Personality Chapter) can also lead to burnout. We already know that Burnout is characterised by:

♦ Emotional Exhaustion - anxiety, depression, and with poor stress coping abilities.

♦ De-personalisation of others - evidenced by a lack of empathy or care.

♦ Cynicism.

♦ Feelings of reduced personal accomplishment - poor self-esteem.

♦ An affected person is usually dysfunctional (abusing alcohol and drugs, having difficulty maintaining relationships, addictive behaviours, etc.).

The presence of burnout in a person is a marker of mental illness and can be an immediate precursor of suicidal ideation and suicide. Burnout is the main signifier of risk for our vets.

The effects of Competition on depression, burnout and suicide.

Vets are competitive. They are the intellectual equivalent of top-class athletes - our high-achievers. Veterinary University course designers actively use this competitive trait in their students to encourage them to pursue excellence in their studies. But in fact 'competition' is cited by many mentally ill and stressed students as being a major cause of their problems. (Along with the more obvious worries about money, workload, relationships, poor recreation opportunities, health issues, and the lack of a McSnackley on campus!) In one UK research project, as many as 25% of vet students reported they had suffered from 'clinical depression'.

This trait of competitiveness also means that vets and vet students often fail to *reveal* that they are ill to others. Universities and employers lazily assume affected people will *self-refer* for help. But they are ignoring the fact that most will stay quiet in order to avoid being judged as less than perfect by their peers: Most vets have high cognitive ability and many mistakenly think they can *work their own way through it*. This becomes a vicious circle: The more ill they become, the poorer their self-esteem, the poorer their sense of belongingness (isolation) and so the less likely they are to ask for help. So they become more ill.

Work Factors in the genesis of suicidal behaviour

A vet's training is arduous and challenging. Many students report they feel extremely pressured and *overwhelmed* during their training.

The vet industry is mostly made up of small physical units - many practices only have 1 to 3 vets working in them. Thus professional and social isolation are common - and these are significant factors in the development of depression and burnout.

Mass Psychogenic Illness. History is littered with examples of people within *close knit communities* suffering from what appears to be a form of 'infectious' psychogenic illnesses. Vets work very closely with each other, and local communities of vets spend time together. Some vet suicides appear in clusters. In his book *The Tipping Point (2000)*, Malcolm Gladwell suggests high profile suicides can somehow give permission to others to take their lives too. The figures confirm that the simple act of talking about suicide in a closed population results in a spike in suicide numbers.

Socially proscribed perfectionism. Vets are trained to be perfect. Society expects the medical professions to be perfect - anything less is construed as abuse. As Rosie

McAllister points out in her blog (2015),

> *"Our occupational culture encourages an almost unique combination of perfection, self-sacrifice, independence and omni-competence, which is totally unachievable."*

Long work hours. Heavy and repetitive workload.

Autonomy is a very powerful *protector* of burnout. Many young vets have little or none in their daily lives - poor managers, heavy workload, proscribed and enforced codes of work. In the same vein, many vets have little control over their environments - the ability to change their hours of work, to choose their team, to go part-time. Also, because of the gradual de-professionalization of vets, and the advent of strict management guidelines, many don't have the opportunity to fully practise and so develop their potential skills.

Maladjusted personal approaches to work such as physical and emotional over-commitment contributes to exhaustion - high effort with low rewards. Poor support from colleagues and management is compounded by a poorly developed personal social-life - which is a commonly reported state of affairs in a vet's early years at work. Remember that our vets have low Openness to Experience trait scores - meaning they stay close to home. Professional isolation is increasingly evident in young vets especially those working in corporate and small practices.

Some researchers report that over 80% of practising vets say their jobs are stressful: They report the main causes of this stress to be the fear of making mistakes; of receiving client complaints; and also trying to meet raised client expectations.

There has been a lot of talk about the influence of repeatedly performing animal euthanasia on the mental health of vets. This psychological process is called *habituation* and some researchers feel that by deliberately causing the deaths of animals, a vet's fear of death is diminished. Thus making them more sanguine about suicide. But then again, other researchers have discovered that performing euthanasia can be *protective*. They surmise this happens through the vets' realization of the *finality of death*. These same researches *do* concede that performing many euthanasias can be a factor in the development of depression - i.e. it is a stressor that leads to a *tipping point* where an *already* mentally stressed vet considers suicide.

The availability of the *means* to commit suicide: Again this is often cited as one of the causes of the 'high' suicide rates in vets. This term refers to a vet's ready access to the implements of death - namely drugs and firearms. But there is little convincing evidence that having unlimited access contributes to a vet's *decision* to commit suicide. It *does* contribute to the success of their suicide attempt once they have made that decision.

Support and Understanding

It is important to recognise that when a vet *ideates* (thinks about or creates images in their mind), or attempts, or actually commits suicide, they are not responding to just one bad factor in their lives. Suicide is the end-point of a very long and twisty road. That person has been pushed and pulled along that particular road of misery over a period of time. And therefore it should be possible for them to turn around, or step aside before they reach a crisis point.

Over 15 years ago, the Behavioural health departments of the *Henry Ford Health System* in Detroit decided to institute a systematic approach that would reduce the suicide rate in their mental-health patients (Coffey, 2007, 2016). To zero! They called their improved health delivery system, Henry Ford's *"Perfect Depression Care"*, and they based it around the idea that,

All suicides are Preventable

Their approach consisted of little that was new or unique. They simply instituted systems of management that ensured their existing strategies were watertight: They bolstered their caring staff's morale and well-being. They removed the patients' *means* to commit suicide. They assumed that *every* case of mental illness presented to them was a suicide risk:- It was their setting a ZERO goal that had the greatest impact on the success of their system. This ZERO goal is their great innovation. And there is no reason why their philosophy should not be applied to the veterinary profession. And we should make it soon... Zero is possible.

Appendix VIII

Compassion fatigue

A discussion thread on vetsurgeon.org vet forum in 2015 - by kind permission of Arlo Guthrie.

The thread starts with a practice owner (we'll call her Anony Mouse) revealing her state of mind:

Anony Mouse:

All this recent talk on the forums about hours worked and jaded veterinary surgeons couldn't have come at a better time for me. I'm having a really difficult time at present and I can't see a way out.

The main problem is that I'm a sole charge vet in my own practice so time off is not an option. Unfortunately, trying to get locums just causes even more stress and this alone can keep me awake at night.

My days are too busy. I run 10 minute appointments for 1.5 hours in the morning and 2.5hours in the evening and do ops and admin in the hours in between. My appointments aren't always 100% filled but almost. We try to allocate 20minute appointments for things like blood sampling and first vaccination consults but when appointments are so busy it can be difficult to find a free double slot and we have lost potential clients by not being able to offer them something within 48 hours.

I feel like I'm always playing catch up with insurance forms, health and safety, trying to telephone clients, send accounts and just general maintenance of equipment and all the other background things that come with being the boss.

I'm worn out. I don't have a lot left to give.

If I were an employee, I would probably be signed off with stress by now but this really isn't an option. I've been thinking about changing my appointment length but if I have longer appointments, I have fewer to offer and I'm already struggling to fit everyone in! Also, for those who run longer appointments, do you charge a proportionally higher fee or just take a hit on income? How do you see everybody who wants seen?

I finish at 6.30pm most days, I'd love to finish at 6pm but my competitors close by are open until 7 every day so I feel like this would cost me again in terms of client numbers and, while I'd like to be not quite as busy, I don't want to go out of business either.

Can anyone help?

Anony Mouse: Next day

I read an article recently which cited compassion burn-out as being a major factor in increased risk of addictive dependency and suicide within the veterinary profession. Other veterinary journals are decrying the lack of suitably qualified applicants for jobs, or the lack of desire of recent graduates to work late or out of hours. It seems to me this also is leading to a loss of highly skilled vets to other roles outside the profession.

I have been experiencing the feeling for a while that whilst I care deeply about individual animals and do everything I can to prevent suffering and ensure successful treatment outcomes, I feel that I no longer have what it takes to put on the "front" and give the compassionate and caring approach to all of the owners, al all hours of day and night. Maybe it's because I have become cynical to the sob stories about why they can't pay bills or afford more than the very basic treatment for their animals. There are still clients of whom I am very fond, and not all of those are the insured or wealthy ones so the financial aspect is not a main factor in this, but perhaps more the shift in attitudes I have seen over the time since graduation in what clients expect, versus what the RCVS and our morals expect of us.

I personally have reached the point at which I no longer hold any desire to do clinical work because it brings with it the pain of having to explain the same things, over and over again while all the time feeling that any attempt to educate the client about their pet's needs and welfare is useless as it will only take second place to the latest holiday or gadget. Perhaps a sweeping generalisation I know but explaining over and over again to people the benefits of preventative healthcare when in many cases you know they will fail to heed your advice because it's not what their breeder/sister/aunt/dog walker has told them, is just getting too demoralising. In addition there appear to be a whole new "breed" of owner, (no pardon of pun needed), who see their vet as a public information service, there 24-7 to provide convenience to them and absolve them of any responsibility to actually learn about their pets' needs whatever time of day or night they call.

I write this post mainly because I feel I need to get it off my chest, and in the light of recent studies suggesting over half of recently qualified vets no longer feel that their profession is what they anticipated, I wonder if it is time to look at shifting the focus of entry and qualification requirements of veterinary colleges to include some form of psychometric test to ensure that not only are vets equipped with the clinical knowledge, but with the personality type which would be more resilient and adaptable to the demands of modern day practice.

Perhaps it really is time that the RCVS also looked at the Out of Hours issue with a more realistic approach too, and realised that the honourable intention of an individual and personal obligation to relieve suffering in animals with such a broad generalisation of "under my care" is leading to exploitation of vets both by pet owners and by practices, but with no recourse on either of those parties where that obligation becomes significantly detrimental to the welfare of the individual vet concerned.

For obvious reasons I have chosen to remain anonymous, however please be assured I am not doing so because I am at the addictive or suicidal stage, but I have decided to distance myself from clinical work for a while, and concentrate on other areas of the business.

I realise that the RCVS tries with it's limited exposure to educate clients about what they can expect from their vet, and I recognise that there are vets out there who are so good at combining both clinical excellence and client care that they seemlessly move through their careers, perhaps even ending up opening up a Special Cancer Centre along the way to Supervet status. But these types of people are seemingly in the minority as many of my colleagues and other VetSurgeon posters have expressed similar views to myself, i.e. that they are feeling hopelessly torn between the demands of running a business and their ethical and moral obligations to the animals they treat.

Perhaps other Vetsurgeon members would like to contribute to a discussion, anonymous or otherwise, about how they REALLY feel about the pet owning public as a means to generate business, and whether I'm alone in thinking that client attitudes to their pets and their vets has really taken a turn for the worse over the last few years, leading to me feeling that no matter what I try, they drain me of compassion and still it's not always good enough...

I realise James Herriot died in the public's eyes many years ago, but are we all ready to be Cancer-centre-opening-sleeping-in-my-office-operating-till-the-early-hours type vets? Because I'm genuinely terrified that the pubic perception of our profession is heading that way.

BigBoy:

Thanks for sharing this with us. It is an issue that has been given considerable thought in the VetFutures project, and there are several threads that deserve further consideration (the issue of trying to balance animal welfare and veterinary out of hours responsibilities has recently been given a very thorough airing at the (Royal) College (of Vets).

I think one point that has come out of our deliberations are the realisations that first-ly, societal expectations are changing both in regard to what we expect from a life as a professional but also about the concept of a career for life, and secondly that a veteri-nary degree is a grounding for many different career paths, and there is a tendency to assume that someone in clinical practice is not a "proper" vet.

There are many who expect one or more career changes even with a vocational degree, and many who very successfully change career paths as their needs and expectations alter. Just because they are no longer in clinical practice does not mean they have failed in some way, and our research has shown that many are very happy with their move.

However, for its own good the practising arm of the profession also needs to exam-ine the career paths it is able to offer to veterinary graduates to try and keep them engaged and content.

Jonny Stalker:

IMO people have changed over the last 25 years. The difference is that many people are not prepared to take responsibilities for their own life and actions any more. This makes my life more difficult and miserable and I do have to confess it really pisses me off sometimes. As I'm the owner (of the practice) I can always tell them to hike off, which I am actually very happy to do when needed. Otherwise I'm sure I wouldn't do clinical work anymore.

HappyVet35:

I have been watching the debate over the future of the profession with some interest. Particularly "how do we continue to attract the brightest and best into the profession"

I might get shot down in flames for this... but are the "brightest" necessarily the "best" for the profession?

I accept that the degree is academically fairly demanding, but perhaps in continually selecting for the "straight A's" trait, our educational establishments are also unwittingly selecting for other traits which are far less useful in a clinical setting. I have seen so many students who I genuinely thought would make excellent veterinary surgeons, turned down because they were ever so slightly short of the lofty academic standard set by admissions, but had so many other attributes that in my view, would have made them fantastic vets.

Jonny Stalker:

One of my favourite topics, mainly due to the fact that I've done some research and written several articles on this topic. The last one involved me interviewing a professor who runs a clinic dealing with people from the medical profession with addiction, mental illness, suicide attempts. Very interesting interview, as he also thinks medical professions attract a certain kind of personality. Unfortunately most of the time it is not the kind of personality that would be needed to be able to cope with what awaits you in everyday practice. The ones who seem to cope well are the ones able to detach themselves emotionally while still enjoying what they do, ... Anyway, he also said that he is really worried for many medical professionals and that the kind of heroism that has been promoted by many and consequently asked of everyone who entered the profession up to (or over!!) the brink of self-exploitation contributes to the amount of mental issues and suicides in our profession. He for one applauded the so called generation y for finally doing things differently, for looking for something else beneath being a "hero in whites" and for getting the opportunity to spend time with their children (although he admits they might be overdoing it a bit at the moment, but hey, that's how change gets started!). Because this contributes to possible changes in society, if children grow up with parents living the life many of us do now, nothing will ever change he thinks. We -doing what we do for 25 or 30 years - may think it's a good way to do things, but honestly, why are there so many suicides, addictions and mental issues in our profession then? I still enjoy my job most of the time, I still feel the highs of a cesarian but I also feel burned out by certain aspects. And I don't see why changing working hours to something more moderate would do any harm? Why is it so bad if people want to have time to do something else but work? There's not many of us who are able to cycle 100km plus after returning from work at 8pm while the phone might ring every minute. I admit I am not and I don't feel inferior because I don't. It's just they way I am.

Anony Mouse:

Thank you for all the offers of help and your kind words.

I think this year has been particularly difficult following a bereavement. Going back to work three days after burying a parent was really hard and it was exceptionally busy at that time too (of course). This led to a lot of the build up of tasks like insurance claims piling up and bills needing paid. I've done my best to catch up but it feels like I'm just firefighting. It's only ever enough to just keep things under control. I never really feel like I've got a handle on it.

I've felt very trapped by my practice. I can't take time off easily, I can't quit, I can't phone in sick. Locums are like hen's teeth here, especially at short notice. I would have liked more time off after the funeral but had nobody to cover for me. It's like a background stress knowing that, no matter what, I have to be in the next day. As an employee I only ever had two days off sick in four years but, still, I had that option. I have a holiday booked in a few weeks time - I can't wait!

My usual day is consult to 10.40 or so, start ops, finish ops, deal with questions from reception that have built up in that time, check prescriptions, type up notes and then away for lunch at about 2pm. I know I'm lucky to get a lunch break as many don't! Then it's insurance forms, lab results, emails etc. until about 3.30 when it's time to start sending animals home before consults start again in the afternoon (If they're sleepy or need some explanation they stay until later to go home through appointment if possible).

I think, on reflection, that I can probably change my work practices somewhat to extend appointment times and still have sufficient time to operate and allow for emergencies. I suppose starting consults earlier in the afternoon and having a break later would be a possibility. It just leaves a bit less time for dealing with emergencies, but there's never really enough time in the day for those anyway, is there?!

The practice is profitable and I'm not unhappy with the money I make. Cash flow is good, so at least I don't have to worry about that.

I don't want to expand my empire particularly but having a part time vet might give me enough flexibility to have some breathing space every now and then if I can figure out the practicalities.

I have an amazingly supportive husband who helps me in every way he can but he can't do my work for me.

I think I'm just tired and I just need to figure out how to stop chasing my tail and actually get on top of things.

Many thanks again for all your kind words. They have been genuinely appreciated.

I'm a Metron:

To Anony Mouse:

> *So time off is not an option?*
>
> *Time off HAS to be an option - if you don't take holiday, you will later be forced to take time off sick.*

Anony Mouse:

> My days are too busy.
>
> It is clear that the current situation is not sustainable - it might be that the only way to run this business is to run yourself into the ground - most likely it isn't but you need to find out. You need to change the business to something that works for you or learn (sooner rather than later) that it won't/can't work - in that case you need to kill the business before it kills you.

Anony Mouse:

> I'm worn out. I don't have a lot left to give.
>
> If I were an employee,

I'm a Metron:

> *If you were an employee, you could probably command a salary in the region of £65k which is around what the corporates are paying their clinical directors. You can go and do vet work and still make a decent living, so it is the business that is damaging, not specifically the vet work. The business needs to be changed to make it work for you.*
>
> *You say that the business is profitable and that cash flow is good so the potential exists to increase your prices - if you have more money coming in, you have more options. You might kill your caseload (you almost certainly won't) but in the unlikely event that that does happen, take comfort in knowing that you killed the business before it killed you.*
>
> *Next, review your accounts. Make sure that there is proper provision in there for rental/mortgage payments on any business premises; make sure that you are being paid for the risk you are taking in putting personal guarantees against any borrowings that the business has; make sure that any work done by spouse/partner is properly rewarded (I am not talking minimum wage); add in your own salary costs - start at £65k. Add on a sensible pension contribution (10% of salary if you are less than 30 and more*

than 25% salary if you are more than 40) - once you have resolved the present crisis, you might not want to keep vetting until your dotage - a decent pension pot opens up all kinds of options later. If you can do all of that and still leave a bit in the till for the ongoing good of the business, then you are right in surmising that the profitability and cash flow are adequate and that is great. If not, then you are in the same boat as most owners of "lifestyle" businesses.

Three things that helped me:

1. Finally acknowledging the cold financial facts outlined above rather than continuing to spout the plethora of excuses that others used before me and yet more have used since.

2. The realisation that there are two good reasons for doing thins on the cheap. 1. You have no choice - in fact you almost always have a choice. 2. You really, really want to. By that, I mean that the money you are about to give away in discount/ under-charging is better spent on that particular client than either you or your family and, even more importantly, the time you invest on that discounted/undercharged/ complementary/charity case was time that you didn't want to spend with your family.

3.As a self-employed person, never, ever go on holiday without first booking another holiday to follow it - that way you get time to make locum arrangements etc. and get to enjoy the holiday you need, when you need it and not a half-holiday at the first opportunity after your burn-out gets serious.

DudleyRox:

I'm not sure i will help much other than to speak to someone in exactly the same position.

I am sole charge in a practice I took over 5 years ago. Working 6 days/week, finishing at 7pm mon-fri getting home for 7.30pm, putting kids to bed, eating at 9pm then sitting down for 60min before bed.

Where are you?

Appendix IX

The Ten Minute Appointment

0.0 mins Read clinical history

Vet: "Hello, how's Billy doing?"

Vet: "Yes - put his box on the table would be great."

Owner: "Billy's been a bit quiet. He wouldn't come out from under the bed this morning." "We called you to come and help us, but the nurse said we had to get him ourselves and bring him in." "Look at what he did to my arm."

Vet: "It might be worth going to the doctor about that. Some of those scratches look a bit deep."

Owner: "Should I go now?" Vet: "No. I will print out a sheet on cat scratches. We'll check Billy now you're here and you can go afterwards"

2.0 mins

Vet: Let's put his basket on the scales so we can weigh him. Owner: Shall I get him out first? Vet: No that's fine. We'll weigh the two together first, then get Billy out.

Vet: 5.1 Kilos

Owner: What's that in pounds?

Vet: No. That's not Billy's weight. We need to get him out first. Can you just hold the box please?

Vet: Hello Billy. Shall we get you - oooh. That's not so friendly. You must be poorly. Let's take the top off the box. Yes you undo those clips on your side.

Owner: I can never get this box to go back together. 'Takes me ages.

Vet: How long's he been poorly?

4.00 mins

<u>Owner</u>: He wouldn't come out from under the bed this morning. <u>Vet</u>: Was he normal yesterday?

 <u>Owner</u>: Oh no! he's been different since last Sunday. That was when he started staying under the bed. Although he came out and eat the fish I boiled up for him 2 days ago. But he left it yesterday - I got some of that frozen Coley from Iceland.

<u>Vet</u>:   Could you put the basket back on the scales please so we can see if he's lost any weight.

<u>Vet</u>:   What day did he stop eating?

<u>Owner</u>: Oh. Don't hold him like that. Billy hates being touched by strangers. We're the only one's he'll let stroke him aren't we Eric? Oh bless. Billy. Purr purr.

<u>Vet</u>:   What day did you first notice him eating less? <u>Owner</u>:   I ' m not sure. A few days.

<u>Vet</u>:   Last Friday?

<u>Owner</u>: Yes. Maybe. The Wednesday before maybe. Eric reckons Wednesday. <u>Vet</u>:   A week then. What's his drinking like. 2.1 Kg. Hmmm. Lost some weight. Sorry. What's his drinking like?

<u>Owner</u>: He's always drunk a lot. He's on that Yams. Dry food. It says on the advert they drink more. Mr OldVet said he would drink more and that it was OK. Vet: Has his drinking changed?

<u>Owner</u>: Oh yes! He's drinking a lot more now. He's got really bad teeth. Mr OldVet said don't worry so we let them be. We give him seaweed powder every day. In his food. For his breath.

<u>Owner</u>: It might be the seaweed powder that makes him sick.

6.00 Mins.

<u>Vet</u>:   I'm afraid it looks like he may be quite ill. He's lost weight. Over a quarter of his weight since we last saw you. How many times is he being sick?

Owner: Not much. Mainly after he eats.

Vet: How many times was he sick yesterday?

Owner: Four times. Five times. Really Eric? I only cleaned up four lots.

Vet: This could be caused by several things. There's nothing obvious on my examination, so we probably should do a blood sample first.
Owner: Oh. Mr OldVet did a blood sample on Billy's sister. Then she got cancer and Mr Oldvet had to put her to sleep. Did Mr OldVet tell you about Mollie. He said she was a very unusual…

Vet: Would you like me to take a blood sample so we can see what's wrong? If you like, we can take the sample, and you can wait for the results. It takes about an hour.

Receptionist: Mr Vet, here's Billy's estimate.

Vet: Thanks Receptionist.

Vet: Here's an estimate. With this consultation, it will come to about £125.

Owner: Oh. That's a lot. What do you think Eric? I suppose Billy's never cost us much. And if it means he'll get better.

Vet: This is just for the samples. If he needs treatment, then it'll be more.

Owner: How much more?

7.00 Mins

Vet: Well, I can't tell you that yet until we find out what's going on. But as soon as we find out, we can work out how much treatment will cost.
Owner: I suppose we have to have the tests. We have to find out what's wrong at least. Shall we get them done Eric?

Vet: Ok. I'll just take him through the back and get someone to hold him for me. You take a seat and I'll bring him back in a minute.

8.00 Mins

Vet: Can someone hold this cat for a blood please?

Nurse: I'll be with you in a minute. I'm just getting *another* Brodger for Mr NewVet. [*Whispers*] - it's his fourth one for one cat spay!

Vet: Is there anyone else?

Nurse: N2 is on her break. N3 is at the branch. I'm it. Sorry.

11.00 Mins.

Vet: There we go. He was very good for his test. If you'd like to wait here it'll be about 2 hours for the results. We're a bit short staffed. Sorry. Or you can go home and I'll call you during lunch.

Vet: If you wouldn't mind settling up with Receptionist before you go. Thanks. I'll give you a call later.

12.00 Mins

Read clinical history.

13.00 Minutes

Vet: Ben Thompson please. Sorry for your wait. 'Been a few emergencies in today...

Appendix X

A Day in the life of a Companion-Animal Vet

08.30: Cup of tea.

08.35: Consult room. Boot up computer- it's slow.

08.40: Scroll through list of expected consults in the session to come.

Open the difficult looking ones to read previous histories.

08.52: The 9 o'clock appointment is early.

10.30: Fully booked surgery - seen 9 animals in 9 ten-minute appointments. Now running 13 minutes late because two turned out to be difficult.

Break: 2 minutes.

10.45: First appointment of next session. 14 appointment slots.

Thankfully 2 didn't turn up - last client left at

13.13: Go through to 'the back' (prep area) prior to lunch. Practice owner asks for help with an x-ray.

14.05: Lunch in car driving to branch surgery. Roads are awful.

14.34: First appointment been waiting ten minutes.

15.01: Receptionist makes a cup of coffee. Phew.

16.00: Client misses appointment - check that this morning's histories have all been written up. Sign off some repeat prescriptions. Try to telephone a referral specialist about a case.

16.38: Seen 11 appointments. Due back at main surgery -support duty as 'second vet' due to finish at 18.00.

18.48: Say good night to receptionists. Seen 11 cases in 8 appointment slots. Appointment system stretched and double booked.

Home by **19.32:**

Tomorrow...

Appendix XI

Personality Trait Tests

There are some ethical reasons why I am not offering you information on how to access to Personality Trait Testing. The main reason for my caution is discussed in an earlier Appendix. Namely the issue of self-selection. It is thought that many people who are suffering from mental stress will often pursue data and information that relates directly to their condition. And as we have discovered, Personality Traits are closely linked with many of our 'problems'. We have to take care to consider any risks associated with offering stressed people the means for them to confirm their self-image. These people may be better off seeking medical professional help rather than pursuing Dr Google's opinion and advice. So my advice to you is consider your mental state / health before taking any tests. Consider seeking advice from a medical professional on your feelings and issues before attempting to self-cure. (See Appendix IV on *Self-Actualization*.)

On the other hand, many readers of Chapter 1 are going to be screaming at me to let them take the VPP (Veterinary Personality Project survey) which ran in 2015. This I can't do as it was delivered as a project and then closed (scientific rigour!). Suffice it to say, all the tests used within the VPP are freely available online:

I used a *Big5* Personality Trait test made available online for general personal use by a senior academic in an American University. It forms part of this academic's research and is an ongoing project. Be warned that there are numerous personality trait tests online and very few have academic vigilance applied. I would also caution against completing an MBTI (Myers-Briggs Trait Indicator) assessment. See Chapter 1 and the Appendices to remind you why. Well-being (Mood) and Kessler Tests which measure mental health and suicide risk are similarly available - generally from National health organisations such as the NHS, NHS Scotland, etc.

Appendix XII

So-You-Want-2-Be-a-Vet Test

Part 1 : What are your Big5 Personality Trait Scores.

N   Score (%)   =

C   =

E   =

O   =

A   =

Part 2 : What is your General Mental Ability (GMA) Assessment score

Part 3 : Tenacity Assessment. How tenacious are you?

Part 4 : Resilience. How thick-skinned are you. How quickly do you recover from 'insults' and injury?

Part 5 : What is your relationship with animals?

Part 6 : Empathy - a debatable skill. Possibly makes being a vet easier, but...

Part 7 : Are you physically able - strong even?

Part 8 : How flexible and adaptable are you - especially regarding your daily needs?

Part 9 : Are you a team player?

Part 10 : Are you self-actualized

Part 11 : Do your parents have spare income to invest in you?

Part 12 : Why do you want to be a vet?

Part 13 : *add your own ideas here*

Etc.

Glossary

- Buying Group - This is an organisation that acts as middle-man between its member veterinary practices and the drug manufacturers. The buying group negotiates bulk discounts from the drug companies and passes them onto its members. It charges its members for this service.

- BVA: British Veterinary Association - member based organisation with the aim to be the voice of the profession nationally in the UK.

- Cert AVP: Advanced Practitioner - Certification by RCVS acknowledging a higher academic attainment than normal vets.

- CPD - Continuing Professional Development. A legal requirement enforced by the Royal College of Veterinary Surgeons for all vets who wish to remain registered. The RCVS stipulate the number of hours every year to be spent in a combination of activities that will professionally develop the vet. Examples are research; lecturing; being lectured to; writing; practising new techniques; discussions; etc. Failure to complete their CPD requirement can lead to a vet being removed from the register of vets.

- EBVM - Evidence Based Veterinary Medicine. A theoretical approach to vet practice that involves collating as much data and evidence from academics and specialists as possible in order to enact a series of guidelines for diagnoses, treatment choices and outcomes. The EBVM approach to medicine enables a vet to rely less on their own intuition and guesswork in a case, and to rely more on what the EBVM guidelines suggest. STOP PRESS: Interestingly, a somewhat panicked meeting was held in late 2018 to discuss EBVM and its affect on the vet industry. The Vet-Times newspaper (David Woodmansey, Dec. 17th 2018) reported that it is now recognized that as veterinary practise is increasingly EBVM-driven, proportionately fewer owners seek veterinary advice and treatment (Stull, 2018). Which means vet businesses may make less money. The term "Spectrum of Care" has been coined and refers to a situation where EBVM gold-standard approaches can be moderated or ignored altogether. So vets may be given 'permission' by the 'elite decision-makers' to offer clients treatments that aren't necessarily the best available. This sounds great for clients (and their animals), but unfortunately many of the younger vets working away in vet practices have only been trained in EBVM - not in EBVM-lite. More change coming...)

- EMS - Extra Mural Studies : Time spent in training within 'academic areas' of the vet profession in order to progress the under-graduate qualification (usually focused on more practical skills). EMS is usually completed outside university formal training / establishments.

- FNA - Fine Needle Aspirate - a type of biopsy where a small fine needle is inserted into the tissue (skin/lump/organ) and negative pressure applied. The cells collected within the needle are viewed using microscopy. Can usually be carried out conscious, but sometimes sedation is required.

- Millennials - (aka. GenY) - people born between the early 1980s and the turn of the century (<2000).

- NICE - National Institute for Care and Health Excellence. A government body that determines the value and availability of medicines and treatments available to the NHS and to patients. It dictates which medicines and treatments should be used by medical practitioners.

- PDP - Professional Development Phase - a voluntary phase of a Vet's education which essentially measures the development of their clinical and 'soft' skills in their first years post-graduation. No teaching is involved.

- Psychologist vs. Psychiatrist: Psychologists study behaviour and interpret deviations from the norm. They can perform psychological testing. They practise psychotherapy (the Freud/Jung thing - and modern improvements of course). Psychiatrists are qualified medical doctors and so can prescribe drugs in addition to psychotherapy. Most are focused on monitoring drug and medication in their patients.

- Pyometra - a disorder of the uterus that can be life-threatening.

- Perineal Hernia - a hernia in the perineum. My favourite piece of surgery.

- RCVS - Royal College of Veterinary Surgeons. The Royal-Chartered body authorised by Parliament to regulate and monitor the work done by vets. All vets have to be entered into the RCVS register of members of the RCVS in order to practice. Their two responsibilities are 1) To protect the public's interests (from any vet's action), and 2) to ensure the animal's interests are preserved.

- SPVS: Society for Practising Veterinary Surgeons - a more business orientated organisation.

- VPP: Veterinary Personality Project 2015

- Vet Times: A weekly 'newspaper' sent to all vet practices weekly.

References

Akirav, I. & Maroun, M. (2006) *The Role of the Medial Prefrontal Cortex-Amygdala Circuit in Stress Effects on the Extinction of Fear:* Hindawi Publishing Corporation Neural Plasticity

Anonymous. (2006) *Thinking of owning your own practice: which path to choose?* Vet Times.

BVA: British Veterinary Association - Press release. 25 April 2017

Bear, J.B. & Williams Woolley, A. (2011) *The Role of Gender in Team, Collaboration and Performance.* INTERDISCIPLINARY SCIENCE REVIEWS, Vol. 36 No. 2, June, 2011, 146–53

Brennan, N. et al (2010) *The transition from medical student to junior doctor: today's experiences of Tomorrow's Doctors.* Medical Education 2010: 44: 449–458

Baxter, N. et al (1996) *The Impact of Gender on the Choice of Surgery as a Career.* p374 AJS Vol 172 Oct. 1996

Beeston: Thanks To David Beeston writing in the Vet Times October 2017 for these reading book / reference book suggestions.

Brown, SE. & Katcher, A.H, (2001) *Pet Attachment and Dissociation:* Society & Animals

BEVA (2018) Equine vets have the highest injury risk of all civilian professions. Quoting from Labour Force Survey (LFS) and Health and Safety Executive (HSE) Table.

BVA: (2017) *85% of vets report they have been exposed to intimidating language or behaviour.* Survey of over 1600 BVA members. Younger vets and female vets are more likely to be a target. https://www.bva.co.uk/news-campaigns-and-policy/newsroom/news-releases/9-out-of-10-vets-report-intimidation-from-clients/

Chamorro-Premuzic, T. et al (2010) *The Psychology of Personnel Selection.* Cambridge University Press

Cobb-Clark, D.A. et al (2012) *"The stability of big-five personality traits".* Economics Letters.

Coffey, C.E. (2007) *Building a System of Perfect Depression Care in Behavioral Health.* The Joint Commission Journal on Quality and Patient Safety

Coffey, J.E. & Coffey, C.E. (2016) *How We Dramatically Reduced Suicide: Case Study 2016* https://catalyst.nejm.org/dramatically-reduced-suicide/

Constantine, et al (2003) *Measuring Protective Factors and Resilience Traits in Youth: The Healthy Kids Resilience Assessment.* Adolescent resilience: a concept analysis. Journal of Adolescence

McCrae, R. & Costa, P. (2003) *Personality in adulthood: A five-factor theory perspective.* 2003 .2nd Ed. RR - Guilford Press

Ferguson, N. (2014) The Great Degeneration. Penguin.

Ganai, M.Y. & Maqbool, M. (2003) *"A study of values of male and female veterinary science doctors"* Global Journal of Arts Humanities and Social Sciences Vol. 1, No. 2, pp.10-18, June 2013

Grandin, T. et al (2010) *The use of therapy animals with individuals with autism spectrum disorders.* Handbook on Animal-Assisted Therapy: Theoretical Foundations and Guidelines. 3rd Ed. 2010 ...edited by Aubrey H. Fine

Hagedorn, W. & Hartwig Moorhead, H.J. (2010) The God-Shaped Hole: Addictive Disorders and the Search for Perfection: Pub. 2010 by the American Counseling Association

Hanchon, T.A. (2010) *Examining Perfectionism through the Lens of Achievement Goal Theory.* North American Journal of Psychology, 2011, Vol. 13, No. 3, 469-490.

Johnson, S.W. et al (2009) *A Descriptive Analysis of Personality and Gender at the Louisiana State University School of Veterinary Medicine.* J Vet Med Educ. J Vet Med Educ 2009 ;36(3):284-90:

Kennedy, D. and Stiglitz, J. (2013) *Law and Economics with Chinese characteristics: Institutions for Promoting Development in the Twenty First Century.* Oxford University press.

Krause-Parello, C.A. (2008) *The Mediating Effect of Pet Attachment Support Between Loneliness and General Health in Older Females Living in the Community.* 2008. JCHN

Martin, C.R. (1997) *Looking at Type: The Fundamentals.* The Myers & Briggs Foundation. http://www.myersbriggs.org

Maslach, C. (1982) *Burnout: The Cost of Caring.* New York : Prentice.Hall

Maslow, A.H. (1954) *Motivation and Personality.*

Mastenbroek, N.J.J.M. et al (2010) *Suicidality in the Veterinary Profession 2012; Interview Study of Veterinarians With a History of Suicidal Ideation or Behavior; V*R

Also (2013) Measuring potential predictors of burnout and engagement among young veterinary professionals. Published Veterinary Record | February 15, 2014

Also (2013) *Burnout and engagement, and its predictors in young veterinary professionals: the influence of gender.* Veterinary Record.

Mathews, S. https://sherrimatthewsblog.com/2013/08/27/the-love-of-animals-and-aspergers-syndrome/

McAllister, R. (2015) *Mental health – to help our colleagues, do we need to change ourselves? .* https://helpline.vetlife.org.uk/

Meadow, R. (1995) *What is, and what is not, 'Munchausen syndrome by proxy'?* 1995. Archives of Disease in Childhood

Mellanby, R.J. et al (2011) *Perceptions of clients and veterinarians on what attributes constitute 'a good vet'.* The Veterinary Record.

Ming, V. (2017) 'Ted Talk'. Making a better person

NHS Protect Tables showing the number of reported physical assaults on NHS staff in 2015/16, broken down by health body: https://www.nhsbsa.nhs.uk/sites/default/files/2017-03/Reported_Physical_Assaults_2015-16_Final.pdf

Okólsk, M. & Salt, J. (2014) *Polish Emigration to the UK after 2004; Why Did So Many Come?* Central and Eastern European Migration Review.

Piedmont, R. (1993) *A Longitudinal Analysis of Burnout in the Health Care setting: The role of the personal dispositions.* JPA 1993 61(3)

Platt, B. et al (2010) *Suicidal behaviour and psychosocial problems in veterinary surgeons: a systematic review.* Soc Psychiat Epidemiol.

Powys-White, K. et al (2010) *Trust, expertise, and the philosophy of science. Democracy and Distrust.* John Hart Ely. 2010

RCVS (2014) RCVS Survey of the Veterinary Profession, 2014

Reevya, M. et al (2014) *Are Emotionally Attached Companion Animal Caregivers Conscientious and Neurotic? Factors That Affect the Human–Companion Animal Relationship.* : Journal of Applied Animal Welfare Science

Robinson, D. & Buzzeo, J. (2013) *RCVS Survey of Recent Graduates*

Rosenberg, D.A. (1987) *Web of deceit: A literature review of Munchausen syndrome by proxy.* Child Abuse & Neglect

Rubenstein, G. (2005) *The Big 5 among male and female students of different faculties.* Personality and Individual Differences 38 (2005) 1495–1503

Rubinstein, G. (2005) *The Big 5 among male and female students of different faculties.*Personality and Individual Differences 38 (2005) 1495–1503

Page-Jones,S. & Abbey, G. (2015) *Career identity in the veterinary profession.* Veterinary Record. 10.1136/vr.102784

Shulte, B (2014) *Overwhelmed: Work, Love, And Play When No One Has The Time.* Sarah Crichton Books

SimplyHealth: Vet Times Choices reprint of an article by Simplyhealth Professionals 2018.

Sinek: Simon Sinek on Millennials in the Workplace: https://www.youtube.com/watch?v=hER0Qp6QJNU

Soto, C.J. et al (2011) *"Age differences in personality traits from 10 to 65: Big Five domains and facets in a large cross-sectional sample".* Journal of Personality and Social Psychology. 2011.

Srivastava, S. et al (2003) *Development of personality in early and middle adulthood: Set like plaster or persistent change?".* Journal of Personality and Social Psychology.

Stevens, P.D. (2015) V*eterinary Personality Project* (VPP)

Stoltz, K., & Ashby, J. S. (2007). *Perfectionism and lifestyle: Personality differences among adaptive perfectionists, maladaptive perfectionists, and non-perfectionists.* Journal of Individual Psychology, 63(4)

Tran, L. et al (2014) *The Distinct Role of Performing Euthanasia on Depression and Suicide in Veterinarians.* Journal of Occupational Health Psychology 2014 American Psychological Association

Westgate, J. (2014) *There's nothing you can't do as a vet.* J Vet Times 16 October 2014. Quoting Callum Blair.

Van der Velde, S. (2010) *Gender differences in depression in 23 European countries. Cross-national variation in the gender gap in depression.* Social Science & Medicine.

Wariboko, N. (2008) *God and Money: A Theology of Money in a Globalizing World.* Lexington Books

Bibliography

By Subject

Burnout

American Association of Critical-Care Nurses, the American College of Chest Physicians, the American Thoracic Society, and the Society of Critical Care Medicine. (2016) *A call for action Against Burnout* - http://humanizandoloscuidadosintensivos.com/en/a-call-for-action-against-burnout/

Anon. (2015) *I'm sorry, I can't face being a doctor any more*. The Guardian, Oct. 22nd 2015.

Bakker, A. et al. (2009)*The Job Demands-Resources model: state of the art*. JMP

Collins, H. & Foote, D. (2005) *Managing Stress in Veterinary Students*. JVME

Constantine, N.A. et al. (1999) *Measuring Protective Factors and Resilience Traits in Youth: The Healthy Kids Resilience Assessment.* . Society for Prevention Research

Mastenbroek, N. J. J. M. et al. (2015) *Measuring potential predictors of burnout and engagement among young veterinary professionals; construction of a customised questionnaire (the Vet-DRQ).* . Vet Record.

Mastenbroek, N. J. J. M. et al. (2014) *Burnout and engagement, and its predictors in young veterinary professionals: the influence of gender*. Vet Record.

Mastenbroek, N. J. J. M. et al. (2012) *The role of personal resources in explaining well-being and performance: A study among young veterinary professionals*. EJWOP

Nedrow, A. et al. (2012) *Physician Resilience and Burnout*. A. Nedrow et al. 2012. American Academy of Family Physicians

Piedmont, R. (1993) *A longitudinal study of burnout in the health care setting: the role of personal dispositions*. JPA.

Whipp, C. (2015) *Ten Ways to mental Strength*. Veterinary Practice.

Suicide

Anon. *(2016)By the end of my first year as a doctor, I was ready to kill myself.* The Guardian, Jan. 5th 2016

Bartram, D. and Baldwin, D. (2008). *Suicide by veterinary surgeons*. Veterinary Record

Bartram, D. and Baldwin, D. (2015) *Veterinary surgeons and suicide: a structured review of possible influences on increased risk*. Vet Record.

Bartram, D. et al (2010) *Veterinary surgeons and suicide: a structured review of possible influences on increased risk*. Vet Record.

Coffey, M.J. and Coffey, C.E. (2016) *How We Dramatically Reduced Suicide*. The Menninger Clinic, Houston, Texas

Gladwell, M. (2000) *The Tipping Point*. Little, Brown. Chapter 7.

Hampton, T (2010) *Depression Care Effort Brings Dramatic Drop in Large HMO Population's Suicide Rate*. JAMA

Ling, V.J. et al (2011) *Toxoplasma gondii seropositivity and suicide rates in women.* JNMD

McAllister, R (2015) *Mental health – to help our colleagues, do we need to change ourselves?* https://helpline.vetlife.org.uk/

Platt, B. et al (2010) *Suicidal behaviour and psychosocial problems in veterinary surgeons: a systematic review*. Soc Psychiat Epidemiol.

Platt, B. et al (2012) *Suicidality in the Veterinary Profession. Interview Study of Veterinarians With a History of Suicidal Ideation or Behaviour*. Crisis.

Platt, B. et al (2010) *Systematic review of the prevalence of suicide in veterinary surgeons*. Occupational Medicine

Stark, C. and Dougall, N. (2012) *Effect of attitudes to euthanasia on vets' suicide risk*. Vet Record.

Tran, L. et al (2014) *The Distinct Role of Performing Euthanasia on Depression and Suicide in Veterinarians*. JOHP

Witte, T.K. et al (2012) *Experience with Euthanasia is Associated with Fearlessness about Death in Veterinary Students*. The American Association of Suicidology

Well-Being

Bartram, D. et al. (2009). *Psychosocial working conditions and work-related stressors among UK veterinary surgeons.* Occupational Medicine.

Bartram, D. & Boniwell, I. (2007). *The science of happiness: achieving sustained psychological well-being.* Vet Record In Practice

Bourne, T. et al. (2015)*The impact of complaints procedures on the welfare, health and clinical practise of 7926 doctors in the UK: a cross-sectional survey.* BMJ.

Collins, H. & Foote, D. (2005) *Managing Stress in Veterinary Students.* JVME

Fritschi, L. et al. (2009) *Psychological well-being of Australian veterinarians.* AVJ

Larkin, M. (2013) *When it's not the patient who needs a wellness check, but the veterinarian.* JAVMA

Miller,L. (2013) *The wellness bucket.* . CVJ

Rix, J. (2015). *How anxiety scrambles your brain and makes it hard to learn.* The Guardian Nov. 21st 2015

Mental health

Baron-Cohen, S. et al. (2014) *Attenuation of Typical Sex Differences in 800 Adults with Autism vs. 3,900 Controls.* Plos One

Bartram, D. (2009) *A cross sectional study of mental health and well-being and their associations in the UK veterinary profession.* RCVS

Cardwell, J.M. et al (2014) *A cross-sectional study of mental health in UK veterinary undergraduates.* Vet Record

Gibson-Beverly, G. & Schwartz, J. (2008) *Attachment, Entitlement, and the Impostor Phenomenon in Female Graduate Students.* . JCC

Olsson, C.A. et al. (2002) *Adolescent resilience: a concept analysis.* Journal of Adolescence.

Sakulku, J. & Alexander, J. (2011) *The Impostor Phenomenon.* . IJBS

Shirangi, A. et al. (2013) *Mental health in female veterinarians: effects of working hours and having children.* AVJ

Perfectionism

Ashby, J. et al. (2012) *Differences between "Normal" and "Neurotic" Perfectionists: Implications for Mental Health Counselors.* . Journal of Mental Health Counseling.

Bryce Hagedorn, W. and Hartwig Moorhead, H.J. (2010) *The God-Shaped Hole: Addictive Disorders and the Search for Perfection.* American Counseling Association.

Grzegorek, J.L. et al. (2004) *Self-Criticism, Dependency, Self-Esteem, and Grade Point Average: Satisfaction Among Clusters of Perfectionists and Nonperfectionists.* JCP

Hanchon, T.A. (2011) *Examining Perfectionism through the Lens of Achievement Goal Theory.* NAJP

Lacher, E. (2013) *4 ways to stop being a perfectionist veterinarian.* Veterinary Economics

Performance

Brennan, N. et al (2015) *The transition from medical student to junior doctor: today's experiences of Tomorrow's Doctors.* Medical Education

Busch, F. (2008) *Veterinary ethical dilemmas: underfeeding and euthanasia.* Vet Times

Busch, F. (2008) *Considering ethics and aesthetics.* Vet Times

Busch, F. (2008) *Why ethical debates are necessary.* Vet Times

Coombes, R. (2005) *Do vets and doctors face similar ethical challenges?* . BMJ.

Frank, M. (2015) *Why things fall apart.* New Scientist. Aug. 12th 2015

Ganai, M.Y. & Maqbool, M. (2013) *A Study of values of male and female veterinary science Doctors of SKUAST-K.* - Global Journal of Arts Humanities and Social Sciences

GVS. *Working as a Government Vet.* (2014).

Halligan, P.W. (2015) *Consciousness isn't all about you, you know.* New Scientist.

Linz, S.J. & Semykina, A. (2007) *Personality traits as performance enhancers? A comparative analysis of workers in Russia, Armenia and Kazakhstan.* Elsevier B.V.

Mellanby, R.J. et al (2015) *Perceptions of clients and veterinarians on what attributes constitute 'a good vet'.* Vet Record

Norring, M. et al (2014) *Empathic veterinarians score cattle pain higher.* VJ

Rawlins, M.D. (2011) *The death of clinical freedom.* IJE

Robinson, D. & Williams, M. & Buzzeo, J. (2014) *RCVS Survey of the Veterinary*

Professions. Synthesis Report. RCVS

Ross,I. (2014) *It's no longer James Herriot in wellies: the harsh reality of becoming a modern vet.* New Statesman July 14th, 2014

Westgate, W. (2015) *Big players smooth the way for new graduates.* VBJ

Vet Futures (2015) *Voices from the future of the profession.* (RCVS)

VIN New graduate Survival manual. Unattributed. Undated. VIN

Business

AAVMC (2006) *Envisioning the Future of Veterinary Medical Education.* A report.

AVMA (2015) *Workforce Needs in Veterinary Medicine.*

Bernays, E. (1947) *The Engineering of Consent.* University of Oklahoma Press

BVA. *Information on Accreditation of Veterinary Medicine Programmes for Veterinary Employers.*

Chamorro-Premuzic, T. et al. 2010 *The Psychology of Personnel Selection.* CUP

Clenfield, J. (2017) *When Big Business Happens to Your Pet.* . Bloomberg

Fernandez-Mehler, P. et al. (2013) *Veterinarians' role for pet owners facing pet loss.* Vet Record.

Feakes, A. et al (2014) *Re-shaping veterinary business curricula to improve graduates' business skills: a shared resource for educators.* DoE Sydney

Ferguson, N. (2013) The Great Degeneration. Penguin Press

Fleming, P. (2015) *We are no longer paid what we are worth – just look at dog walkers.* The Guardian. 26 May 2015

Gibbs, E.P.J. (2005) *Emerging zoonotic epidemics in the interconnected global community.* Vet Record

Heath, T.J. & Niethe, G.E (2001) *Effect of gender on ownership and income in veterinary practice.* Aust Vet J. Vol 79, No 8,

Henry, C. & Treanor, L. (2012) *The Veterinary Business Landscape: Contemporary Issues and Emerging Trends.* A Bird's-Eye View of Veterinary Medicine

Mellanby, R et al. (2011) *Perceptions of clients and veterinarians on what attributes constitute 'a good vet'.* Vet Record

Ming, V. (2017) *AI for Good: Augmented Intelligence.* DreamForce. Salesforce.com

NHS Protect. Tables showing the number of reported physical assaults on NHS staff in 2015/16.

2016. NHS Protect.

RCVS (2016) *Managing expectations: a vastly underutilised skill.*

Reevya, G. & Delgadob, M. (2014) *Are Emotionally Attached Companion Animal Caregivers Conscientious and Neurotic? Factors That Affect the Human–Companion Animal Relationship.* JAAWS

Prince, J. (2006). *Future demand, probable shortages, and strategies for creating a better future in food supply veterinary medicine.* JAVMA

Vet Futures Project Board. (2015) *Taking Charge of our future.*

Education

Adams, C. & Kurtz, S. (2006) *Building on Existing Models from Human Medical Education to Develop a Communication Curriculum in Veterinary Medicine.* JVME

Admissions Testing Service (2014) *Biomedical Admissions Test.(BMAT).*

Australian NTA. (2012) *Enhancing the capabilities of Vet Professionals.*

Brodbelt, T et al (2010) *Influences on the decision to study veterinary medicine: variation with sex and background.* Vet Record.

Ely, J.H. (1980) *Democracy and Distrust.* Harvard University Press.

Evans, L. (2008) *Professionalism, Professionality and the Development of Education Professionals.* BJES

Hargreaves, L. et al. (2006) *The Status of Teachers and the Teaching Profession: Views from Inside and Outside the Profession.* University of Cambridge Press

Heath, T. (2007) *Longitudinal study of veterinary students and veterinarians: family and gender issues after 20 years.* AVJ

Ioannidis, J. (2005) *Why Most Published Research Findings Are False.* JPA

Johnson, S. et al. (2009) *A descriptive analysis of personality and gender at the Louisiana State University School of Veterinary Medicine.* JVME

Jones, M.L. et al (2014) *Level of and motivation for extracurricular activity are associated with academic performance in the veterinary curriculum.* J Vet Med Educ.

Jones, M. et al. (2014) *Influences on the decision to study veterinary medicine: variation with sex and background.* JVME

Kurtz, S. (2006) *Teaching and Learning Communication in Veterinary Medicine.* JVME

Lincoln, A.E. (2010) *The Shifting Supply of Men and Women to Occupations: Feminization in Veterinary Education.* The University of North Carolina Press

Lounsbury, J. (2009) *An investigation of the construct validity of the personality trait of self-directed learning.* Learning and Individual Differences.

NAVMEC. (2010) *Roadmap for Veterinary Medical Education in the 21st Century: A Report.*

Powers, D. (2010) *Student Perceptions of the First Year of Veterinary Medical School.* JVME

Powys Whyte, K. & Crease, R. (2010) *Trust, expertise, and the philosophy of science.* Synthese

RCVS. (2014) *Guidance on the Professional Development Phase (PDP).*

Rubinstein, G. (2010) *The big five among male and female students of different faculties.* Personality and Individual Differences.

Serpell, J. (2005) *Factors Influencing Veterinary Students' Career Choices and Attitudes to Animals.* JVME

Strand, E. (2006) *Enhanced Communication by Developing a Non-anxious Presence: A Key Attribute for the Successful Veterinarian.* JVME

Gender

Baxter, N. (1996) *The Impact of Gender on the Choice of Surgery as a Career.* AJS

Bear, J. & Williams Woolley, A. (2011) *The Role of Gender in Team Collaboration and Performance.* Interdisciplinary Science Reviews

Heath, T. and Niethe, G. (2001) *Effect of gender on ownership and income in veterinary practice.* AVJ

Mastenbroek, N.J.J.M. et al. (2013) *Burnout and engagement, and its predictors in young veterinary professionals: the influence of gender.* Vet Record

Merrill, J. et al (1994) *Gender: Measurements of its influence on senior medical students "Professional Personality" and career choice.* AJM

Professionalism

Buzzeo, J et al (2014) *The 2014 RCVS Survey of the Veterinary Profession.* RCVS

Cardif, R. et al. (2008) *'One medicine—one pathology': are veterinary and human pathology prepared?.* Laboratory Investigation

Gibbs, P. (2014) *The evolution of One Health: a decade of progress and challenges for the future.* Vet Record

Judge, T. & Kammeyer-Mueller, J. (2012) *On the Value of Aiming High: The Causes and Consequences of Ambition*. JAP

Lewis, R. & Klausner, J. (2003) *Nontechnical competencies underlying career success as a veterinarian*. JAVMA

Linz, S. & Semykina, A. (2009) *Personality traits as performance enhancers? A comparative analysis of workers in Russia, Armenia and Kazakhstan*. JAP

Osburn, B. et al (2009) *One World – One Medicine – One Health: emerging veterinary challenges and opportunities*. RSTO

Rawlins, M. (2011) *The death of clinical freedom*. IJE

RCVS (2017) *RCVS Facts 2016*.

RCVS (Constantly updated) *Code of professional Conduct*.

Robinson, D. & Buzzeo, J. (2013) *RCVS Survey of Recent Graduates*. RCVS

Shaw, J. (2006) *Four Core Communication Skills of Highly Effective Practitioners*. VCSA

Timmins, R. (2006). *How Does Emotional Intelligence Fit into the Paradigm of Veterinary Medical Education?* JVME

Williams, S. (2015) *Veterinary futures: the drivers of change: A review of the literature*. RCVS

Zenne, D. (2005) *Veterinary Students as Elite Performers: Preliminary Insights*. JVME

Personality Typing

Boudreau, J. & Boswell, W. (2001) *Effects of Personality on Executive Career Success in the United States and Europe*. JVB

Coulston, C. et al (2012) *Female medical students: Who might make the cut?* Psychiatry Research

Costa, P. & McCrae, R. (1992) *Normal personality assessment in clinical practice: The NEO Personality Inventory*. Psychological Assessment

Costa, P. & McCrae, R. (1998) *Personality in Adulthood: A Six-Year Longitudinal Study of Self-Reports and Spouse Ratings on the NEO Personality Inventory*. JPSP

Costa, P. & McCrae, R. (1992) *Revised NEO Personality Inventory (NEO-PI-R) and NEO Five-Factor Inventory (NEOFFI) professional manual*. Psychological Assessment

Gelissen, J. et al (2006) *Personality, social background, and occupational career success*. Social Science Research

Howard, P & J. (1995) *Buddy Can You Paradigm?* Training and Development

Johnson, John A. (2016) *Personal Communications.* Professor Emeritus of Psychology. Pennsylvania State University.

Kessler, R.C. et al. (2003) *Screening for Serious Mental Illness in the General Population.* Archives of General Psychiatry

Komarraju, M. et al (2009) *Role of the Big Five personality traits in predicting college students' academic motivation and achievement.* Learning and Individual Differences

Myers-Briggs Type Indicator Manual. 2012. WC Personality

RCVS (2014) *Veterinary graduate numbers and new veterinary schools in the UK.*

Rubinstein, G. (2005) *The big five among male and female students of different faculties.* Personality and Individual Differences

Quenk, N. (2009) *Essentials of Myers-Briggs Type Indicator® Assessment.* John Wiley & Sons

Tennant, R. et al (2007) *Warwick-Edinburgh Mental Well-being Scale* (WEMWBS)

Tennant, R. et al. (2007)*The Warwick-Edinburgh Mental Well-Being Scale* (WEMWBS): Development and UK validation. Health and Quality of Life Outcomes. *A measure of mental well-being* - the Kessler6

Tokar, D. et al (1998) *Personality and Vocational Behavior: A Selective Review of the Literature,* 1993–1997. JVB

Vet Times. (2015) *Is the Veterinary Profession for you?.* Vet Times. 22nd Feb 2015

Psychology

Akirav, I. & Maroun, M. (2007) *The Role of the Medial Prefrontal Cortex-Amygdala Circuit in Stress Effects on the Extinction of Fear.* Neural Plasticity

Gibson-Beverly, G. and Schwartz, J.P. (2008) *Attachment, Entitlement, and the Impostor Phenomenon in Female Graduate Students.* Journal of College Counseling

Maslow, A.H. (1954) *Motivation and Personality.*

Matthews, S. (2013) *The Love of Animals and Asperger's Syndrome.* Pub.sherrimatthewsblog. com

Sze, D. (2015) *Post Self Actualisation.* Huffington Post

The Client

RCVS. (2016) *Managing expectations: a vastly underutilised skill.*

Vet Futures Project Board. (2015) *Taking charge of our future: A vision for the veterinary profession for 2030.*

Author Biography

Paul D. Stevens has been a vet for over 30 years. His extensive knowledge of the veterinary sector has been built from working in many different areas of vet work. Starting as an assistant vet in Yorkshire, he now lives in Derbyshire. In the intervening years, he has worked for the UK Government, owned three veterinary practices and has spent much of the last decade as a clinical locum-vet in many businesses across the UK.

In 2005 he was awarded a BA(Hons) in Contemporary Art from NTU and he has exhibited his work across the world.

Thanks to

ood104 and *Juhele* at "openclipart.org" for the fun figures

Yvonne for being so Vonnio

Richard Watts - illustrator - for being so chilled about the whole thing

Dr. John A. Johnson Professor Emeritus of Psychology Pennsylvania State University for his support and advice on the Big5, its applications, interpretation and implementation. I love the way Americans make so much effort to respond in good time.

Susan P Cohen for being available to chat. Another American.

Everyone who completed the VPP survey and who remained in touch.

T'end

Ask yourself these questions once every 12 months.

Keep doing it until you are very old (30 years old +)

1) Why do I want to be a vet ?

2) How am I doing?

BEING A VET IN THE 21ST CENTURY

Boo !!